THE 1994 ANNUAL: DEVELOPING HUMAN RESOURCES

(The Twenty-Third Annual)

Edited by

J. WILLIAM PFEIFFER, Ph.D., J.D.

**Johannesburg • Oxford
San Diego • Sydney • Toronto**

Copyright © 1994 by Pfeiffer & Company

Looseleaf ISBN: 0-88390-412-8
Paperbound ISBN: 0-88390-413-6
ISSN: 1046-333X

Library of Congress Catalog Card Number 86-643030

The materials that appear in this book *(except those for which reprint permission must b obtained from the primary sources)* may be freely reproduced for educational/training activ ties. There is no requirement to obtain special permission for such uses. We do, however, a that the following statement appear on all reproductions:

> Reproduced from
> *The 1994 Annual:*
> *Developing Human Resources*
> J. William Pfeiffer, Editor
> San Diego, California: Pfeiffer & Company, 1994

This permission statement is limited to the reproduction of materials for educational/trainin events. *Systematic or large-scale reproduction or distribution (more than one hundred copie per year)—or inclusion of items in publications for sale—may be done only with prior writte permission. Also, reproduction on computer disk or by any other electronic means require prior written permission.*

Printed in the United States of America.

Published by

Amsterdam	San Diego
Pfeiffer & Company	Pfeiffer & Company
Roggestraat 15	8517 Production Avenue
2153 GC Nieuw-Vennep	San Diego, California 92121
The Netherlands	United States of America
31-2526-89840, FAX 31-2526-86885	1-619-578-5900, FAX 1-619-578-2042
Johannesburg	Sydney
Pfeiffer & Company	Pfeiffer & Company
P.O. Box 4684, Randburg, 2125	6/1 Short Street
9 Langwa Street, Strijdom Park, Randburg, 2194	Chatswood NSW 2067
Republic of South Africa	Australia
27-11-792-8465/6/7, FAX 27-11-792-8046	61-2-417-5551, FAX 61-2-417-5621
London	Toronto
Pfeiffer & Company	Pfeiffer & Company
862 Garratt Lane	4190 Fairview Street
London, SW17 0NB	Burlington, Ontario L7L 4Y8
England	Canada
44-81-307-7788, FAX 44-81-307-7699	1-416-632-5832, FAX 1-416-333-5675

This book is printed on acid-free, recycled stock that meets or exceeds the minimum GPO and EPA specifications for recycled paper.

PREFACE

One central purpose of the *Annual* always has been to keep readers aware of and involved in the current developments in the field of human resource development (HRD). Consequently, each year the contents of the *Annual* are selected and edited to reflect these developments as we at Pfeiffer & Company perceive them. The HRD function in most organizations has grown in visibility and has exerted a stronger and more valuable influence in such efforts as strategic planning. The individual pieces selected for this *Annual* exemplify the depth of the field today. They not only serve as cause for optimism about HRD's future but also offer food for thought about what that future may require.

The 1994 Annual: Developing Human Resources is the twenty-third volume in our series; its contents reflect our intention to continue in the forefront of this field. Our philosophy remains that the *Annual* be strongly user oriented and that everything in it be potentially useful to the professional trainers, consultants, and facilitators who read it. The contents of this *Annual* focus on increasing each reader's professional competence and, therefore, his or her impact on the field of HRD. In keeping with this objective, users may duplicate and modify materials from the *Annuals* for *educational and training purposes,* as long as each copy includes the credit statement found on the copyright page of the particular volume. However, reproducing Pfeiffer & Company materials in publications for sale or for large-scale distribution (more than one hundred copies in twelve months) requires *prior written permission.* Also, reproduction of material that is copyrighted by some source other than Pfeiffer & Company (as indicated in a footnote) requires written permission from the designated copyright holder.

The success of the *Annual* as a clearinghouse for HRD professionals depends on the continuing flow of materials from our readers. We at Pfeiffer & Company encourage our readers to submit materials for publication—especially those with a clear organizational focus and those that reflect the changing nature of the HRD field. For the *Annual* series, we are interested in receiving presentation and discussion resources (articles that include theory along with practical application); inventories, questionnaires, and surveys (paper-and-pencil inventories, rating scales, and other response tools); and experiential learning activities (group learning designs based on the five stages of the experiential learning cycle—experiencing, publishing, processing, generalizing, and applying). These materials should be those that would be immediately useful to practicing professionals in the HRD field. Contact the Editorial Department at the San Diego office for guidelines for contributors, and send submissions to the *Annual* editor at the same address.

I want to express my appreciation to the dedicated people at Pfeiffer & Company who have produced this volume: Marian K. Prokop, project manager;

Carol Nolde and Arlette C. Ballew, senior developmental editors; Socorro F Gonzalez, editor; Marion Mettler, managing editor; Dawn Kilgore, production editor; Judy Whalen, graphic designer and page compositor; and Lee Ann Hubbard, illustrator, p. 36. Also, I am especially grateful to Dr. Beverly Byrum Robinson, who has again reviewed all of our experiential learning activities. He perspective as a facilitator and her insightful recommendations contribut significantly to the usefulness of these training designs. As always, I extend m sincere gratitude to our authors for their generosity in sharing their profes sional ideas, materials, and techniques so that other HRD practitioners ma benefit.

J. William Pfeiffer

San Diego, California
October, 1993

About Pfeiffer & Company

Pfeiffer & Company is engaged in publishing, training, and consulting in the field of human resource development (HRD). The organization has earned an international reputation as the leading source of practical publications that are immediately useful to today's facilitators, trainers, consultants, and managers. A distinct advantage of these publications is that they are designed by practicing professionals who are continually experimenting with new techniques. Thus, readers benefit from the fresh but thoughtful approach that underlies Pfeiffer & Company's experientially based materials, resources, books, workbooks, instruments, and tape-assisted learning programs. These materials are designed for the HRD practitioner who wants access to a broad range of training and intervention technologies as well as background in the field.

The wide audience that Pfeiffer & Company serves includes training and development professionals, internal and external consultants, managers and supervisors, team leaders, and those in the helping professions. For its clients and customers, Pfeiffer & Company offers a practical approach aimed at increasing people's effectiveness on an individual, group, and organizational basis.

TABLE OF CONTENTS

Preface	v
General Introduction to the 1994 *Annual*	1

EXPERIENTIAL LEARNING ACTIVITIES

Introduction to the Experiential Learning Activities Section	3
Experiential Learning Activities Categories	5
509. First Impressions: Examining Assumptions: *Steven E. Aufrecht*	9
510. Parole Board: Exploring Individual and Group Values: *Arlette C. Ballew and Charles A. Beitz, Jr.*	17
511. Let Me: Introducing Experiential Learning: *J. Allan Tyler*	31
512. Alpha/Beta: Exploring Cultural Diversity in Work Teams: *Steven R. Phillips*	37
513. Needs, Features, and Benefits: Exploring the Sales Process: *Bonnie Jameson*	47
514. Diversity Quiz: Viewing Differences As Resources: *Linda Eschenburg*	55
515. Wreck Survivors: Operating from Strategic Assumptions: *Virginia E.B. Prosdocimi*	67
516. Assignment Flexibility: Comparing Negotiation Styles: *John E. Oliver*	75
517. Hats "R" Us: Learning About Organizational Cultures: *Catherine J. Nagy*	93
518. Parsley, Garlic, Ginger, Pepper: Introductions: *Marian K. Prokop*	107
519. Disability Awareness: Providing Equal Opportunities in the Training Environment: *Robert William Lucas*	115
520. The Employment Case: Exploring Organizational Value Conflicts: *Joann Keyton*	123

*See Experiential Learning Categories, p. 5, for an explanation of the numbering system.

INVENTORIES, QUESTIONNAIRES, AND SURVEYS

Introduction to the Inventories, Questionnaires, and Surveys Section ... 13

Value-System Instrument: *Michele Stimac* ... 13?

Studying Organizational Ethos: The OCTAPACE Profile: *Udai Pareek* ... 15?

Organizational-Type Inventory: *Manfred F.R. Kets de Vries, Danny Miller, and Gaylord Reagan* ... 16?

PRESENTATION AND DISCUSSION RESOURCES

Introduction to the Presentation and Discussion Resources Section ... 18?

Danger—Diversity Training Ahead: Addressing the Myths of Diversity Training and Offering Alternatives: *Paula Grace* ... 189

Behavior-Management Interventions: Getting the Most Out of Your Employee Assistance Program: *Robert T. Brill* ... 201

Fostering the Effectiveness of Groups at Work: *Patrick J. Ward and Robert C. Preziosi* ... 213

Using Mentoring for Professional Development: *J. Barton Cunningham* ... 227

The Enneagram: A Key to Understanding Organizational Systems: *Michael J. Goldberg* ... 243

Journey to Excellence: One Path to Total Quality Management: *Donald T. Simpson* ... 257

Theme Development: Finally Getting Control of the Design Process: *H.B. Karp* ... 273

Evaluating the Effectiveness of Training Programs: *Patricia E. Boverie, Deanna Sánchez Mulcahy, and John A. Zondlo* ... 279

Why Job and Role Planning Is Critical to the Future: *Edgar H. Schein* ... 295

Contributors ... 307

GENERAL INTRODUCTION TO THE 1994 *ANNUAL*

The 1994 Annual: Developing Human Resources is the twenty-third volume in the *Annual* series. The series is a collection of practical and useful materials for human resource development (HRD) practitioners—materials written by and for professionals. As such, the series continues to provide a publication outlet for HRD professionals who wish to share their experiences, their viewpoints, and their procedures with their colleagues.

This year marks several changes for the *Annual* series. In conjunction with the twenty-fifth anniversary of Pfeiffer & Company, we reexamined all of the materials that had been published in the *Annuals* and in the *Handbooks of Structured Experiences*. We updated and reorganized these materials to form the *Pfeiffer & Company Library,* a twenty-eight-volume set of activities, instruments, and articles that chronicle the evolution of human resource development (HRD).

This reorganization resulted in a simpler system of categorization than we had used previously. The new categories are Individual Development, Communication, Problem Solving, Groups, Teams, Consulting, Facilitating, and Leadership. Each category is further divided into logical subcategories. The categories, the subcategories, and the distribution of activities within them can be found on page 5. We believe that these changes will make it even easier for our readers to access information from our *Annuals* and *Handbooks*.

Another change affects how we refer to materials in the *Annuals*. In place of the term "structured experiences," we are using "experiential learning activities." The Instrumentation section has been retitled "Inventories, Questionnaires, and Surveys." The materials that had been previously labeled as Lecturettes, Theory and Practice, Resources, or Professional Development now can be found in the section entitled "Presentation and Discussion Resources." The new titles are more descriptive of the contents of the sections and allow greater flexibility in meeting the needs and interests of HRD practitioners.

One feature of the individual *Annuals* in the series has remained consistent over the years: the quality of content. As has been the case with each volume, the materials for the 1994 *Annual* have been selected for the quality of their ideas, their applicability to real-world concerns, their relevance to current HRD issues, their clarity of presentation, and their ability to add to our readers' professional development. In addition, we chose experiential learning activities that will create a high degree of enthusiasm among the participants and add enjoyment to the learning process. As in the past several years, the contents span a range of subject matter, which reflects the range of interests of our readers.

The "Introduction to the Experiential Learning Activities Section" describes the experiential learning activities selected for this volume. Their order follows the revised categorization scheme, which also is used in our *Reference Guide to Handbooks and Annuals*. We believe that this order will prove to be logical and easy to use for our readers, particularly those who regularly use experiential learning activities in their work.

The Inventories, Questionnaires, and Surveys section of this *Annual* contains three new paper-and-pencil, instrumented-feedback inventories. These pieces are described in the "Introduction to the Inventories, Questionnaires, and Surveys Section."

The purpose of the Presentation and Discussion Resources section is to assist readers of the *Annual* in their own professional development. The "Introduction to the Presentation and Discussion Resources Section" describes the pieces that were chosen. The editor and the editorial staff continue to be pleased with the high quality of submitted materials. Nevertheless, just as we cannot publish every manuscript that is submitted, readers may find that not all of the works we include in the *Annual* are equally useful to them. We actively solicit reactions from our readers so that we may continue to select manuscripts that meet their needs.

Pfeiffer & Company follows the stylistic guidelines established by the American Psychological Association, particularly concerning the use and format of references. Potential contributors to our publications may wish to purchase copies of the APA's Publication Manual from: Order Department, American Psychological Association, 1200 Seventeenth Street, N.W., Washington, DC 20036. Pfeiffer & Company also publishes guidelines for potential authors, which were revised in 1993; they are available from Pfeiffer & Company's Editorial Department in San Diego, California.

Biographies of *Annual* authors appear at the end of each experiential learning activity, instrument, and article. In addition, at the end of each *Annual* is a list of contributors' names, affiliations, addresses, and telephone numbers. This information is intended to contribute to the networking function that is so valuable in the field of human resource development.

INTRODUCTION TO THE EXPERIENTIAL LEARNING ACTIVITIES SECTION

Andragogy, or adult learning, differs from *pedagogy*, or children's learning. One key difference is that adults need more active involvement in the learning process. Research studies estimate that adults remember 10 percent of what they hear and 25 percent of what they see. However, they remember 90 percent of what they do—which is the basis of Pfeiffer & Company's emphasis on experiential learning.

The experiential learning activities in the 1994 *Annual* are presented in an order that reflects their classification into categories, according to their focus and intent. A list of the eight major categories and their subcategories follows this introduction, and an explanation of the categorization scheme appears in the *Reference Guide to Handbooks and Annuals* (1994 Edition).

The first and second experiential learning activities reflect the Individual Development category. In "First Impressions," the participants have the opportunity to identify behaviors or characteristics by which they judge others and by which they themselves might be judged. "Parole Board" allows participants to examine their own values within the framework of choosing prisoners to be paroled. In the process, they also explore how those values affect both individual and group decisions.

The next three activities have to do with communication. "Let Me" demonstrates the positive effects of experiential learning through the mechanism of teaching American Sign Language. In the next activity, a simulation called "Alpha/Beta," the participants experience the impact of cultural diversity and practice communicating and problem solving in a culturally diverse setting. "Needs, Features, and Benefits," the fifth activity, is designed to give the participants an understanding of how needs, features, and benefits differ. They also explore how these factors affect "selling," whether it be products, organizations, or ideas.

The sixth and seventh activities represent the Problem Solving category. "Diversity Quiz" presents a nonthreatening introduction to the topic of diversity. This activity creatively links the concepts of diversity and collaboration, allowing participants to compare the results of their individual work with those of a diversified group. The next activity, "Wreck Survivors," begins with a shipwreck situation; as a result of their problem-solving discussions, participants learn the differences between "strategy" and "tactics" and learn the importance of clarifying strategic assumptions before making decisions.

The eighth activity belongs to the Groups category. "Assignment Flexibility" allows participants to experience and compare the effects of "hardball" and "win-win" stances in the context of union/management contract negotiations.

"Hats 'R' Us" represents the Consulting category. In this activity, th participants become acquainted with four general types of organizational cu ture, identify the culture of their own organization, and explore their persona alignment—or misalignment—with that culture.

The tenth and eleventh activities fit the Facilitating category. "Parsley Garlic, Ginger, Pepper" is a lighthearted introductory activity that eases learn ing by building norms of openness and encouraging interaction. The nex activity, "Disability Awareness," is designed for use with practicing or prospec tive facilitators. Beyond being a model activity for disability-awareness training the activity raises the participants' awareness of the need to provide equal acces to training opportunities for people with disabilities.

The final activity, "The Employment Case," offers the participants th opportunity to clarify personal and professional values using a value-base(group decision-making task. In the process, the activity reinforces the impor tance of making legal hiring decisions.

All experiential learning activities in this *Annual* include a description o the goals of the activity, the size of the group and/or subgroups that can b(accommodated, the time required to do and *process*[1] the activity, the material and handouts required, the physical setting, step-by-step instructions for facili tating the experiential task and discussion phases of the activity, and variation of the design that the facilitator might find useful. All of these activities are complete; the content of all handouts is provided.

Other activities that address certain goals can be located by using ou comprehensive *Reference Guide to Handbooks and Annuals*. This book, which i updated regularly, indexes all of the *Annuals* and all of the *Handbooks o Structured Experiences* that we have published to date. With each revision, th(*Reference Guide* becomes a complete, up-to-date, and easy-to-use resource fo selecting appropriate materials from *all* of the *Annuals* and *Handbooks*.

---

[1] It would be redundant to print here a caveat for the use of experiential learning activities, but HRD professionals who are not experienced in the use of this training technology are strongly urged to read the "Introduction to the Structured Experiences Section" of the 1980 *Annual* or the "Introduction" to the *Reference Guide to Handbooks and Annuals* (1994 Edition). Both articles present the theory behind the experiential-learning cycle and explain the necessity of adequately completing each phase of the cycle to allow effective learning to occur.

STRUCTURED EXPERIENCE CATEGORIES

Numbers of Structured Experiences		Numbers of Structured Experiences	
1-24	Volume I, *Handbook*	293-316	Volume VIII, *Handbook*
25-48	Volume II, *Handbook*	317-328	1982 *Annual*
49-74	Volume III, *Handbook*	329-340	1983 *Annual*
75-86	1972 *Annual*	341-364	Volume IX, *Handbook*
87-100	1973 *Annual*	365-376	1984 *Annual*
101-124	Volume IV, *Handbook*	377-388	1985 *Annual*
125-136	1974 *Annual*	389-412	Volume X, *Handbook*
137-148	1975 *Annual*	413-424	1986 *Annual*
149-172	Volume V, *Handbook*	425-436	1987 *Annual*
173-184	1976 *Annual*	437-448	1988 *Annual*
185-196	1977 *Annual*	449-460	1989 *Annual*
197-220	Volume VI, *Handbook*	461-472	1990 *Annual*
221-232	1978 *Annual*	473-484	1991 *Annual*
233-244	1979 *Annual*	485-496	1992 *Annual*
245-268	Volume VII, *Handbook*	497-508	1993 *Annual*
269-280	1980 *Annual*	509-520	1994 *Annual*
281-292	1981 *Annual*		

INDIVIDUAL DEVELOPMENT

Sensory Awareness

	Vol.-Page
Feelings & Defenses (56)	III-31
Lemons (71)	III-94
Growth & Name Fantasy (85)	'72-59
Group Exploration (119)	IV-92
Relaxation & Perceptual Awareness (136)	'74-84
T'ai Chi Chuan (199)	VI-10
Roles Impact Feelings (214)	VI-102
Projections (300)	VIII-30

Self-Disclosure

	Vol.-Page
Johari Window (13)	I-65
Graphics (20)	I-88
Personal Journal (74)	III-109
Make Your Own Bag (90)	'73-13
Growth Cards (109)	IV-30
Expressing Anger (122)	IV-104
Stretching (123)	IV-107
Forced-Choice Identity (129)	'74-20
Boasting (181)	'76-49
The Other You (182)	'76-51
Praise (306)	VIII-61
Introjection (321)	'82-29
Personality Traits (349)	IX-58
Understanding the Need for Approval (438)	'88-21
The Golden Egg Award (448)	'88-89

Sex Roles

	Vol.-Page
Polarization (62)	III-57
Sex-Role Stereotyping (95)	'73-26
Sex-Role Attributes (184)	'76-63
Who Gets Hired? (215)	VI-106
Sexual Assessment (226)	'78-36
Alpha II (248)	VII-19
Sexual Values (249)	VII-24
Sex-Role Attitudes (258)	VII-85
Sexual Values in Organizations (268)	VII-146
Sexual Attraction (272)	'80-26
Sexism in Advertisements (305)	VIII-58
The Promotion (362)	IX-152
Raising Elizabeth (415)	'86-21
The Problem with Men/Women Is....(437)	'88-9
The Girl and the Sailor (450)	'89-17
Tina Carlan (466)	'90-45

Diversity

	Vol.-Page
Status-Interaction Study (41)	II-85
Peer Perceptions (58)	III-41
Discrimination (63)	III-62
Traditional American Values (94)	'73-23
Growth Group Values (113)	IV-45
The In-Group (124)	IV-112
Leadership Characteristics (127)	'74-13
Group Composition (172)	V-139
Headbands (203)	VI-25
Sherlock (213)	VI-92
Negotiating Differences (217)	VI-114
Young/Old Woman (227)	'78-40
Pygmalion (229)	'78-51
Race from Outer Space (239)	'79-38
Prejudice (247)	VII-15
Physical Characteristics (262)	VII-108
Whom To Choose (267)	VII-141
Data Survey (292)	'81-57
Lifeline (298)	VIII-21
Four Cultures (338)	'83-72
All Iowans Are Naive (344)	IX-14
AIRSOPAC (364)	IX-172
Doctor, Lawyer, Indian Chief (427)	'87-21
Life Raft (462)	'90-17
Zenoland (492)	'92-69
First Impressions (509)	'94-9
Parole Board (510)	'94-17

Life/Career Planning

	Vol.-Page
Life Planning (46)	II-101
Banners (233)	'79-9
Wants Bombardment (261)	VII-105
Career Renewal (332)	'83-27
Life Assessment and Planning (378)	'85-15
Work-Needs Assessment (393)	X-31
The Ego-Radius Model (394)	X-41
Dropping Out (414)	'86-15
Roles (416)	'86-27
Creating Ideal Personal Futures (439)	'88-31
Pie in the Sky (461)	'90-9
What's in It for Me? (463)	'90-21
Affirmations (473)	'91-9
Supporting Cast (486)	'92-15
Career Visioning (498)	'93-13

COMMUNICATION

Awareness

	Vol.-Page
One-Way, Two-Way (4)	I-13
Think-Feel (65)	III-70
Ball Game (108)	IV-27
Re-Owning (128)	'74-18
Helping Relationships (152)	V-13
Babel (153)	V-16
Blindfolds (175)	'76-13
Letter Exchange (190)	'77-28
Dominoes (202)	VI-21
Blivet (241)	'79-46
Meanings Are in People (250)	VII-28
Mixed Messages (251)	VII-34
Gestures (286)	'81-28
Maze (307)	VIII-64
Feelings (330)	'83-14
Synonyms (341)	IX-5
In Other Words (396)	X-55
Taking Responsibility (397)	X-62
Pass It On (398)	X-68
Shades of Difference (417)	'86-35
E-Prime (440)	'88-39
Words Apart (464)	'90-29
Supportive Versus Defensive Climates (474)	'91-15
Let Me (511)	'94-31

Building Trust

	Vol.-Page
Dyadic Encounter (21)	I-90
Nonverbal Communication I (22)	I-101
Intimacy Program (70)	III-89
Dialog (116)	IV-66
Dimensions of Trust (120)	IV-96
Dyadic Renewal (169)	V-116
Disclosing & Predicting (180)	'76-46
Current Status (196)	'77-57
Dyadic Risk Taking (220)	VI-130

Conflict

	Vol.-Page
Frustrations & Tensions (75)	'72-5
Conflict Fantasy (130)	'74-22
Escalation (219)	VI-127
Defensive & Supportive Communication (238)	'79-24
Conflict Management (242)	'79-54
Resistance (309)	VIII-75
Conflict Role Play (340)	'83-80

The 1994 Annual: Developing Human Resources

	Vol.-Page		Vol.-Page		Vol.-Page
The Company Task Force (352)	IX-84	Marzilli's Fine Italian Foods (454)	'89-55	Structures (308)	VIII-69
The Decent but Pesky Co-Worker (400)	X-80	Cooperative Inventions (467)	'90-61	Team Planning (351)	IX-74
VMX Productions, Inc. (441)	'88-43	Greenback Financial Services (470)	'90-83	Group Sell (357)	IX-114
Quality Customer Service (475)	'91-27	Puzzling Encounters (481)	'91-97	Four Corners (442)	'88-51
The Parking Space (476)	'91-35	The Real Meaning (502)	'93-39	Orientations (443)	'88-57
Time Flies (499)	'93-19			Whirlybird (491)	'92-63
Alpha/Beta (512)	'94-37	**Information Sharing**			
		Energy International (80)	'72-25	**Competition/Collaboration**	
Feedback		Pine County (117)	IV-75	Model-Building (32)	II-29
Group-on-Group (6)	I-22	Farm E-Z (133)	'74-44	Prisoners' Dilemma (61)	III-52
Coins (23)	I-104	Sales Puzzle (155)	V-34	Decisions (83)	'72-51
Behavior Description Triads (50)	III-6	Room 703 (156)	V-39	Wooden Blocks (105)	IV-18
Psychomat (84)	'72-58	Al Kohbari (178)	'76-26	World Bank (147)	'75-56
Puzzlement (97)	'73-30	Murder One (212)	VI-75	Testing (164)	V-91
Analyzing & Increasing Open Behavior (99)	'73-38	Farmers (284)	'81-16	X-Y (179)	'76-41
The Gift of Happiness (104)	IV-15	The Sales Manager's Journey (359)	IX-125	Blue/Green (189)	'77-24
Sculpturing (106)	IV-21	The Welsh Boothouse (383)	'85-67	Circle in the Square (205)	VI-32
The Portrait Game (107)	IV-24	Society of Taos (432)	'87-57	Balance of Power (231)	'78-63
Party Conversations (138)	'75-10	Dust Pan Case (482)	'91-107	Paper Box (243)	'79-60
Adjectives (168)	V-114	Diversity Quiz (514)	'94-55	Trading Cards (263)	VII-112
Introspection (209)	VI-57			War Gaming (264)	VII-117
Cards (225)	'78-34	**Consensus/Synergy**		Move to Newtown (278)	'80-60
Developing Trust (303)	VIII-45	Top Problems (11)	I-49	High Iron (280)	'80-78
Giving and Receiving Feedback (315)	VIII-125	Residence Halls (15)	I-72	Cross-Group Negotiation and Cooperation (302)	VIII-41
Feedback (355)	IX-107	NORC (30)	II-18	Risk Game (311)	VIII-93
Pin Spotter (377)	'85-11	Kerner Report (64)	III-64	Intertwine (319)	'82-20
Feedback on Nonverbal and Verbal Behaviors (379)	'85-35	Supervisory Behavior/Aims of Education (69)	III-84	Block Buster (320)	'82-24
Gaining Support (380)	'85-39	Shoe Store (102)	IV-5	Stock Exchange (384)	'85-75
I Am, Don't You Think? (390)	X-8	Consensus-Seeking (115)	IV-51	Assignment Flexibility (516)	'94-75
Two Bags Full (391)	X-22	Hung Jury (134)	'74-64		
Seeing Ourselves as Others See Us (426)	'87-17	Kidney Machine (135)	'74-78	**Conflict**	
The Art of Feedback (449)	'89-9	Lost at Sea (140)	'75-28	Conflict Resolution (14)	I-70
Feedback Awareness (487)	'92-29	Cash Register (151)	V-10	Lindell-Billings Corporation (144)	'75-46
A Note to My Teammate (497)	'93-9	Letter Occurrence/Health Professions Prestige (157)	V-44	Conflict Styles (186)	'77-15
		Wilderness Survival (177)	'76-19	Controversial Issues (224)	'78-28
Listening		Pyramids (187)	'77-20	Budget Cutting (323)	'82-35
Listening Triads (8)	I-31	Admissions Committee (223)	'78-15	Trouble in Manufacturing (374)	'84-67
Rumor Clinic (28)	II-12	Alphabet Names (236)	'79-19	Datatrak (375)	'84-74
Not-Listening (52)	III-10	What's Important on My Job? (244)	'79-71	Winterset High School (435)	'87-79
Peter-Paul (87)	'73-7	Lists (255)	VII-57		
Active Listening (252)	VII-39	Values for the 1980s (271)	'80-20	**Negotiating/Bargaining**	
I'm All Ears (395)	X-46	Ranking Characteristics (429)	'87-31	Unequal Resources (78)	'72-17
Poor Listening Habits (428)	'87-25	People Are Electric (501)	'93-35	Monetary Investment (265)	VII-124
In Reply (465)	'90-35			Creative Products (279)	'80-69
Needs, Features, and Benefits (513)	'94-47	**Action Planning**		Territory (314)	VIII-120
		Force-Field Analysis (40)	II-79	Bargaining, United Nations Style (471)	'90-95
Styles		Wahoo City (73)	III-100		
Building Open & Closed Relationships (93)	'73-20	Dhabi Fehru (259)	VII-91	**TEAMS**	
Submission/Aggression/ Assertion (206)	VI-36	Island Commission (260)	VII-99	**How Groups Work**	
Organizational TA (310)	VIII-83	Missiles (275)	'80-43	System Problems (111)	IV-38
The Human Bank Account (399)	X-76	Robbery (334)	'83-40	Top Secret Contract (194)	'77-47
The Candy Bar (457)	'89-73	The Impact Wheel (458)	'89-83	Team Development (208)	VI-54
Stating the Issue (503)	'93-43	Coping Strategies (485)	'92-9	Slogans (276)	'80-51
		Wreck Survivors (515)	'94-67	Project Colossus (288)	'81-43
PROBLEM SOLVING				Group Identity (299)	VIII-25
Generating Alternatives		**GROUPS**		Chips (322)	'82-31
Broken Squares (7)	I-25	**How Groups Work**		Meetings Audit (325)	'82-49
Brainstorming (53)	III-14	Committee Meeting (9)	I-36	Work-Group Review (327)	'82-60
Quaker Meeting (76)	'72-11	Process Observation (10)	I-45	Healthy or Unhealthy? (404)	X-96
Nominal Group Technique (141)	'75-35	Group Tasks (29)	II-16	Sticky Wickets (405)	X-99
Poems (185)	'77-13	Self-Interaction-Task (37)	II-68	Bean Bags (419)	'86-45
Package Tour (192)	'77-35	Towers (54)	III-17	Instant Survey (434)	'87-75
Numbers (221)	'78-9	What To Look for in Groups (79)	'72-19		
Puzzle Cards (240)	'79-41	Greeting Cards (82)	'72-44	**Roles**	
Analytical or Creative? (285)	'81-24	Cog's Ladder (126)	'74-8	Role Nominations (38)	II-72
Vacation Schedule (312)	VIII-100	Faculty Meeting (139)	'75-15	Line-Up & Power Inversion (59)	III-46
Pebbles (335)	'83-45	Tinkertoy Bridge (160)	V-60	Role Clarification (171)	V-136
Bricks (343)	IX-10	LEGO Bridge (161)	V-73	Baseball Game (270)	'80-14
Departmental Dilemma (350)	IX-66	Word-Letter (200)	VI-15	The Car (326)	'82-55
QC Agenda (370)	'84-44	Spy (218)	VI-117	The Seven Pieces (366)	'84-16
Water Jars (392)	X-26	Homesell (228)	'78-46	Role Power (368)	'84-26
		Line of Four (237)	'79-21	Kaleidoscope (408)	X-122
		Slingshots (256)	VII-69	Position Power (420)	'86-51
		Four-Letter Words (287)	'81-34	America's Favorite Pastime (455)	'89-61
		Dynasell (290)	'81-50	Symbols (469)	'90-73
				Multiple Roles (480)	'91-85

	Vol.-Page		Vol.-Page		Vol.-Page
Yours, Mine, and Ours (500)	'93-31	Prairie General Hospital (479)	'91-65	Empty Chair (51)	III-8
Problem Solving/Decision Making		The Hundredth Monkey (505)	'93-75	Nonverbal Communication III (72)	III-97
Lutts & Mipps (31)	II-24	Hats "R" Us (517)	'94-93	Medial Feedback (92)	'73-17
Joe Doodlebug (103)	IV-8	**Consulting: Diagnosing/Skills**		Participant-Staff Expectations (96)	'73-29
Planning Recommendations or		Roxboro Electric Company (131)	'74-24	Group Leadership Functions (148)	'75-63
Action (132)	'74-32	Consulting Triads (183)	'76-53	Training Philosophies (363)	IX-159
The Lawn (337)	'83-65	Tri-State (193)	'77-39	Good Workshops Don't	
Threats to the Project (373)	'84-62	HELPCO (211)	VI-66	Just Happen (495)	'92-97
Unscrambling the Bank		Willington (230)	'78-55	Up Close and Personal	
Accounts (431)	'87-51	Elm Street Community		with Dr. Maslow (496)	'92-111
Control or Surrender (453)	'89-47	Church (347)	IX-34	Zodiac for Trainers (508)	'93-97
		Inquiries (348)	IX-48	Disability Awareness (519)	'94-115
Feedback		Measuring Excellence (385)	'85-81		
Leveling (17)	I-79	Client Concerns (412)	X-148	**Facilitating: Closing**	
Dependency-Intimacy (18)	I-82	The Client-Consultant		Symbolic Closing Exercise (86)	'72-61
Group Development (39)	II-76	Questionnaire (424)	'86-79	Closure (114)	IV-49
Group Self-Evaluations (55)	III-22	City of Buffington (460)	'89-101	Payday (146)	'75-54
Nominations (57)	III-33	Metaphors (484)	'91-125	Symbolic Toast (176)	'76-17
Dividing the Loot (60)	III-49	Working at Our Company (493)	'92-79	Bread Making (201)	VI-19
Team-Building (66)	III-73	Help Wanted (494)	'92-87	Golden Awards (222)	'78-12
Organizational Mirror (67)	III-78	International Equity Claims		Kia Ora (318)	'82-12
Team Identity (77)	'72-13	Department (506)	'93-85	Aloha (389)	X-5
Twenty-Five Questions (118)	IV-88				
Agenda Setting (166)	V-108	**Facilitating: Opening**		**LEADERSHIP**	
Cups (167)	V-111	Listening & Inferring (1)	I-3	**Ethics**	
Person Perception (170)	V-131	Two-Four-Eight (2)	I-5	What Do You See? (137)	'75-7
Affirmation of Trust (216)	VI-110	Who Am I? (5)	I-19	Ideal Cards (143)	'75-43
Stones, Bands, & Circle (254)	VII-53	Group Conversation (25)	II-3	Who Killed John Doe? (235)	'79-15
I Hear That You... (291)	'81-54	Jigsaw (27)	II-10	Personal Identity (246)	VII-11
Group Effectiveness (297)	VIII-18	First Names, First Impressions (42)	II-88	Louisa's Problem (283)	'81-13
Group Sociogram (316)	VIII-131	"Who Am I?" Variations (49)	III-3	Values and Decisions (361)	IX-146
Constructive Criticism (345)	IX-28	"Cold" Introductions (88)	'73-9	The Gold Watch (411)	X-142
Messages (356)	IX-110	Getting Acquainted (101)	IV-3		
Sharing and Supporting		Hum-Dinger (125)	'74-7	**Interviewing/Appraisal**	
Goals (386)	'85-87	Energizers (149)	V-3	Live Case (142)	'75-40
Smackers (388)	'85-95	Limericks (173)	'76-7	Sunglow (257)	VII-73
Power and Affection		Labeling (174)	'76-10	Assistant Wanted (333)	'83-31
Exchange (402)	X-88	Best Friend (197)	VI-3	Interviewing (358)	IX-122
Yearbook (403)	X-92	Choose an Object (198)	VI-7	Inquiries and Discoveries (365)	'84-9
Group Sociogram II (418)	'86-41	Tea Party (245)	VII-5	Constructive Discipline (371)	'84-49
The Advertising Firm (444)	'88-69	Autographs (269)	'80-11	BARS (423)	'86-73
Images (445)	'88-73	Alliterative Names (281)	'81-9	Performance Appraisal (425)	'87-11
It's in the Cards (456)	'89-67	Birth Signs (282)	'81-11	What's Legal? (451)	'89-23
The Genie's Wish (468)	'90-67	Name Tags (293)	VIII-5		
Bases of Power (477)	'91-43	Learning Exchange (294)	VIII-7	**Motivation**	
Group Calendar (489)	'92-47	Rebus Names (317)	'82-9	Motivation (100)	'73-43
Strengths and Needs (490)	'92-51	Just the Facts (329)	'83-11	Motivation (204)	VI-28
		News Bulletin (342)	IX-8	Darts (210)	VI-61
Conflict and Intergroup Issues		Group Savings Bank (376)	'84-92	Penny Pitch (253)	VII-46
Conflict		Daffodil (387)	'85-91	People on the Job (295)	VIII-10
Ajax Appliance Corporation (406)	X-106	Getting To Know You (413)	'86-11	The Manager's Guidebook (354)	IX-102
Sharing Perspectives (409)	X-126	I Represent (436)	'87-87	MACE (367)	'84-22
Conflict Management (483)	'91-119	Color Me (507)	'93-93	There's Never Time To Do It	
Intergroup Issues		Parsley, Garlic, Ginger, Pepper		Right (430)	'87-45
Win as Much as You Can (36)	II-62	(518)	'94-107	Four Factors (452)	'89-39
Intergroup Meeting (68)	III-81				
Intergroup Model-Building (81)	'72-36	**Facilitating: Blocks to Learning**		**Diversity/Stereotyping**	
Win What, Lose What? (145)	'75-51	Gunnysack (89)	'73-11	Hollow Square (33)	II-32
Riddles (150)	V-5	Perception of Task (91)	'73-15	Hampshire In-Basket (34)	II-41
Intergroup Clearing (289)	'81-48	The "T" Test (112)	IV-41	Absentee (158)	V-49
The Value Profile (407)	X-118	Communication Analysis (191)	'77-32	When To Delegate (304)	VIII-52
		Buttermilk (234)	79-13	Reviewing Objectives	
CONSULTING & FACILITATING		Resistance to Learning (301)	VIII-37	and Strategies (328)	'82-65
Consulting: Awareness		Needs, Expectations, and		Vice President's In-Basket (336)	'83-49
Strategies of Changing (98)	'73-32	Resources (324)	'82-46	Meeting Management (421)	'86-55
Organization Structures (110)	IV-34			Raises (422)	'86-65
Coloring Book (163)	V-85	**Facilitating: Skills**		Delegation (447)	'88-81
Marbles (165)	V-98	Fantasies (16)	I-75	The Robotics Decision (459)	'89-89
Tug O'War (188)	'77-22	Awareness Expansion (19)	I-86	Termination (472)	'90-103
MANDOERS (232)	'78-71	Assumptions About Human		The Employment Case (520)	'94-123
Organizational Blasphemies (339)	'83-77	Relations Training (24)	I-107		
Matrix (360)	IX-136	Miniversity (26)	II-7	**Styles**	
The Shoe-Distribution Company		Verbal Activities Within Groups (43)	II-91	T-P Leadership Questionnaire (3)	I-7
(372)	'84-55	Nonverbal Communication II (44)	II-94	Choosing a Color (12)	I-56
The People of Trion (410)	X-132	Helping Pairs (45)	II-97	Auction (35)	II-58
Dos and Don'ts (446)	'88-77	Microlab (47)	II-113	Toothpicks (121)	IV-99
		Process Intervention (48)	II-115	Styles of Leadership (154)	V-19

	Vol.-Page
Fork-Labyrinth (159)	V-53
Pins & Straws (162)	V-78
Executive Pie (195)	'77-54
Staff Meeting (207)	VI-39
Power Personalities (266)	VII-127
Managerial Characteristics (273)	'80-31
Choosing an Apartment (274)	'80-37
Power & Affiliation (277)	'80-54
Boss Wanted (296)	VIII-15
Tangram (313)	VIII-108
Manager's Dilemma (331)	'83-19
Power Caucus (346)	IX-31
Management Skills (353)	IX-93
Follow the Leader (369)	'84-38
Management Perspectives (381)	'85-45
Chipping In (382)	'85-57
Choose Me (401)	X-85
Quantity Versus Quality (433)	'87-69
Rhetoric and Behavior (478)	'91-51
The Good Leader (488)	'92-37
Organizational Structures (504)	'93-63

509. FIRST IMPRESSIONS: EXAMINING ASSUMPTIONS

Goals
- To develop the participants' awareness of the ways in which they judge people and the ways in which others might judge them.
- To help the participants to see how their judgments about people cause them to make discriminatory decisions.
- To offer the participants an opportunity to discuss the implications of their first impressions and the judgments they make.

Group Size
A minimum of ten participants to ensure a variety of different responses; a maximum of thirty participants so that everyone has a chance to participate in the discussion.

Time Required
One hour and ten minutes to one and one-half hours.

Materials
- A copy of First Impressions Form A for each participant.
- A copy of First Impressions Form B for each participant.
- A pencil and a portable writing surface for each participant.
- A newsprint flip chart and a felt-tipped marker.
- Masking tape for posting newsprint.

Physical Setting
Any room in which the participants can be seated comfortably. It is preferable, but not essential, to seat the participants in a circle so that they can see one another.

Process
1. The participants are given copies of First Impressions Form A, portable writing surfaces, and pencils and are asked to read the instructions and to complete the form accordingly. The facilitator emphasizes that they should not spend a lot of time thinking about their responses and clarifies that the forms will not be collected. (Five minutes.)

2. After everyone has completed Form A, the facilitator distributes copies of Form B and again asks the participants to read the instructions and to complete the form. Again, the participants are told that the forms will not be collected. (Five minutes.)

3. The participants are asked to look through both completed forms and to note which items they rated as "1." The facilitator writes the numbers of the instrument items on newsprint (1, 2, 3a, 3b, 3c, 3d, 4a, 4b, and so on) and asks for a show of hands indicating which items were rated as "1." (If there are very few or no "1" votes, the facilitator should complete the same process for items rated as "2.") The number of "1" responses for each item is recorded, and then the facilitator asks the following questions about a few of the items that received a large number of "1" votes:

- What is it about this characteristic/behavior that bothers you so much?
- Where/how did you learn to regard the characteristic/behavior negatively?
- How is this characteristic/behavior a valid consideration in assessing a person's qualifications for employment?
- What are some different or opposing thoughts about this characteristic/behavior? If you rated this item as "3," "4," or "5," how do you react to what people have been saying?

(Fifteen to twenty minutes.)

4. The participants are asked to look through both completed forms and note which items they rated as "5." The facilitator writes the numbers of the instrument items on a new sheet of newsprint and asks for a show of hands indicating which items were rated as "5." (If there are very few or no "5" votes, the facilitator should complete the same process for items rated as "4.") After recording the number of "5" responses for each item, the facilitator asks the following questions about a few of the items that received a large number of "5" votes:

- What is it about this characteristic/behavior that you like so much?
- Where/how did you learn to regard the characteristic/behavior positively?
- How is this characteristic/behavior a valid consideration in assessing a person's qualifications for employment?
- What are some different or opposing thoughts about this characteristic/behavior? If you rated this item as "1," "2," or "3," how do you react to what people have been saying?

(Fifteen to twenty minutes.)

5. The facilitator asks the participants to look through both forms for items on which they rated the male and the female differently, calls for a show of hands, and lists these items and their corresponding numbers of votes on

another sheet of newsprint. Then the participants are asked the following questions about each of these items:
- Why would a man and a woman be judged differently on this characteristic/behavior? Why *should* they be?
- How do the female participants feel about this difference in judgment? How do the male participants feel?

(Ten minutes.)

6. The facilitator elicits reactions to the activity and then asks questions such as these:
   - How might your responses to this activity be different from the actual judgments you make when you meet someone?
   - How do you feel knowing that someone may judge you in the same ways based on a first impression?
   - How are the judgments you made related to discrimination based on race, ethnicity, or sex? How do you feel about those judgments? What do they tell you about yourself? What do they tell you about what you expect of people in your own work environment?
   - What have you learned about the first impressions of others?
   - How do first impressions help us in our daily lives? How do they hinder us?
   - How might this experience impact you the next time you meet someone? How might you view that person differently? What might you say or do differently?

   (Twenty to thirty minutes.)

7. Before concluding the activity, the facilitator congratulates the participants on the risks that they took in participating actively.

Variations

- The items on the forms may be made more relevant to the specific group involved.
- The situation presented in the forms may be changed from a professional to a social one. Or the activity may make use of one professional situation and one social situation, with the differences examined afterward.
- The facilitator may conclude the activity with role plays of positive first impressions, based on what the participants have learned.
- The activity may be concluded with the construction of a list of "dos and don'ts" for meeting people or creating first impressions.

Submitted by Steven E. Aufrecht.

Steven E. Aufrecht, Ph.D., *is an associate professor of public administration at the University of Alaska, Anchorage. His current research involves problems of comparative research, Chinese civil-service reform, and public accountability and ethics. He is a former Peace Corps volunteer (Thailand), is a Fulbright Scholar (Hong Kong), has worked in the personnel department of the Municipality of Anchorage, and is a former National Association of Schools of Public Affairs and Administration (NASPAA) Fellow at the National Oceanic and Atmospheric Administration.*

FIRST IMPRESSIONS FORM A

Instructions: Assume that you are meeting a *male* friend of a friend for lunch. This person is looking for a job and wants to talk with you about your own place of work. Following is a list of various characteristics and behaviors. Think about the impression that your lunch companion would make on you if he displayed each of the characteristics or behaviors listed. Then rate the impression produced by each characteristic or behavior by circling the appropriate number on the 1-to-5-scale that follows, where 1 = extremely negative, 3 = neutral, and 5 = extremely positive. Indicate what *your actual response* would be, not what you think would be the politically correct response.

Characteristic or Behavior	Extremely Negative		Neutral		Extremely Positive
1. Is five minutes early	1	2	3	4	5
2. Is ten minutes late	1	2	3	4	5
3. Has an accent					
a. Brooklyn	1	2	3	4	5
b. Southern	1	2	3	4	5
c. French	1	2	3	4	5
d. Korean	1	2	3	4	5
4. Attire/Grooming					
a. latest style	1	2	3	4	5
b. shoes need polish	1	2	3	4	5
c. casual	1	2	3	4	5
d. dressy	1	2	3	4	5
e. fingernails dirty	1	2	3	4	5
f. out of style but neat	1	2	3	4	5
g. hair styled	1	2	3	4	5
h. wears a backpack	1	2	3	4	5

Characteristic or Behavior	Extremely Negative		Neutral		Extremely Positive
5. Is forty pounds overweight	1	2	3	4	5
6. Wears a "Save the Whales" button	1	2	3	4	5
7. Wears a National Rifle Association hat	1	2	3	4	5
8. Looks you in the eye while talking	1	2	3	4	5
9. Looks down while talking	1	2	3	4	5
10. Is six feet tall	1	2	3	4	5
11. Is five feet, two inches tall	1	2	3	4	5
12. Smokes	1	2	3	4	5
13. Leaves no tip	1	2	3	4	5
14. Pays for you both	1	2	3	4	5
15. Has a baby with him	1	2	3	4	5
16. Has a cocktail/wine with lunch	1	2	3	4	5
17. Has a front tooth missing	1	2	3	4	5
18. Is a picky eater	1	2	3	4	5
19. Carries a Bible	1	2	3	4	5
20. Makes a few off-color remarks during lunch	1	2	3	4	5

FIRST IMPRESSIONS FORM B

Instructions: Assume that you are meeting a *female* friend of a friend for lunch. This person is looking for a job and wants to talk with you about your own place of work. Following is a list of various characteristics and behaviors. Think about the impression that your lunch companion would make on you if she displayed each of the characteristics or behaviors listed. Then rate the impression produced by each characteristic or behavior by circling the appropriate number on the 1-to-5-scale that follows, where 1 = extremely negative, 3 = neutral, and 5 = extremely positive. Indicate what *your actual response* would be, not what you think would be the politically correct response.

Characteristic or Behavior	Extremely Negative		Neutral		Extremely Positive
1. Is five minutes early	1	2	3	4	5
2. Is ten minutes late	1	2	3	4	5
3. Has an accent					
a. Brooklyn	1	2	3	4	5
b. Southern	1	2	3	4	5
c. French	1	2	3	4	5
d. Korean	1	2	3	4	5
4. Attire/Grooming					
a. latest style	1	2	3	4	5
b. shoes need polish	1	2	3	4	5
c. casual	1	2	3	4	5
d. dressy	1	2	3	4	5
e. fingernails dirty	1	2	3	4	5
f. out of style but neat	1	2	3	4	5
g. hair styled	1	2	3	4	5
h. wears a backpack	1	2	3	4	5

Characteristic or Behavior	Extremely Negative		Neutral		Extremely Positive
5. Is forty pounds overweight	1	2	3	4	5
6. Wears a "Save the Whales" button	1	2	3	4	5
7. Wears a National Rifle Association hat	1	2	3	4	5
8. Looks you in the eye while talking	1	2	3	4	5
9. Looks down while talking	1	2	3	4	5
10. Is six feet tall	1	2	3	4	5
11. Is five feet, two inches tall	1	2	3	4	5
12. Smokes	1	2	3	4	5
13. Leaves no tip	1	2	3	4	5
14. Pays for you both	1	2	3	4	5
15. Has a baby with her	1	2	3	4	5
16. Has a cocktail/wine with lunch	1	2	3	4	5
17. Has a front tooth missing	1	2	3	4	5
18. Is a picky eater	1	2	3	4	5
19. Carries a Bible	1	2	3	4	5
20. Makes a few off-color remarks during lunch	1	2	3	4	5

510. PAROLE BOARD: EXPLORING INDIVIDUAL AND GROUP VALUES

Goals

- To provide participants with an opportunity to explore their values concerning characteristics of individuals.
- To explore how individual values affect individual and group decisions.
- To explore the impact of group values on decision making.

Group Size

Twelve to twenty-four participants (three subgroups of three to six members each, plus one or two additional participants per subgroup who serve as observers).

Time Required

One hour and forty-five minutes to two hours.

Materials

- A copy of the Parole Board Candidates Sheet for each participant.
- A copy of the Parole Board C Background Sheet for each member and each observer of Parole Board C.
- A copy of the Parole Board L Background Sheet for each member and each observer of Parole Board L.
- A copy of the Parole Board M Background Sheet for each member and each observer of Parole Board M.
- A copy of the Parole Board Observer Sheet for each observer.
- A pencil for each observer.
- A clipboard or other portable writing surface for each observer.
- A newsprint flip chart and a felt-tipped marker.
- Masking tape for posting newsprint.

Physical Setting

A room with movable chairs and sufficient space to accommodate the meetings of the three subgroups without any subgroup's disturbing the others. It is preferable to have a large room for the total group and three separate rooms in which the subgroups can meet.

Process

1. The participants are requested to form two subgroups, based on whether they typically consider themselves to be "liberal" or "conservative." They are asked to make this decision quickly and not to spend too much time worrying about labels. The facilitator then forms *three* subgroups of approximately equal size, one of "conservative" members, one of "liberal" members, and the last of a mixture of liberal and conservative (or those who could not decide). In the case of a group in which nearly all participants label themselves the same way, the facilitator may ask some members to role play a different tendency. Depending on the total number of participants, one or two members of each subgroup may be designated as observers. (Five minutes.)

2. Each subgroup is told that it is an official board of inquiry for a correctional facility. The subgroup is serving as a "parole board" to determine which prisoners should be let out of the facility early, before serving their full terms of imprisonment. Participants are encouraged to enter into the spirit of the activity (especially if they are in a subgroup that does not reflect their real tendencies) and not question the factual validity of the information provided. Each participant is given a copy of the Parole Board Candidates Sheet. In addition, each member and observer of the liberal subgroup receives a copy of the Parole Board L Background Sheet, each member and observer of the conservative subgroup receives a copy of the Parole Board C Background Sheet, and each member and observer of the "mixed" subgroup receives a copy of the Parole Board M Background Sheet. In addition, each observer is given a copy of the observer sheet, a pencil, and a clipboard or other portable writing surface. Time is allowed for the participants to read the sheets. (Fifteen minutes.)

3. The facilitator announces that it is time for the parole boards to meet and directs each one to a separate area of the room (or to a separate meeting room). The subgroup members are told that they will have forty-five minutes in which to determine their individual choices and to discuss the candidates with the other subgroup members and reach consensus on which ones will be granted parole. Observers are instructed to record observations on their copies of the observer sheet. The subgroups are told to return to the primary meeting space at the end of the allotted time. (Five minutes.)

4. The subgroups conduct their meetings simultaneously. After ten minutes, the facilitator suggests that the participants conclude their individual decision making and move on to the consensus phase of the activity. He or

she also notifies the participants when they have ten minutes left, when they have five minutes left, and then calls time. (Forty-five minutes.)

5. When the total group has reconvened, each "parole board" is asked to announce its decisions: the names of the three candidates that it nominated for parole and any special conditions of parole for each of the three. The facilitator writes each subgroup's decisions on newsprint. (Ten to fifteen minutes.)

6. The facilitator asks the participants to try to step out of their advocacy positions and to try to put their focus on what happens in a group when its members must reach consensus on a serious issue. The facilitator then initiates a discussion of the activity, keeping the focus on learning themes generated by the activity, not on the "rightness" or "wrongness" of any subgroup's decisions. After the participants respond to each of the following questions, observers are asked to report their recorded observations.

   - How did you feel about the responsibility of determining the fate of the six candidates? If some members felt differently from others, why do you think this happened?
   - What values seemed to be operating within each subgroup? How did the subgroup's values differ from one another?
   - What processes did you use in your subgroups to guide your discussions and reach your conclusions? How did these processes typify the values each subgroup represented?
   - How did the fact that subgroup members' values were similar or different affect the decision-making process?
   - Did any one subgroup fail to nominate three candidates for parole? If so, what happened during that subgroup's deliberations that prevented a decision?

   (Fifteen to twenty minutes.)

7. The facilitator leads a concluding discussion based on these questions:
   - What did you learn from this experience about how personal values affect individual and group decision making?
   - How can these learnings be applied to future decision-making situations, both individual and group?

   (Five to ten minutes.)

Variations

- Three subgroups can be formed, with each being given the task of designing a new correctional facility (prison). Each subgroup is to generate a description of the physical facility, staffing needs, equipment needs, and a list of training programs for employees. On the role sheets, one of the subgroups is designated "liberal," one "conservative," and one "mixed," but the subgroups are not told that they have been given different orientations. The results of each subgroup's planning session are depicted on newsprint and posted, so that differences in design, staffing, equipment, and training are apparent. Processing includes the differences in the results, how the subgroup's orientation affected its process and its results, each subgroup's significant issues, and learnings and applications.

- The activity in the previous variation can be amended as follows: At the beginning of the activity, the facilitator verbally and graphically presents a model of organizational subsystems (for example, Jones' "Organizational-Universe Model").[1] Time is allowed for questions and clarification. (The first learning goal then becomes "To present a model of organizations and their subsystems.") The subgroup's tasks include descriptions of organizational structure, unit tasks, authority, work flow, and special rules and regulations.

- With smaller groups, just the liberal and conservative designations can be used to highlight potential contrasts.

Submitted by Arlette C. Ballew, based on variations submitted by Charles A. Beitz, Jr.

Arlette C. Ballew *is a developmental senior editor at Pfeiffer & Company in San Diego, California. She is co-author of* University Associates Training Technologies *and associate editor of* Theories and Models in Applied Behavioral Science. *Ms. Ballew specializes in developing, writing, and editing HRD materials for professional consultants and trainers.*

Charles A. Beitz, Jr., D.P.A., *is chairperson of the Department of Business and Economics at Mount Saint Mary's College. He teaches in both the graduate and undergraduate business programs. Dr. Beitz is also the senior associate in Life and Career Transitions Associates, based in Carlisle, Pennsylvania. He has extensive experience in designing and facilitating in-house education series for private- and public-sector executives and senior managers, focusing on the areas of life and career transitions, executive self-assessment skills, and leadership.*

---

[1] See *Theories and Models in Applied Behavioral Science* (Vol. 4: Organizational) by J.W. Pfeiffer and A.C. Ballew (Eds.), 1991, San Diego, CA: Pfeiffer & Company.

PAROLE BOARD C BACKGROUND SHEET

In this location, people who have been convicted of serious crimes typically are sent to a correctional facility (prison) for periods of time ranging from five years to life. However, not all prisoners remain imprisoned for the full length of their terms; some, whose conduct while imprisoned has been good and who are believed to be capable of being rehabilitated, are released early or "paroled."

A paroled person must meet certain conditions in order to remain at liberty outside the correctional facility. These conditions relate to conduct, use of addictive substances, employment, housing, area in which the person may travel, and so on. In addition, a person who is "on parole" must report once each month to a "parole officer," who monitors the person's conduct, employment, housing, associates, and so on. If the parole officer determines that the person has exceeded the conditions of his or her parole, that person is apprehended and returned to a correctional facility.

You are a member of a parole board, a group that meets at regular intervals of time to determine which, if any, of the prisoners who have been incarcerated long enough to be eligible for parole will, in fact, be released before completing their full terms of imprisonment.

Obviously, you do not want to recommend anyone for parole who may engage in criminal behavior or in any way be a menace to society when he or she is released. Also, you do not want to increase the strain on the already-overloaded parole officers by assigning people to them who are apt to violate their conditions of parole.

On the other hand, the correctional facilities all over the country are overfilled, and the parole system is a way of releasing the prisoners who may be able to lead normal, productive lives while keeping the more dangerous ones "locked up."

Six prisoners currently are eligible—and have been recommended by the prison authorities—for possible parole. Your task is to nominate three candidates for parole; then your subgroup must reach consensus on *which three* of these six candidates will be released on parole. You may nominate only three people.

Keep the following guidelines in mind as you try to reach consensus:

1. Avoid arguing for your individual judgments. Approach the task on the basis of logic.

2. Avoid changing your mind simply to reach agreement and to avoid conflict, but support solutions with which you are able to agree to some extent.

3. Avoid "conflict-reducing" techniques such as majority vote, averaging, or trading in reaching your decision.

4. View differences of opinion as a help rather than a hindrance in decision making.

The parole board on which you serve is "conservative."
You will have forty-five minutes to complete these tasks.

PAROLE BOARD L BACKGROUND SHEET

In this location, people who have been convicted of serious crimes typically are sent to a correctional facility (prison) for periods of time ranging from five years to life. However, not all prisoners remain imprisoned for the full length of their terms; some, whose conduct while imprisoned has been good and who are believed to be capable of being rehabilitated, are released early, or "paroled."

A paroled person must meet certain conditions in order to remain at liberty outside the correctional facility. These conditions relate to conduct, use of addictive substances, employment, housing, area in which the person may travel, and so on. In addition, a person who is "on parole" must report once each month to a "parole officer," who monitors the person's conduct, employment, housing, associates, and so on. If the parole officer determines that the person has exceeded the conditions of his or her parole, that person is apprehended and returned to a correctional facility.

You are a member of a parole board, a group that meets at regular intervals of time to determine which, if any, of the prisoners who have been incarcerated long enough to be eligible for parole will, in fact, be released before completing their full terms of imprisonment.

Obviously, you do not want to recommend anyone for parole who may engage in criminal behavior or in any way be a menace to society when he or she is released. Also, you do not want to increase the strain on the already-overloaded parole officers by assigning people to them who are apt to violate their conditions of parole.

On the other hand, the correctional facilities all over the country are overfilled, and the parole system is a way of releasing the prisoners who may be able to lead normal, productive lives while keeping the more dangerous ones "locked up."

Six prisoners currently are eligible—and have been recommended by the prison authorities—for possible parole. Your task is to nominate three candidates for parole; then your subgroup must reach consensus on *which three* of these six candidates will be released on parole. You may nominate only three people.

Keep the following guidelines in mind as you try to reach consensus:

1. Avoid arguing for your individual judgments. Approach the task on the basis of logic.

2. Avoid changing your mind simply to reach agreement and to avoid conflict, but support solutions with which you are able to agree to some extent.

3. Avoid "conflict-reducing" techniques such as majority vote, averaging, or trading in reaching your decision.

4. View differences of opinion as a help rather than a hindrance in decision making.

The parole board on which you serve is "liberal."
You will have forty-five minutes to complete these tasks.

PAROLE BOARD M BACKGROUND SHEET

In this location, people who have been convicted of serious crimes typically are sent to a correctional facility (prison) for periods of time ranging from five years to life. However, not all prisoners remain imprisoned for the full length of their terms; some, whose conduct while imprisoned has been good and who are believed to be capable of being rehabilitated, are released early, or "paroled."

A paroled person must meet certain conditions in order to remain at liberty outside the correctional facility. These conditions relate to conduct, use of addictive substances, employment, housing, area in which the person may travel, and so on. In addition, a person who is "on parole" must report once each month to a "parole officer," who monitors the person's conduct, employment, housing, associates, and so on. If the parole officer determines that the person has exceeded the conditions of his or her parole, that person is apprehended and returned to a correctional facility.

You are a member of a parole board, a group that meets at regular intervals of time to determine which, if any, of the prisoners who have been incarcerated long enough to be eligible for parole will, in fact, be released before completing their full terms of imprisonment.

Obviously, you do not want to recommend anyone for parole who may engage in criminal behavior or in any way be a menace to society when he or she is released. Also, you do not want to increase the strain on the already-overloaded parole officers by assigning people to them who are apt to violate their conditions of parole.

On the other hand, the correctional facilities all over the country are overfilled, and the parole system is a way of releasing the prisoners who may be able to lead normal, productive lives while keeping the more dangerous ones "locked up."

Six prisoners currently are eligible—and have been recommended by the prison authorities—for possible parole. Your task is to nominate three candidates for parole; then your subgroup must reach consensus on *which three* of these six candidates will be released on parole. You may nominate only three people.

Keep the following guidelines in mind as you try to reach consensus:

1. Avoid arguing for your individual judgments. Approach the task on the basis of logic.

2. Avoid changing your mind simply to reach agreement and to avoid conflict, but support solutions with which you are able to agree to some extent.

3. Avoid "conflict-reducing" techniques such as majority vote, averaging, or trading in reaching your decision.

4. View differences of opinion as a help rather than a hindrance in decision making.

The parole board on which you serve contains some members who regard themselves as liberal, some who tend to be conservative, and some whom you have not been able to label.

You will have forty-five minutes to complete these tasks.

PAROLE BOARD CANDIDATES SHEET

The following prisoners have served the required amount of time and have met the prison criteria to be eligible for parole. The task of your group is to approve *three* of the candidates for parole and specify any special conditions of parole for each of the three selected. It is suggested that you read the following descriptions individually, make your own individual choices, and then discuss the issues in your subgroup.

Candidates

James Johnson, age 28. Johnson was convicted on two counts of armed robbery. On both occasions, he entered a small food store and forced the cashier (at gunpoint) to give him money from the cash register. He did not fire the gun on either occasion. He has served ten years of a fifteen-year prison term.

Johnson was eighteen years old at the time he committed both offenses. He comes from a poor, lower-class family that was abandoned by the father. He dropped out of high school at the age of sixteen. Although he did not join an organized street gang, he kept company with several gang members as well as with other high school dropouts (several of whom had been convicted of misdemeanors).

Johnson was surly and uncommunicative for the first three years of his prison term. Then he began to work in the prison library and, with the encouragement of the librarian, joined a program to learn how to read. He began to show an interest in reading and learning and, in his fifth year in prison, passed an examination that qualified him for a high school equivalency degree. Since that time, he has continued his education, with the guidance of the prison counselors. He hopes to enroll in a community college, to work part-time, to receive a degree, and to pursue a career as a medical technician.

Johnson blames his previous conduct on his family background and lack of role model. He says that he now has developed better values and has realistic goals and a sense of direction, which were lacking in his youth.

Norman Jennings, age 40. Jennings is an accountant who was convicted of embezzling $10,000 from his employer. He has served three years of a five-year sentence.

Jennings is from a middle-class background. He received a college degree in accounting. At the time of his offense, he was thirty-seven years old, a bachelor who lived alone. He was described by his associates as "quiet," "shy," and "not very sociable." Six months prior to the discovery of his embezzlement, he met a thirty-year-old woman in a restaurant near his home. They began to see each other regularly, and Jennings believed that he was "in love" for the first time.

At his trial, Jennings said that the woman asked him to steal the money to provide "for their life together." Unfortunately, she left town soon after his arrest, so could not be questioned about her part in the affair. The fact that the police were unable to locate her, although it is known that she was seen and in good health just after Jennings was arrested, led his attorney to depict Jennings as an unsophisticated "puppet" of an experienced, scheming woman.

Jennings says that he has learned his lesson. While in prison, he studied advanced accounting and kept informed of new accounting procedures. He expects to be able to pass the examination to become a certified public accountant when he is released. He believes that his chances of employment are good, once he has had an opportunity to explain himself.

Frederick Upjohn, Jr., age 38. Upjohn was convicted of selling cocaine and has served ten years of a fifteen-year sentence.

The only son of a wealthy entrepreneur, Upjohn holds a university degree in music education. Following his graduation, he became a member of a rock-music band, which made several successful recordings and became quite popular. Upjohn received critical acclaim for his talent and had many fans. During seven years of touring worldwide with the band, Upjohn experimented with drugs and eventually became addicted to cocaine. He was arrested for selling cocaine to an undercover agent who was posing as a recording-studio technician. He was twenty-eight years old at the time.

While Upjohn was incarcerated, his father passed away, leaving him with a substantial private income.

Upjohn says that now that he is drug free, he has no intention of becoming involved with drugs again. He intends to resume his career as a musician.

Lucille DuBois, age 38. DuBois was convicted of soliciting for prostitution, which is a felony in this location. This is her second conviction. She previously served a full, five-year prison term as the result of a similar conviction. She has served five years of an eight-year term for the most recent offense.

DuBois is from an upper-middle-class family. When she was eight years old, her father (a successful professional man) was convicted of sexually abusing her and sent to prison. The mother subsequently suffered a series of nervous breakdowns; when the mother was unable to care for them, DuBois and her brother were taken in by a series of aunts and uncles. DuBois ran away from home at the age of sixteen and apparently drifted into prostitution as the only way she could find to support herself. From the age of twenty-one to the time of her first conviction (at age twenty-four), she often worked as a waitress, returning to prostitution when she was out of work.

A relative who owns a successful restaurant has offered DuBois a job as a waitress on her release from prison. If she is paroled, she plans to accept this offer. She says that she is "too old" to return to her former life, and believes that she can work her way up in the family business.

Emilia Cumo, age 55. Cumo has served twenty years of a thirty-year sentence for manslaughter. She was convicted of administering an overdose of medication to her mother.

At the time of her conviction, Cumo was thirty-five years old and unmarried. She had lived with her widowed mother for her entire life. Her mother, who was sixty-nine years old at the time of her death, had suffered from Alzheimer's Disease for the previous six years.

At Cumo's trial, the prosecution portrayed her as a scheming woman who had tired of the responsibility of caring for her parent and who wished to live without responsibility on her mother's money.

The defense maintained that Cumo's mother had previously begged her to "help her to die" if and when she became so incapacitated that she would be an embarrassment to herself. In the last eighteen months of her life, the mother's condition had deteriorated so that she did not know who or where she was, did not recognize anyone, and was frequently confused and distraught. The defense pointed out that although Cumo had agreed to her mother's request to ease the mother's mind, she had not acted on her promise for a year and a half while she agonized over the moral consequences of taking a human life versus not keeping her promise and allowing her mother to suffer.

Cumo's brother and sister, both married, are divided in their view of her actions. The brother calls Cumo a "cold-blooded murderess." The sister supports Cumo, maintaining that their mother's life was a "living hell." She has invited Cumo to live with her family if Cumo is released on parole.

Jacob Knowles, age 46. Knowles has served eleven years of a twenty-year sentence for vehicular manslaughter. He was convicted of killing a twelve-year-old girl while driving under the influence of alcohol.

Prior to his conviction, Knowles had been cited repeatedly for driving while drunk, and his license had been suspended. When he was arrested at the scene of the girl's death, he had been driving without a license or insurance coverage.

Knowles had been employed as a sales manager for a nationwide building-parts firm but had lost his job six months prior to his conviction for showing up at work while drunk.

While in prison, Knowles entered an Alcoholics Anonymous group. He is a vehement spokesperson for the benefits of such programs in helping addicted people to recover. He says that prison "saved my life even though it was too late to save the little girl's."

If released on parole, Knowles hopes to find a job as a counselor in a program for alcohol and drug abusers.

PAROLE BOARD OBSERVER SHEET

Instructions: Use the following questions to guide your observations of the interactions within your subgroup, writing answers in the spaces provided. You will be asked to share these observations as part of the concluding discussions.

1. What discussion took place regarding the subgroup's responsibilities? What individual differences were evident in terms of accepting these responsibilities?

2. What values were articulated within the subgroup? (Focus on values that might be labeled "liberal" or "conservative.")

3. How did the subgroup reach its conclusions? Did the processes reflect the values that the subgroup members were espousing?

4. How did similarities or differences in individual values affect the discussion and the decisions?

5. Did your subgroup complete the task? If not, what behaviors prevented completion?

511. LET ME: INTRODUCING EXPERIENTIAL LEARNING

Goals
- To acquaint the participants with the concept of experiential learning.
- To demonstrate the positive effects of learning by doing.

Group Size
As many as fifteen participants of a newly formed training group.

Time Required
Thirty to thirty-five minutes, plus prework for the facilitator (learning the American Sign Language on the Let Me Illustration Sheet).

Materials
- One copy of the Let Me Instruction Sheet (for the facilitator's use).
- One copy of the Let Me Illustration Sheet (for the facilitator's use).
- A newsprint flip chart and a felt-tipped marker.

Physical Setting
A room with chairs positioned so that the participants can see one another, the facilitator, and the newsprint flip chart. Plenty of space should be left between chairs so that the participants can practice American Sign Language without interfering with one another's movement.

Process
1. The facilitator explains the goals of the activity and makes comments such as the following:

    "Many different methods are used to teach. All of us are familiar with the lecture method, in which the instructor conveys information while the students passively absorb. In another method the instructor demonstrates a particular skill or concept, and again the students passively absorb. Still another method—one that has been used successfully with adult learners for many years now—is known as experiential learning, or *learning by doing*. An old saying, attributed to Confucius, illustrates the impact of experiential learning as opposed to learning by other methods: '*Tell me* and I forget. *Show me* and I remember. But *let me* and I understand.'"

As the facilitator quotes the Confucius saying, he or she writes it on newsprint and then continues:

"Obviously, experiential learning is dependent on some previous input in the form of information or instructions; for example, the student may read a book, listen to a lecture, or watch an instructor's demonstration. But the critical part of the learning occurs after the input has taken place, once the student tries to complete a related task—to learn by doing."

2. The facilitator informs the participants that they are going to be offered proof of the Confucius saying by learning that saying in American Sign Language: First they will learn by being told, then by being shown, then by doing.

3. The participants are told that they may only listen for the first phase of the activity; they may not practice using the American Sign Language on their own. Then the facilitator reads the Let Me Instruction Sheet to the participants.

4. The facilitator chooses a volunteer or recruits a participant to demonstrate how well he or she has learned by attempting to sign the saying.

5. The participants are informed that now they will see the signs, but again they will not be allowed to practice. Then, using the content of the Let Me Illustration Sheet, the facilitator signs the entire saying before the total group, saying the words while signing them.

6. The facilitator chooses a new volunteer or recruit to demonstrate how well he or she has learned by attempting to sign the saying. (This participant probably will do better than the first.)

7. The participants are told that now they will be shown the correct signs and will be permitted to practice while the facilitator demonstrates. The facilitator demonstrates each sign in the sequence and assists the participants in producing each sign correctly. The participants continue practicing, with the facilitator leading, until the entire group is able to perform each sign correctly in sequence.

8. The facilitator chooses a new volunteer or recruit to demonstrate how well he or she has learned by attempting to sign the saying. (It is likely that this participant will do the signing perfectly.)

9. The facilitator leads a discussion by asking questions such as the following:

- What was your reaction to having the signs read to you and trying to learn them? What was your reaction to having them demonstrated for you and trying to learn them?
- How many wanted to try to produce the signs when you were instructed not to do so in the first two steps?
- What was your reaction to trying the signing for yourself?

- What does this activity suggest about the efficacy of learning by hearing? By seeing? By doing? What similar experiences in these types of learning come to mind?
- How will you apply what you have learned to your work or home life?

Variations

- After step 7 subgroups may be formed. Each subgroup is then given the task of practicing until it can do the signing correctly as a team.
- This activity may be used as an introduction to a communication-skills experience to demonstrate how words can be misinterpreted.
- Instead of the facilitator's lecturing and demonstrating, the participants may be given copies of the instruction sheet and the illustration sheet to review for five minutes each. A participant volunteer or recruit is still chosen to perform at the end of each step.
- The facilitator may form two subgroups. One subgroup is given the instruction sheet and the illustration sheet and is not allowed to practice. The other subgroup is given both sheets and is allowed to practice. Subsequently, results in performance are compared. This variation would be good for a focus on self-directed learning in addition to experiential learning.
- The facilitator may make copies of the instruction sheet and the illustration sheet and distribute them at the conclusion of the activity.

Submitted by J. Allan Tyler.

J. Allan Tyler is the director of training and services for WAVE, Inc. (Work, Achievement, Values and Education), a national youth-service organization that provides training and technical assistance to schools and community-based organizations. He is also the president of Jayden Enterprises, a human resource consulting group based in Alexandria, Virginia. He delivers workshops on communication, training trainers, creative problem solving, team building, and managing the multicultural work force.

LET ME INSTRUCTION SHEET

1. TELL: Put your right index finger to your chin. Then move your finger away from your chin, leaving your finger pointed upward.
2. ME: Use your right index finger to point to your chest.
3. AND: Place your right hand, with the fingers open and the palm facing you, in front of the left side of your chest. Draw that hand from the left side of your chest to the right, bringing your fingertips and thumb together.
4. I: With your right hand, make a fist and extend your little finger. Tap your chest with that fist, keeping the side with the little finger away from your body.
5. FORGET: Using your open right palm, wipe your forehead from left to right. End with a hitchhiker's sign close to your right temple.
6. SHOW: Extend your left hand with the palm facing outward. Point to the palm with your right index finger and push both hands a few inches away from your body.
7. ME: Use your right index finger to point to your chest.
8. AND: Place your right hand, with the fingers open and the palm facing you, in front of the left side of your chest. Draw that hand from the left side of your chest to the right, bringing your fingertips and thumb together.
9. I: With your right hand, make a fist and extend your little finger. Tap your chest with that fist, keeping the side with the little finger away from your body.
10. REMEMBER: Make two fists with the thumbs exposed. Touch your right thumb to your forehead and hold your left fist at chest height. Bring the two fists together in front of you and touch your right thumb to your left thumbnail.
11. BUT: Make two fists but extend your index fingers. Quickly cross your index fingers; then move them apart a few inches.
12. LET: Extend both of your hands, held flat, with the palms facing each other. Then raise your hands together, keeping your elbows tight to your body, until your hands are at chest height with your fingers pointed slightly outward.
13. ME: Use your right index finger to point to your chest.
14. AND: Place your right hand, with the fingers open and the palm facing you, in front of the left side of your chest. Draw that hand from the left side of your chest to the right, bringing your fingertips and thumb together.

15. I: With your right hand, make a fist and extend your little finger. Tap your chest with that fist, keeping the side with the little finger away from your body.
16. UNDERSTAND: Make a fist with your right hand. Then bring your fist in front of your forehead and flick your index finger upward.

LET ME ILLUSTRATION SHEET

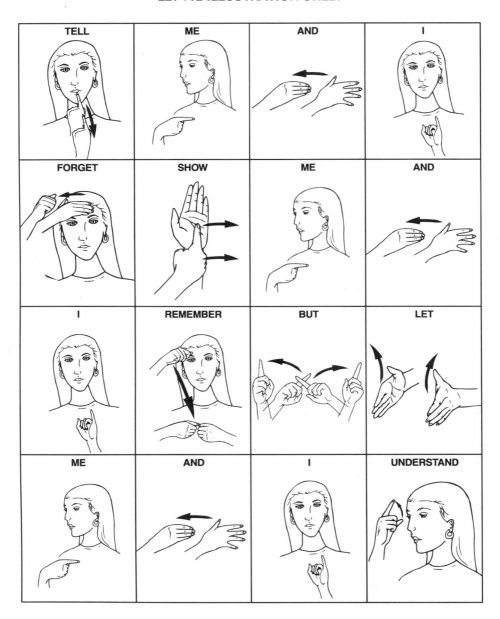

512. ALPHA/BETA: EXPLORING CULTURAL DIVERSITY IN WORK TEAMS

Goals
- To develop the participants' understanding of the complexities of working in culturally diverse work teams.
- To provide the participants with an opportunity to understand how culturally diverse work teams operate in a simulated environment.
- To encourage the participants to explore the problems and the possibilities that exist in culturally diverse work teams.

Group Size
Thirty-five participants (seven teams, each of which has four role players and one observer). If there are more than thirty-five participants, the extra participants may be assigned as extra observers.

Time Required
Approximately two hours.

Materials
- A copy of the Alpha/Beta Work-Team Configuration for each participant.
- Twenty copies of the Alpha/Beta Culture Sheet for Alphas (enough for the thirteen participants who play Alphas plus one for each of seven observers). If there are more than seven observers, extra copies must be available for the additional observers.
- Twenty-two copies of the Alpha/Beta Culture Sheet for Betas (enough for the fifteen participants who play Betas plus one for each of seven observers). If there are more than seven observers, extra copies must be available for the additional observers.
- A copy of the Alpha/Beta Observer sheet for each observer.
- A pencil for each observer.
- A clipboard or other portable writing surface for each observer.
- Fourteen magazines (two per team).
- Fourteen pairs of scissors (two pairs per team).
- A large supply of blank $8\frac{1}{2}$" x 11" paper (enough so that each team can have approximately thirty sheets, if necessary).

- Glue, paste, and/or tape for each team.
- At least thirty-six name tags:
  - Four name tags labeled "Alpha Leader";
  - Nine name tags labeled "Alpha Worker";
  - Three name tags labeled "Beta Leader";
  - Twelve name tags labeled "Beta Worker";
  - Seven name tags labeled "Observer" (or more, if there are more than seven observers); and
  - One name tag labeled "President (Alpha)" (for the facilitator's use).
- A sign for each of the work stations, posted prominently on the wall by each station or on the table at that station. The signs read "Work Station 1," "Work Station 2," "Work Station 3," and so on up to "Work Station 7."

Physical Setting

A large room in which the teams can work without disturbing one another. A separate work station, consisting of table and chairs, should be provided for each of the seven teams. In addition, a separate room or area should be provided where the Betas can meet (see step 5).

Process

1. The facilitator makes the following introductory remarks:

   "The activity that you are about to participate in is intended to provide you with an opportunity to understand how culturally diverse work teams operate in a simulated environment. The two cultures involved, the Alphas and the Betas, interact on work teams. The activity will simulate two work assignments.

   "Alpha and Beta are fictitious representations that may have incidental likenesses to real cultures. By participating in fictitious cultures rather than real ones, you should be able to break away from your preconceived notions of 'correct behavior' more fully. The simulation is meant to be fun. As with any learning experience, however, the more effort you put forth and the more closely you follow the instructions, the more you and those around you are likely to learn from the experience.

   "Please listen carefully to all instructions as we move along. You will be told everything you need to know at the appropriate time."

2. The facilitator distributes copies of the Alpha/Beta Work-Team Configuration and explains this handout:

   "Please look at the work-team configuration. We will number off in just a moment. When the simulation begins, I will be serving as president of the organization in which the Alphas and Betas work.

"As you can see, aside from the role of the president, the organization consists of seven work teams of four members each. Each team has a designated *leader,* whose job is to coordinate the team's activities and keep the team headed in the right direction. The other members of the team are simply referred to as *workers.* Also, each team will have at least one person who does not participate but observes its activities.

"This chart indicates which team you will be on; whether you will be a leader, a worker, or an observer; and, if you are a leader or a worker, whether you will be an Alpha or a Beta. The circled numbers represent the Beta culture, while the numbers that are not circled indicate the dominant Alpha culture. You will be provided the specifics of your particular culture in a few moments."

3. The facilitator asks the participants to number off and to remember their numbers. Each participant calls out his or her number in succession up to number thirty-five. (If there are more than thirty-five participants, the facilitator assigns those above number thirty-five to be extra observers.)

4. The facilitator continues the explanation of the activity, noting the location of each work station. Then the facilitator makes these comments:

"Soon you will receive some materials, including a handout describing your culture. When I signal for you to split into the two cultures, the Alphas will stay in this room and the Betas will assemble in a separate area. After you have read and studied your handout and talked briefly among yourselves about your culture and how you can represent your culture's behavior in your team, you will be asked to go to your appropriate work stations."

5. The Alphas are given copies of the culture sheet for Alphas and Alpha name tags (for the leader and the workers), and the Betas are given copies of the culture sheet for Betas and Beta name tags (for the leader and the workers). The observers are given copies of both culture sheets, copies of the observer sheet, pencils, clipboards or other portable writing surfaces, and observer name tags. All participants are instructed to put on their name tags and to wear them for the duration of the activity. After showing the Betas where to meet, the facilitator asks the two groups to meet separately and to read, study, and discuss their culture sheets and how they will role play behavior until further notice. In addition to the culture sheets, the observers are told to read their observer sheets but not to discuss the contents with anyone. (Fifteen minutes.)

6. The Betas are called back to the main assembly room. The facilitator asks the participants to go to their work stations, puts on his or her name tag labeled "President (Alpha)," announces the beginning of the simulation, and then makes these comments:

"Welcome, all of you Alphas and Betas! I hope you'll enjoy your first work assignment. Before I tell you about the assignment, though, I'd like to make some brief comments about the kind of environment we want to promote around here. Some of you are Alphas, like me, and others of you are Betas. Although the Alphas and Betas come from different backgrounds, I'm sure we can still find a way to work together productively.

"In the past some of the Betas have accused our staff of not being caring enough. So, even though it may seem strange to you Alphas, I want all team leaders to go out of their way to give workers a pat on the back when they're working well. Just literally come up behind them and give them a good, old-fashioned pat on the back! I'm sure that will motivate them to work harder.

"Now here's some information about your first work assignment. In your teams you are to cut out letters of the alphabet from magazines and secure them, in their A-to-Z order, to a sheet of paper. Then begin another sheet in the same way. Complete as many sheets of the alphabet as you can.

"You will get your supplies from me. Once you have your supplies, start working."

The facilitator distributes the magazines; the pairs of scissors; the blank paper; and the glue, paste, and/or tape. Then the participants are told to begin.

7. After the participants have worked for approximately ten minutes, the facilitator asks them to stop and to listen to the second assignment:

"Thanks for all of your hard work on the first assignment. Now, for your second assignment, I'd like you to cut out pictures of people's heads and place them on sheets of paper, with three heads on each sheet.

"This assignment represents a large contract that could make or break our company's survival in the coming months, so it's extremely important that every team do its best work. Start now."

8. After the participants have worked for ten minutes, the facilitator breaks in with an announcement:

"I regret to inform you that the market has taken a significant, downward shift. Every team leader must now lay off one person from the team. The company can only survive if we get rid of the deadwood. After laying off one member, return to your assignment and strive for higher productivity."

9. After ensuring that every team has laid off one member, the facilitator monitors the team activities for another ten minutes.

10. At the end of the ten-minute period, the facilitator asks the participants to stop their work and to come out of their roles as leaders and workers to discuss the experience.

11. The facilitator asks one person who role played an Alpha and one person who role played a Beta to read the contents of their respective culture sheets to the total group. Then the facilitator asks the observers to take turns sharing the contents of their observer sheets, making sure that each ob-

server clarifies whether he or she observed an all-Alpha, an all-Beta, or a mixed team. (Twenty minutes.)

12. The facilitator leads a debriefing based on the following questions:
    - How did you react to playing your cultural role? How did you react to interacting with people who played a different cultural role?
    - What real-life experiences have you had that you can relate this experience to? When have you faced communication difficulties because of cultural differences?
    - What have you learned about cultural diversity in work teams? What would you have done differently if you could?
    - What practical insights from this activity will you apply to real-life interactions with people from different cultures?

Variations

- The facilitator may create a shortage of materials so that the teams must negotiate for supplies.
- Rather than having leaders, the facilitator may stipulate that all four participants on each work team are of equal status.
- To simplify the simulation, the facilitator may omit certain portions of the culture sheets.
- After step 12 the participants may be asked to return to their teams to practice what they would have done differently. The facilitator may instruct them to do their best to understand the other culture before proceeding to work.

Submitted by Steven R. Phillips.

Steven R. Phillips, Ph.D., received his doctorate in organizational communication from the University of Southern California in 1989. Since that time he has taught organizational communication at the University of Montana and has received several awards for outstanding teaching, including the university's 1992 award for "Most Inspirational Teacher." In addition to fulfilling his teaching responsibilities, he has conducted numerous workshops and facilitated a variety of groups. He is currently co-principal investigator on a grant from the U.S. Department of Education to provide communication-skills training for professionals and parents who work with children with disabilities.

ALPHA/BETA WORK-TEAM CONFIGURATION

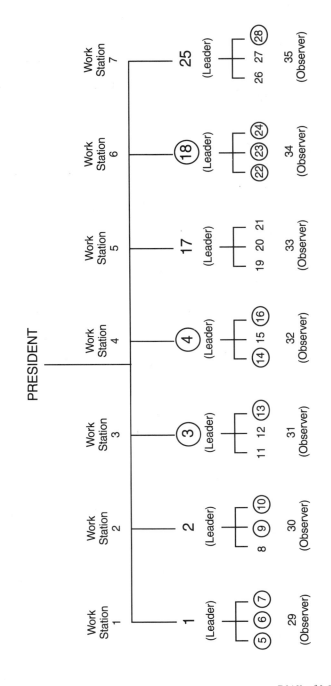

ALPHA/BETA CULTURE SHEET FOR ALPHAS

Instructions: The following is a list of behavioral characteristics of your culture. During the work simulation, be certain that you exhibit these characteristics. If you are a leader, it is even more important that you serve as a model of the cultural behaviors.

1. You are assertive, proud, loud-mouthed, and free-spirited. You love to work hard and play hard.

2. You strive for productivity and quickness, and you concentrate on quantity—not quality!

3. Although you do not like to touch or be touched, you know that Betas love touching. Consequently, you are willing to touch them—briefly—in the belief that they *may* work faster as a result.

4. You demand eye contact from others at all times, especially from your coworkers. Failure to make eye contact shows disrespect.

5. Most of the time you like to keep a distance of at least an arm's length between yourself and others.

6. You do not trust Betas to be alone with scissors, glue, or tape, because they tend to do strange things with them. However, you do trust Betas to have these supplies when they are supervised.

7. Alpha males are very protective of Alpha females. If a Beta male touches an Alpha female, the nearest Alpha males immediately surround the Beta male until he stops touching the Alpha female or leaves the area.

8. When giving instructions or talking about work, especially with a Beta, you check and double-check to make sure that the Beta understands what you are saying. After all, there is an important link between clear communication and productivity.

ALPHA/BETA CULTURE SHEET FOR BETAS

Instructions: The following is a list of behavioral characteristics of your culture. During the work simulation, be certain that you exhibit these characteristics. If you are a leader, it is even more important that you serve as a model of the cultural behaviors.

1. You are submissive.
2. You talk softly. If you are in the presence of an Alpha, out of politeness, you cover your mouth and talk even more softly.
3. You are very intelligent. You are offended if people ask you if you understand what they are saying.
4. You strive to do things slowly, with grace and calmness.
5. You are interested in quality—not quantity.
6. You like to stand close to other people.
7. You love to touch and be touched. You like to hold hands and link arms, even with Alphas. It is a special sign of respect to touch an Alpha female on the cheek.
8. In your culture being touched on the back is a sexual advance. When that happens, you immediately stop what you are doing and sit on the floor without moving.
9. It is very inappropriate to make eye contact with others, especially a coworker. Making eye contact is a form of disrespect.

ALPHA/BETA OBSERVER SHEET

Note here whether the team you are to observe consists of all Alphas, all Betas, or mixed Alpha and Beta members.

_____

Once the simulation begins, observe the team's activity and jot down answers to the following questions. Later you will be asked to share your observations with the total group. When you do so, be sure to mention whether the group you observed consisted of all Alphas, all Betas, or mixed members.

1. How does stereotyping manifest itself?

2. How does the cultural identity of the leader (Alpha or Beta) impact the team's interactions and productivity?

3. What conflicts arise between team members?

4. How successful are the team members in attempting to resolve and work through their conflicts?

5. How would you characterize the interactions of the team members? Are these interactions helpful or not helpful in terms of completing the task?

6. How would you describe the team's cohesiveness?

7. How would you describe the team's productivity?

8. What is the impact of firing one of the team's members?

513. NEEDS, FEATURES, AND BENEFITS: EXPLORING THE SALES PROCESS

Goals
- To introduce the concepts of needs, features, and benefits in creating a "case."
- To provide the opportunity for participants to practice writing and presenting needs, features, and benefits.

Group Size
Six to sixteen participants.

Time Required
One hour and forty-five minutes to two hours.

Materials
- Two copies of the Needs, Features, and Benefits Work Sheet for each participant.
- A copy of the Needs, Features, and Benefits Theory Sheet for each participant.
- A pencil for each participant.
- A newsprint flip chart and felt-tipped markers.
- Masking tape for posting newsprint.

Physical Setting
Either a table surrounded by chairs that will accommodate all participants or chairs for all participants arranged in a circle and a portable writing surface for each participant.

Process
1. The facilitator announces the goal of the experience and gives *one* copy of the Needs, Features, and Benefits Work Sheet and a pencil to each participant. (Five minutes.)
2. The facilitator asks each participant to write down his or her favorite hobby or activity in the first section of the work sheet and, in one sentence, to write how he or she became interested in that hobby or activity. (Five minutes.)

3. The facilitator asks each participant to pass his or her work sheet to the right so that each person has a new work sheet. The facilitator then asks each person to write in the second section of the new work sheet one sentence about why there is a *need* for the hobby or activity listed. (If someone does not know of a need, he or she is to invent one.) (Five minutes.)

4. The participants are instructed to pass their work sheets to the right once more. Each participant is instructed to write, in the third section, one positive *feature* of the hobby or activity listed on the work sheet (something positive that the hobby or activity offers to someone). (Five minutes.)

5. The work sheets are passed to the right once again. Each participant is instructed to write, in the fourth section, one sentence that describes a *benefit* of the hobby or activity listed (what benefit a person will receive by participating in the hobby or activity). (Five minutes.)

6. The work sheets are passed to the right a final time. Each participant is asked to write, in the fifth section, a one-sentence request that convinces someone to join him or her in participating in the hobby or activity listed on the current sheet (Will you join me in...). (Five minutes.)

7. The participants take turns reading the work sheets they are holding to the whole group. (Five to fifteen minutes.)

8. The facilitator explains that the participants have just participated in a basic process. By learning the *needs, features,* and *benefits* of something—a product, service, organization, or charity—they can effectively sell the *case* for that thing. The facilitator explains that, in sales, this process is followed by the *close*, which is a resolution of some kind. Each participant then is given a copy of the Needs, Features, and Benefits Theory Sheet and is allowed time to read it. (Ten to fifteen minutes.)

9. Each participant receives a second copy of the Needs, Features, and Benefits Work Sheet and, working individually, fills in the sentences, using his or her product/organization/favorite cause as the subject for writing a case. (Ten minutes.)

10. The participants are instructed to form pairs. (The facilitator may join in if there is an odd number of participants.) Each pair is instructed to select which member will start by presenting his or her new case to the other, an interested "customer," for ten minutes and then receiving feedback on how he or she did from the "customer" for five minutes. The pairs are told to begin. The facilitator announces when the feedback is to begin. At the end of the feedback period, the facilitator instructs the pairs to change roles and have the second person in the pair present his or her case and the first one act as "customer." Again, the facilitator gives time warnings and tells the pairs when to begin the feedback process. (Thirty minutes.)

11. The facilitator calls time and reassembles the total group. The participants are encouraged to share their reactions to the experience. The facilitator records pertinent points on newsprint, using the following questions as discussion starters:
    - How did you feel about trying to "sell" something to another person?
    - How did you feel about being the customer?
    - What tended to happen during each stage of the process (needs, features, benefits)?
    - What patterns do you notice in these responses? Why do you think that they occurred?
    - In what ways are the steps in the process (needs, features, benefits) important in building a case?
    - What guidelines can you derive from your experiences in the selling process?
    - How and when might you use the process of building a case in your work? In other activities?

    (Twenty to twenty-five minutes.)

Variations

- If participants are affiliated with a nonprofit organization, they can role play presenting their cases to "prospective donors." If they are customer-service representatives or salespeople, they can role play selling their products or services to "prospective customers."
- If participants are managers or trainers, they can discuss ways to teach their employees/volunteers/board members the elements of presenting a case so that they are able to promote their organization's case to customers/prospective donors.
- For a shorter introduction to the selling process, the role playing can be eliminated.

Submitted by Bonnie Jameson.

Bonnie Jameson is a private consultant who has worked as a designer, trainer, and facilitator in human resource development for the past twenty years. Her special areas of expertise are training for trainers, strategic planning, team building, and leadership. She works with a variety of clients in the for-profit and the nonprofit sectors in the San Francisco area. Currently, Ms. Jameson also teaches courses in strategic planning and building effective organizations in the nonprofit program at California State University in Hayward, California.

NEEDS, FEATURES, AND BENEFITS WORK SHEET

Instructions: Please answer each of the following questions when the facilitator instructs you to do so.

1. Write down the name of your hobby or activity. Write one sentence about how you became interested in it.

2. Why is there a need for this hobby or activity? Who needs it? (Please answer in one sentence.)

3. What is a feature of this hobby or activity (something inherent that it offers to someone)? (Please answer in one sentence.)

4. What benefit will someone receive from this hobby or activity? (Please answer in one sentence.)

5. Convince someone to join you in this hobby or activity. (Please write one sentence.)

NEEDS, FEATURES, AND BENEFITS THEORY SHEET

In work and other aspects of life, we all find occasions when we are trying to "sell" something to another person. One may be actually trying to sell a product or service to a potential buyer. One may be "selling" a vision or concept while trying to solicit a donation or support for a worthy cause. Or one may be trying to satisfy a dissatisfied person by "selling" him or her a solution, for example, trying to "sell" an employee the benefits of a job change or trying to "sell" a family member a change of vacation plans. Thus, everyone engages in some type of customer service. Whether or not the customer is being asked to exchange monetary resources for a product or service, good customer service means that the customer winds up being happy with the interaction he or she has had.

The most important concepts to understand in order to help the customer to be satisfied with the exchange are as follows:

- The customer's *needs*;
- The *benefits* the customer will receive as a result of the exchange (for example, purchasing the product or service);
- The *features* of the proposed solution/product or service that make it attractive to the customer; and
- How those *features* provide *benefits* to the customer and meet the customer's *needs*.

A salesperson sells either a product or a service. In order to be successful, the salesperson has several obligations. The most important obligation is to become so familiar with the product or service that it becomes internalized as something familiar and something that the salesperson values a great deal. Without this understanding and sense of importance of the product or service, the salesperson has little chance of convincing anyone that the product or service has value and will satisfy customer needs. Thus, the first and most important obligation is to understand the *case* for the product or service. The case is all of the reasons that anyone would want to buy the product or service.

Consider the case of a consultant who is offering training services. In order to be successful, the consultant must become so familiar with the services offered that they become internalized as something of value. Without this understanding and sense of importance, the consultant has little chance of convincing anyone that the services have value and will satisfy customer needs.

Needs

If a person values something, it is easy to talk about it. However, a more important skill is getting someone else to talk about why he or she *needs* or would value the product or service and actively listening to what the person says. The best way to find out about the customer's needs is to ask the customer. A salesperson must know how to design open-ended questions to find out what the customer needs and then must actively listen by *paraphrasing the answers heard so that the customer knows that he or she is understood.* A good salesperson may spend 80 percent of his or her time eliciting and listening to the customer's needs and communicating his or her understanding of those needs by paraphrasing what the customer has just said.

The salesperson's skill in listening for the customer's needs enables him or her to sell the case so that the case matches the needs of the customer. This is where it is essential for the salesperson to know the product or service well, to value it enough that his or her genuine enthusiasm for it is evident, and to quickly adjust the discussion of features and benefits to match the customer's needs.

In the case of the consultant who is offering training services, an opening question might be to ask, "What is the problem that you want to solve?" If the answer to the question is that supervisors need to learn delegation skills, an active-listening response might be to ask, "Your supervisors don't have time to plan and coordinate because they end up doing the tasks themselves?" If this indeed is the case, the consultant would sell the features of a supervisory training program that are relevant to delegation.

Features

Assuming that the enthusiasm and value for the product or service exist, the salesperson also must have information about the product or service. First, the salesperson must fully understand the product or service: What are the *features* of the product or service that make it valuable? What does it offer that is unique? What makes it different from other products or services that are available to the customer? This may require researching the product or service to find out its history, its purpose, why it is valuable, and how it will benefit the customer. This is learning the features of the product or service. These features must not only be known but also believed by the salesperson, so that when he or she speaks about the product or service, enthusiasm for the features is evident in his or her voice, body language, and whole personality.

The consultant who is selling training services might communicate that his or her training program features teaching an understanding of the supervisory position in the organization and teaching the skills of delegating, planning, and so on. The program may be unique in that it includes role playing. It may differ from other services that are available in that it includes videotaped modeling and writing in journals.

The process of selling is the same no matter what is sold. The ingredient that sets a successful salesperson apart from others is the innate enthusiasm and value the salesperson holds for the product or service. The axiom is "Sell something you value or find a way to value what you sell." The value is contained in the features.

Benefits

The next step is for the salesperson to communicate the value to the customer. This cannot be done in a believable way unless the salesperson takes the time to find out the customer's needs and how the product or service can *benefit* the customer, that is, meet the customer's needs. Only then can the salesperson tell how the features of the product or service will benefit the customer or satisfy the customer's needs. For the consultant who is selling training services, a benefit may be to increase a unit's productivity or to reduce the supervisors' overtime.

Summary

In summary, presenting a case involves finding value for a product or service and learning about it so well that enthusiasm is a natural part of speaking about it. The next step is listening to the customer to discover his or her needs. Third, one must let the customer know how the features of the product or service will benefit the customer better than those of other available products or services. This is accomplished by emphasizing how the customer's needs will be met.

Although the final step is closing, it is not as proactive as the preceding ones. It is important to let the customer make up his or her own mind. The foregoing process should be sufficient to ensure a positive closure.

514. DIVERSITY QUIZ: VIEWING DIFFERENCES AS RESOURCES

Goals

- To introduce the topic of diversity in the workplace in a nonthreatening way.
- To offer the participants an opportunity to compare the results of individual work with those of group work.
- To give the participants a chance to collaborate with others in order to complete a task.
- To link the concepts of diversity and collaboration.

Group Size

Two to six subgroups of five participants each. If necessary, one or more subgroups may have six or seven participants, in which case each extra subgroup member should receive a duplicate of one of the data sheets.

Time Required

Approximately one and one-half hours.

Materials

- A set of five data sheets for each subgroup. Each sheet contains unique data and is coded by the number of periods, from one to five, following the last sentence of the first paragraph. (The facilitator should have extra copies on hand if some subgroups must have more than five members each.)
- A copy of the Diversity Quiz Sheet for each participant.
- A copy of the Diversity Quiz Answer Key for each participant.
- A pencil for each participant.

Physical Setting

A room large enough so that the members of each subgroup may sit in a circle and work without disturbing the other subgroups. Writing surfaces of some type should be provided.

Process

1. The facilitator announces that the activity will consist of completing an "open-book" quiz on the subject of diversity. Then the facilitator assembles

the participants into subgroups of five members each (or six or seven members each, if necessary), ensuring as much as possible that each subgroup consists of members who are diverse in terms of gender, age, and race.

2. The facilitator distributes copies of the data sheets, taking care that all five differently coded data sheets have been distributed in each subgroup. In addition, the facilitator distributes copies of the quiz sheet and pencils and explains that each subgroup's goal is to use the data sheets to find the correct answers to all twenty questions. The facilitator further clarifies that the subgroups have thirty-five minutes to complete the task, stipulating that each participant is to work independently for the first ten minutes and then join forces with his or her fellow subgroup members for the next twenty-five minutes. After eliciting and answering questions about the task, the facilitator asks the subgroups to begin.

3. After ten minutes the facilitator announces the end of the independent work and the beginning of the subgroup work.

4. As the subgroups work, the facilitator monitors their progress, assisting as necessary.

5. After twenty-five more minutes, the facilitator calls time and asks the subgroups to stop their work.

6. The facilitator reconvenes the total group and leads a discussion based on the following questions:
   - How did you go about completing the task when you were working alone? How did your completion of the task change when you were working in your subgroup?
   - How did your subgroup use the information on the data sheets?
   - Which behaviors helped your subgroup to complete the task? Which behaviors hindered your subgroup in its efforts? How did the diversity of your subgroup affect the outcome?
   - What happened if people did not share the information on their data sheets?
   - What would you do differently if you had to repeat the task now? How could you make greater use of the diverse resources in your subgroup?

   (Twenty minutes.)

7. The facilitator distributes copies of the answer key and discusses answers with the participants. (Five minutes.)

8. The facilitator makes the following comments:

    "In the United States the culture is growing more diverse, as the statistics cited in *Workforce 2000*[1] attest. The same is true in many other countries as well. People differ from one another not only in terms of gender, age, ethnicity, sexual orientation, race, and physical ability, but also in terms of background, values, expectations, and preferences.

    "To cope effectively with the differences that exist between ourselves and others, all of us will have to be more conscious of differences and work harder to cooperate with one another. In the work place, for instance, group work may involve more patience, more communication, more negotiation, and greater efforts to understand one another; however, the work of today's diverse groups may also lead to a richness of ideas and a variety of approaches to problem solving that are not possible with more homogeneous groups."

9. The facilitator initiates a discussion on promoting collaboration by asking, "Given what you have just learned about diversity, how could you promote greater collaboration in a diverse workplace?"

Variations

- The activity may be used to introduce a workshop on managing diversity, after which the subgroups' completed quiz sheets are retained. At the conclusion of the workshop, the quiz is repeated as a "posttest" and its results compared with those of the "pretest."

- If there are a large number of subgroups, one data sheet may be given to each subgroup; then the subgroups collaborate to complete the quiz.

- The activity may be used as an icebreaker. Each participant may be given a 3" x 5" index card with a piece of information from the quiz, such as "most competitive country," "percentage of new work force that is female," and so on. In order to complete the quiz, the participants have to obtain information from one another.

Submitted by Linda Eschenburg.

---

[1] *Workforce 2000: Work and Workers for the Twenty-First Century* by W.B. Johnston and A.E. Parker, 1987, Indianapolis, IN: Hudson Institute. See also *Workforce 2000: Gaining the Diversity Advantage* by D. Jamieson and J. O'Mara, 1991, San Francisco: Jossey-Bass, and "The Confucius Connection: From Cultural Roots to Economic Growth" by G. Hofstede and M.H. Bond, 1988 (Spring), *Organizational Dynamics*, pp. 5-21.

Linda Eschenburg *is a trainer, speaker, and management consultant with international experience. Her particular areas of emphasis are personal and organizational effectiveness. Prior to founding her own training and consulting practice six years ago, she worked in the high-technology, service, and public sectors. She also has worked as a management development specialist, a director of hospital social services, and a community college faculty member. Ms. Eschenburg is a founding board member of the Tampa Bay chapter of the Association for Psychological Type and is active in the American Society for Training and Development.*

DIVERSITY QUIZ DATA SHEET

As far as the United States work force is concerned, times are changing. A now-famous white paper that came out in 1987, *Workforce 2000: Work and Workers for the Twenty-First Century,* cited important U.S. population changes that were expected to occur between the years 1985 and 2000. For instance, the paper stated that the labor pool in the U.S. is shrinking. Throughout the decade of the 1990s there will be 4 to 5 million fewer entry-level workers than there were in the 1980s. Candidates for entry-level positions—*new* workers—are scarce in the Nineties.

In addition, the *new* workers include more females, more disadvantaged people, and more people representing diverse groups. In 1985 white males made up 47 percent of the labor force, whereas only 15 percent of the *new* workers are white males.

As a result of these and other developments, organizations can no longer conduct business as usual. As workers are increasingly diverse, one management style cannot be effective for all workers; people's individual needs must be taken into account. Organizations must compete to hire and retain the best talent. And talent is blind to age, gender, nationality, and color.

In addition to age, gender, nationality, and race, issues that account for diversification among workers include education, values, physical ability, mental capacity, personality, experiences, culture, and the way that work is approached. For example, the age of the U.S. work force is increasing. Also, women make up about 66 percent of the *new* workers, and men of color make up about 7 percent. In addition, it is important to note that before 1970, 79 percent of the immigrants to the U.S. were from Canada and Europe; now the majority come from entirely different areas.

Tomorrow's work force, like today's, is characterized by a mix of values. Some employees primarily value their home and family lives, others their careers. Some value loyalty to their companies, others to their professions, and still others to themselves. Often what people have lacked in the past—money, respect, or control—is most highly valued.

Here are some other bits of information that you may find useful in considering the issue of diversity:

- The country that is the size of California is considered the most competitive.

- In cultures that value individuality, chief of which is the U.S., people are promoted on the basis of their individual accomplishments. To stand out from the group by being a leader is considered good, normal, and something to strive for.

- In 70 percent of the world, however, people consider what is best for the group—whether that group is the work group, the company, or the country—to be more important than what is best for the individual person. The group's performance—not individual performance—is the basis for a performance appraisal. Leadership is based on age and seniority rather than on individual performance.

DIVERSITY QUIZ DATA SHEET

As far as the United States work force is concerned, times are changing. A now-famous white paper that came out in 1987, *Workforce 2000: Work and Workers for the Twenty-First Century,* cited important U.S. population changes that were expected to occur between the years 1985 and 2000. For instance, the paper stated that the labor pool in the U.S. is shrinking. Throughout the decade of the 1990s there will be 4 to 5 million fewer entry-level workers than there were in the 1980s. Candidates for entry-level positions—*new* workers—are scarce in the Nineties. .

In addition, the *new* workers include more females, more disadvantaged people, and more people representing diverse groups. In 1985 white males made up 47 percent of the labor force, whereas only 15 percent of the *new* workers are white males.

As a result of these and other developments, organizations can no longer conduct business as usual. As workers are increasingly diverse, one management style cannot be effective for all workers; people's individual needs must be taken into account. Front-line supervisors are the management group most affected by the need for flexibility in management style; they are the ones who deal most directly with diverse entry-level employees. Organizations and their management teams must compete to hire and retain the best talent. And talent is blind to age, gender, nationality, and color.

In addition to age, gender, nationality, and race, issues that account for diversification among workers include education, values, physical ability, mental capacity, personality, experiences, culture, and the way that work is approached. For example, the age of the U.S. work force is increasing. In 1970 the average age was only 28; now it is much higher. Also, people of color made up only 10 percent of the total U.S. labor force in 1985; now that percentage is higher. Since 1970, the countries of origin of immigrants have changed dramatically; now 78 percent of immigrants to the U.S. come from Latin America and Asia.

Tomorrow's work force, like today's, is characterized by a mix of values. Some employees primarily value their home and family lives, others their careers. Some value loyalty to their companies, others to their professions, and still others to themselves. Often what people have lacked in the past—money, respect, or control—is most highly valued.

Here are some other bits of information that you may find useful in considering the issue of diversity:

- People who are considered to be illiterate would have trouble reading traffic signs.
- The largest country discussed in *Workforce 2000* is also the one that most highly values individuality.
- In Japan, authority is respected more than in the U.S.

DIVERSITY QUIZ DATA SHEET

As far as the United States work force is concerned, times are changing. A now-famous white paper that came out in 1987, *Workforce 2000: Work and Workers for the Twenty-First Century,* cited important U.S. population changes that were expected to occur between the years 1985 and 2000. For instance, the paper stated that the labor pool in the U.S. is shrinking. Throughout the decade of the 1990s there will be 4 to 5 million fewer entry-level workers than there were in the 1980s. Candidates for entry-level positions—*new* workers—are scarce in the Nineties...

In addition, the *new* workers include more females, more disadvantaged people, and more people representing diverse groups. In 1985 white males made up 47 percent of the labor force, whereas only 15 percent of the *new* workers are white males.

As a result of these and other developments, organizations can no longer conduct business as usual. As workers are increasingly diverse, one management style cannot be effective for all workers; people's individual needs must be taken into account. Organizations must compete to hire and retain the best talent. And talent is blind to age, gender, nationality, and color.

In addition to age, gender, nationality, and race, issues that account for diversification among workers include education, values, physical ability, mental capacity, personality, experiences, culture, and the way that work is approached. For example, the age of the U.S. work force is increasing. Between 1985 and 2000, the percentage of people over the age of forty-five will increase by 30 percent. Also, 13 percent of the *new* workers will be women of color. In addition, since 1970, 78 percent of the immigrants to the U.S. have come from Latin America and Asia, whereas prior to 1970 the countries of origin were in entirely different parts of the world.

Tomorrow's work force, like today's, is characterized by a mix of values. Some employees primarily value their home and family lives, others their careers. Some value loyalty to their companies, others to their professions, and still others to themselves. Often what people have lacked in the past—money, respect, or control—is most highly valued.

Here are some other bits of information that you may find useful in considering the issue of diversity:

- People who are considered to be illiterate would have trouble reading a McDonald's menu.
- The largest country discussed in *Workforce 2000* is the United States.
- Some countries are oriented toward the values and the needs of the group, whereas others are oriented toward the values and the needs of individual people.

DIVERSITY QUIZ DATA SHEET

As far as the United States work force is concerned, times are changing. A now-famous white paper that came out in 1987, *Workforce 2000: Work and Workers for the Twenty-First Century,* cited important U.S. population changes that were expected to occur between the years 1985 and 2000. For instance, the paper stated that the labor pool in the U.S. is shrinking. Throughout the decade of the 1990s there will be 4 to 5 million fewer entry-level workers than there were in the 1980s. Candidates for entry-level positions—*new* workers—are scarce in the Nineties. . . .

In addition, the *new* workers include more females, more disadvantaged people, and more people representing diverse groups. In 1985 white males made up 47 percent of the labor force, whereas only 15 percent of the *new* workers are white males.

As a result of these and other developments, organizations can no longer conduct business as usual. As workers are increasingly diverse, one management style cannot be effective for all workers; people's individual needs must be taken into account. Organizations must compete to hire and retain the best talent. And talent is blind to age, gender, nationality, and color.

In addition to age, gender, nationality, and race, issues that account for diversification among workers include education, values, physical ability, mental capacity, personality, experiences, culture, and the way that work is approached. For example, the age of the U.S. work force is increasing. By the year 2000, the average age of U.S. workers will be 40. Also, immigrants will increase to almost 25 percent of the new hires. Before 1970, most of the immigrants to the U.S. were from Canada and Europe; now they are from entirely different parts of the world. Also, it is estimated that as many as 25 percent of the people who now graduate from high school are illiterate.

Tomorrow's work force, like today's, is characterized by a mix of values. Some employees primarily value their home and family lives, others their careers. Some value loyalty to their companies, others to their professions, and still others to themselves. Often what people have lacked in the past—money, respect, or control—is most highly valued.

Here are some other bits of information that you may find useful in considering the issue of diversity:

- Japan is about the size of California.
- Hispanics consider their families to be more important than their jobs. Therefore, it might be difficult for a Hispanic to accept a job that would involve a lot of overtime work.
- In Mexico, authority is respected more than in the U.S.

DIVERSITY QUIZ DATA SHEET

As far as the United States work force is concerned, times are changing. A now-famous white paper that came out in 1987, *Workforce 2000: Work and Workers for the Twenty-First Century,* cited important U.S. population changes that were expected to occur between the years 1985 and 2000. For instance, the paper stated that the labor pool in the U.S. is shrinking. Throughout the decade of the 1990s there will be 4 to 5 million fewer entry-level workers than there were in the 1980s. Candidates for entry-level positions—*new* workers—are scarce in the Nineties. . . . .

In addition, the *new* workers include more females, more disadvantaged people, and more people representing diverse groups. In 1985 white males made up 47 percent of the labor force, whereas only 15 percent of the *new* workers are white males.

As a result of these and other developments, organizations can no longer conduct business as usual. As workers are increasingly diverse, one management style cannot be effective for all workers; people's individual needs must be taken into account. Organizations must compete to hire and retain the best talent. And talent is blind to age, gender, nationality, and color.

In addition to age, gender, nationality, and race, issues that account for diversification among workers include education, values, physical ability, mental capacity, personality, experiences, culture, and the way that work is approached. For example, the age of the U.S. work force is increasing. Also, by the year 2000, U.S.-born people of color and immigrants are expected to make up 43 percent of the *new* workers. In addition, since 1970, 78 percent of the immigrants to the U.S. have come from Latin America and Asia, whereas prior to 1970 they came from entirely different parts of the world.

Tomorrow's work force, like today's, is characterized by a mix of values. Some employees primarily value their home and family lives, others their careers. Some value loyalty to their companies, others to their professions, and still others to themselves. Often what people have lacked in the past—money, respect, or control—is most highly valued.

Here are some other bits of information that you may find useful in considering the issue of diversity:

- People who graduate from high school and cannot read or write at the eighth-grade level are considered to be illiterate.
- The largest country discussed in *Workforce 2000* is the United States.
- The majority of cultures respect authority more than the U.S. does; in these cultures it is considered impolite to disagree with or question the boss.
- Asians are members of group-oriented cultures, whereas the culture of the U.S. is oriented toward individuality.

DIVERSITY QUIZ SHEET

1. Throughout the 1900s, the U.S. labor pool of entry-level workers will shrink by _____ million.

2. The management group most affected by the different mix of *new* workers in the U.S. work force is _____.

3. White males make up _____ percent of the *new* workers in the U.S.

4. Talent is blind to _____, _____, _____, and _____.

5. In addition to age, gender, nationality, and race, diversity includes these eight issues:

   _____   _____

   _____   _____

   _____   _____

   _____   _____

6. In 1970 the average age of U.S. workers was _____.

7. By the year 2000, the average age of U.S. workers will be _____.

8. Women make up about _____ percent of the *new* workers in the U.S.

9. People of color made up _____ percent of the 1985 U.S. work force.

10. People of color make up _____ percent of the *new* workers in the U.S.

11. By the year 2000, immigrants will comprise almost _____ percent of the new hires in the U.S.

12. Before 1970, 79 percent of the immigrants to the U.S. were from these areas (be specific): _____ and _____.

Pfeiffer & Company

13. Since 1970, 78 percent of the immigrants to the U.S. have come from these areas (be specific): _____ and _____.

14. It is estimated that as many as _____ percent of the people who graduate from high school cannot read or write at the _____ grade level.

15. Adults who cannot read at this grade level (see item 14 above) would have trouble reading a _____ menu and _____ signs.

16. The most competitive country is _____.

17. The country that values individuality the most is _____.

18. The group is valued more than the individual in _____ percent of the world.

19. In cultures that respect _____, it is considered impolite to _____ or _____ the boss.

20. People in the countries of _____ and _____ respect authority more than do people in the U.S.

The 1994 Annual: Developing Human Resources 65

DIVERSITY QUIZ ANSWER KEY

1. Throughout the 1990s, the U.S. labor pool of entry-level workers will shrink by <u>4 to 5</u> million.
2. The management group most affected by the different mix of *new* workers in the U.S. work force is <u>front-line supervisors</u>.
3. White males make up <u>15</u> percent of the *new* workers in the U.S.
4. Talent is blind to <u>age</u>, <u>gender</u>, <u>nationality</u>, and <u>color</u>.
5. In addition to age, gender, nationality, and race, diversity includes these eight issues: <u>education</u>, <u>values</u>, <u>physical ability</u>, <u>mental capacity</u>, <u>personality</u>, <u>experiences</u>, <u>culture</u>, and <u>the way that work is approached</u>.
6. In 1970 the average age of U.S. workers was <u>28</u>.
7. By the year 2000, the average age of U.S. workers will be <u>40</u>.
8. Women make up about <u>66</u> percent of the *new* workers in the U.S.
9. People of color made up <u>10</u> percent of the 1985 U.S. work force.
10. People of color make up <u>20</u> percent of the *new* workers in the U.S.
11. By the year 2000, immigrants will comprise almost <u>25</u> percent of the new hires in the U.S.
12. Before 1970, 79 percent of the immigrants to the U.S. were from these areas (be specific): <u>Canada</u> and <u>Europe</u>.
13. Since 1970, 78 percent of the immigrants to the U.S. have come from these areas (be specific): <u>Latin America</u> and <u>Asia</u>.
14. It is estimated that as many as <u>25</u> percent of the people who graduate from high school cannot read or write at the <u>eighth</u>-grade level.
15. Adults who cannot read at this grade level (see item 14 above) would have trouble reading a <u>McDonald's</u> menu and <u>traffic</u> signs.
16. The most competitive country is <u>Japan</u>.
17. The country that values individuality the most is <u>the U.S.</u>
18. The group is valued more than the individual in <u>70</u> percent of the world.
19. In cultures that respect <u>authority</u>, it is considered impolite to <u>disagree with</u> or <u>question</u> the boss.
20. People in the countries of <u>Japan</u> and <u>Mexico</u> respect authority more than do people in the U.S.

515. WRECK SURVIVORS: OPERATING FROM STRATEGIC ASSUMPTIONS

Goals
- To explore common patterns found in group problem solving and consensus seeking.
- To enable participants to practice clarifying strategic assumptions.
- To identify the differences between "strategy" and "tactics."

Group Size
Up to seven subgroups of five to seven members each.

Time Required
Two hours to two hours and twenty minutes.

Physical Setting
A room with a chair for each participant and enough space for the subgroups to work without disturbing one another. (One room that will accommodate the total group and smaller rooms in which the subgroups can meet is best.)

Materials
- A copy of Wreck Survivors Situation Sheet for each participant.
- A copy of the Wreck Survivors Individual Task Sheet for each participant.
- A pencil for each participant.
- A copy of the Wreck Survivors Group Task Sheet for each subgroup.
- A copy of the Wreck Survivors Possible Solutions Sheet for each participant.
- A newsprint flip chart and felt-tipped markers for each subgroup.
- Masking tape for posting newsprint.

Process
1. The facilitator introduces the activity as a problem-solving task and distributes a copy of the Wreck Survivors Situation Sheet and a copy of the Wreck Survivors Individual Task Sheet to each participant. The facilitator tells the participants to read their sheets individually and then to begin the task. (Ten minutes.)

2. After ten minutes, the facilitator calls time and divides the total group into subgroups of five to seven members each. Each subgroup receives a copy of the Wreck Survivors Group Task Sheet, a newsprint flip chart, and felt-tipped markers and is directed to a different area of the room or to a separate room. The subgroups are advised that they have forty-five minutes in which to read the group task sheet and to complete the task. (Five minutes.)

3. After thirty minutes, the facilitator warns the subgroups that they have fifteen minutes left. When the time is up, the subgroups are directed to return to the main meeting area with their flip charts. (Fifty minutes.)

4. The facilitator explains that there is not just one correct solution and that each subgroup's implicit survival strategy will have affected its choice of items. The facilitator asks each subgroup, in turn, to post its list of items. The subgroup members then are asked to report what they think their survival strategy was and how they think that strategy affected their choice of items, highlighting the *first three* and the *last three* items on its list as examples. (Ten to twenty minutes.)

5. The facilitator distributes a copy of the Wreck Survivors Possible Solutions Sheet to each participant and allows time for the sheet to be read. (Five minutes.)

6. The subgroups' lists are then reviewed for similarities to the strategies identified on the Wreck Survivors Possible Solutions Sheet. Additional strategies are also identified. If it appears that any subgroup failed to reach a decision about its strategy, the facilitator asks how that affected the subgroup's deliberations, i.e., how did that subgroup's process differ from that of the other subgroups? (Five to ten minutes.)

7. The facilitator says that, in any consensus task, it is usual for some group members to try to "sell" their own assumptions and choices to their groups. The facilitator asks how the focus on group strategy as a task affected this tendency. (Five to ten minutes.)

8. The facilitator asks whether, in attempting to reach consensus, any subgroup members engaged in conflict-reducing strategies such as voting, "horse-trading," averaging, or the like. The participants are encouraged to assess the impact of such behaviors on the strategic quality of the subgroup's decision. (Five to ten minutes.)

9. The facilitator leads a concluding discussion based on the following questions:
   - How often, in real life, do groups start with an analysis of the situation and the task?
   - How often do members stop to consider whether they have different perceptions of the final objective or strategy and, thus, of what tactics are needed to attain it?

- How would you describe your organization's strategy? Can you identify it? How does it affect what is done in your organization?
- What have you learned most from this experience?
- How can you use these learnings with other groups?

(Twenty minutes.)

Variations

- The Wreck Survivors Group Task Sheet can be amended to indicate that a strategy for survival is a key element and that each subgroup is to articulate the strategy for survival on which its final list is based.
- A short lecturette on organizational strategy and how it affects tactics may be provided if appropriate to the group.
- A list of items generally found on boats may be supplied on the Wreck Survivors Individual Task Sheet.

Submitted by Virginia Prosdocimi.

Virginia Prosdocimi, Ph.D.*, is a full professor of general and comparative psychology at universities in Argentina and Italy. She also worked for the Ministry of Public Health in Argentina to coordinate the Plan for Psychiatric Epidemiology for the World Health Organization. For the past several years, Dr. Prosdocimi has worked as a freelance managerial consultant with national and multinational companies such as Finmeccanica, Fedit, and Uniroyal.*

WRECK SURVIVORS SITUATION SHEET

A private yacht, sailing through an archipelago located between the 10th and 20th parallels in the Pacific Ocean, is caught in a sudden storm and runs aground violently on a coral reef. The passengers and crew miraculously reach the sandy shores of one of the islands. Shortly before the wreck, the crew had estimated that the port they were heading for was about 300 nautical miles away. Before abandoning ship, shortly before the impact, they tried a MAYDAY message on the radio with approximate coordinates; it was not possible to repeat the distress message or to receive a reply because of the rush of events. Unfortunately, the chances of the message getting through—in view of the atmospheric conditions, the quality of the transmission, and the distance—were very poor.

The situation can be summarized as follows:

1. The island is small and uninhabited. There is plenty of tropical vegetation, and among the plants abound coconuts, mangoes, and bananas. It rains in the afternoon most days, but the climate is mild and does not require heavy clothing. At low tide, fish and shellfish can be seen just offshore.
2. Nobody had time to pick up any supplies from the yacht. The passengers' and crew members' pockets contain cigarettes, matches, two lighters, and a pocket knife. Among them, they have three watches.
3. The lagoon between the beach and the coral reef where the yacht ran aground is approximately 900 yards in diameter and has an area of deep water.
4. Only a few of the passengers and crew members are good swimmers.
5. Most certainly, all the equipment aboard the yacht (i.e. radio transmitter, radar, generators) was destroyed on impact.
6. The crew predicts that the yacht will be dragged along the reef and will sink at high tide about eight hours later.

The total group has decided that the wrecked yacht must be reached before it sinks in order to recover those items necessary for future survival. Those persons who are the best swimmers will go to analyze the situation on board the yacht and attempt to bring supplies back to the shore. The group needs to prepare a list of those items that it considers most valuable for the group, selecting them in order of priority. Anticipating this, some crew members have compiled lists of items they think will be needed. Because time is valuable, it is decided that the total group's list will include fifteen of these items (the most that can be retrieved in the time available), listed in order of priority. Each person may suggest one alternative item not on the original list, which he or she may place on the list of fifteen if so desired.

WRECK SURVIVORS INDIVIDUAL TASK SHEET

During this task, do not communicate with anyone. Your task is to rank, in order of priority, fifteen items from the following lists. In addition, you have the option to add one item of your choice that in all probability was left on board the yacht. Next to the number "1" on the next page, write the name of the item you believe is the *most* important. Continue until you reach number "15," the *least*-important item. You will have fifteen minutes to complete this task.

These items are the choices of five members of the crew:

Chris:
ax
hammer and nails
knives
fishing tackle
transistor radio
plastic buckets

Pat:
bed sheets
blankets
cooking pots
canned food
beverages
first aid kit

Dale:
suntan lotion
toilet articles
mirror
condensed milk
chocolate bars
mosquito netting

Kelly:
rope
binoculars
water tanks
large plastic sheet
bottles of rum
life preservers

Robin:
marine charts
pistol and ammunition
wooden planks
tool box
flippers and harpoon
shark repellent

Item of your choice, if any:

The 1994 Annual: Developing Human Resources

Individual Ranking

1.

2.

3.

4.

5.

6.

7.

8.

9.

10.

11.

12.

13.

14.

15.

WRECK SURVIVORS GROUP TASK SHEET

The subgroup members now will have to agree on a single list, which they will write on newsprint—fifteen items in order of priority, including those items most likely to ensure survival.

It is important to remember that:

- You must reach a consensus regarding the ranking given to each item.
- "Consensus" means that each member of the subgroup agrees to the plan, at least to some degree. Coercion and methods of conflict avoidance such as averaging, voting, and "horse-trading" are not recommended.
- The subgroup may organize as it wishes to obtain the best results.

The subgroup has forty-five minutes in which to complete this task.

Group Ranking

1.
2.
3.
4.
5.
6.
7.
8.
9.
10.
11.
12.
13.
14.
15.

WRECK SURVIVORS POSSIBLE SOLUTIONS SHEET

There is no single, correct solution regarding the priority listing. What is important is the coherence between the *strategy for survival* adopted and the priority of items to achieve that objective. The key is to decide on an objective or strategy before taking action (such as swimming to the yacht) or engaging in "tactics." Tactics are the actions specifically planned to carry out a strategy. If clarity on objectives is not achieved at the beginning, the group is unlikely to produce a list that will achieve any particular objective.

Some possible group strategies, and the different lists that result, are as follows:

Attempt to be rescued. This strategy requires attracting the attention of potential rescuers who may have heard the MAYDAY transmission, who may be concerned with lack of news from the yacht, or who may be passing by the island. The items of higher priority in this list would be those that indicate the presence of survivors on the island and that attract attention from the sea or air. For instance, the mirror, the binoculars, and signal flares (an added item), which are available on almost any vessel or lifeboat, would be most important to retrieve.

Leave the island. This strategy might include using an inflatable boat or a makeshift raft and sailing from island to island until reaching one that is inhabited or until reaching the yacht's original destination. In this scenario, the priority items would be an inflatable boat and/or the tools and materials to build a raft (from wooden planks or tree trunks), as well as navigational instruments such as nautical charts, a compass, bed sheets and ropes to manufacture sails, water tanks, etc.

Continue on vacation. The island seems hospitable, food and rainwater are available if harvested, and the climate is mild. The decision could be to leave things as they are or to postpone the decision until a later date. In this case, those items that would provide food and shelter and make life most comfortable and enjoyable would have greatest priority. Such items might include mosquito netting, canned food, cooking pots, books, and so on.

516. ASSIGNMENT FLEXIBILITY: COMPARING NEGOTIATION STYLES

Goals

- To allow participants to experience the "hardball" negotiation process.
- To allow participants to practice the "win-win" negotiation process.
- To allow participants to compare the effects of "hardball" negotiation and "win-win" negotiation.
- To provide information about "assignment flexibility" and its perceived advantages and disadvantages in work negotiations.

Group Size

Ten to fifteen participants.

Time Required

Two hours and forty-five minutes.

Materials

- A copy of the Assignment Flexibility Theory Sheet for each participant.
- A copy of the Assignment Flexibility "Hardball" Instructions Sheet for each participant.
- A copy of the Assignment Flexibility "Hardball" Work Sheet for each participant.
- A copy of the Assignment Flexibility "Win-Win" Instructions Sheet for each participant.
- A copy of the Assignment Flexibility "Win-Win" Work Sheet for each participant.
- A copy of the Assignment Flexibility Case Study Sheet for each participant.
- A copy of the Assignment Flexibility Union Role Sheet for half of the participants.
- A copy of the Assignment Flexibility Management Role Sheet for the other half of the participants.
- A pencil and writing surface for each participant.

- A newsprint poster prepared in advance that lists the following rules for negotiation:
    - Only the negotiators may speak during negotiations. Subgroup members may pass notes to their negotiator if communication is necessary.
    - Negotiations will last a maximum of twenty minutes or until an agreement is reached. The facilitator will call time after twenty minutes.
    - If both negotiators agree, the negotiations may pause, allowing the subgroups to caucus before reconvening. However, the clock keeps running so that a period of only twenty minutes, total, elapses from start to finish.
- A newsprint flip chart and felt-tipped markers.
- Masking tape for posting newsprint.

Physical Setting

A room large enough for two subgroups to work without disturbing each other, with two large tables and with movable chairs for the participants. Two separate meeting rooms for the subgroups and a larger room for negotiations would be ideal.

Process

1. The facilitator introduces the goals of the activity and gives each participant a copy of the Assignment Flexibility Theory Sheet. The facilitator goes over the sheet or allows time for the participants to read it and ask questions of clarification. (Five minutes.)

2. The participant group is divided into two subgroups: union and management. All of the participants are given copies of the Assignment Flexibility "Hardball" Instructions Sheet, copies of the Assignment Flexibility "Hardball" Work Sheet, pencils, and portable writing surfaces. Each member of the union subgroup is given a copy of the Assignment Flexibility Union Role Sheet. Each member of the management subgroup is given a copy of the Assignment Flexibility Management Role Sheet. The two subgroups are instructed to move their chairs and to meet in separate areas to develop bargaining strategies. Each subgroup will choose a negotiator and prepare the negotiator to bargain with the other subgroup concerning how assignment flexibility will be implemented in the company. (Five minutes.)

3. The two subgroups are given time to read their materials, develop their bargaining strategies, choose their negotiators, and prepare their negotiators to bargain. While the subgroups prepare, the facilitator arranges the negotiation area: one table with chairs for the negotiators across from each other at the table, and chairs for the subgroup members behind their negotiators (Figure 1). (Twenty-five minutes.)

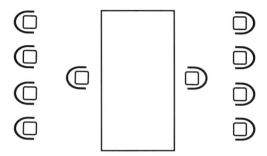

Figure 1. Setup for Hardball Negotiations

4. The facilitator calls time. The negotiators are seated across the table from each other with their subgroups behind them. The facilitator posts the newsprint poster listing the rules for negotiations and reviews the rules with the participants. (Twenty-five minutes.)

5. After twenty minutes or when an agreement is reached, the facilitator stops the activity. The facilitator then leads a group discussion by asking the following questions:
   - How did you feel when preparing for the "hardball" negotiation?
   - How did those of you who were negotiators feel during the "hardball" negotiation? How did the other members feel?
   - What types of behaviors occurred between the negotiators?
   - What are the advantages of hardball negotiation?
   - What are the disadvantages of hardball negotiation?

   (Fifteen minutes.)

6. The union and management subgroups are reconvened. The facilitator distributes copies of the Assignment Flexibility "Win-Win" Instructions Sheet and the Assignment Flexibility "Win-Win" Work Sheet to all participants. The subgroups are told to spend the next twenty minutes completing their Win-Win Work Sheets and preparing for the win-win negotiation. While they are preparing, the facilitator sets up the room for a win-win negotiation: two tables arranged in a V-shape (Figure 2). (Thirty minutes.)

7. The facilitator calls time. The participants are seated so as to alternate members of the union subgroup and members of the management subgroup. A newsprint flip chart is placed at the top of the V where all can see it. (Five minutes.)

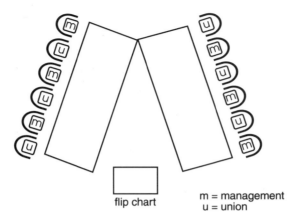

Figure 2. Setup for Win-Win Negotiations

8. For the second round of negotiations, the facilitator again announces the twenty-minute time limit; he or she asks the participants to define the issue and posts the answer on newsprint. Each subgroup is asked for a position statement, which also is written on the newsprint. Then each subgroup is asked to explain its interests. When all interests of both sides are listed and understood, the facilitator asks the participants to generate options that address the interests of both sides. When all available options are listed, the facilitator asks if there are any options or combinations of options that satisfy an acceptable number of the interests of both sides. If so, an agreement is reached. If not, the facilitator asks if there are objective standards that can be brought into the discussion in order to make an acceptable, rational decision. If the final solution is not acceptable, or if one cannot be reached, either side may wish to withdraw from the negotiations, either temporarily or permanently, or exercise its BATNA (Best Alternative to a Negotiated Agreement). After twenty minutes or when an agreement is reached, the facilitator stops the activity. (Twenty minutes.)

9. The facilitator leads a brief discussion of the win-win negotiation process by asking the following questions:
    - How did you feel when preparing for the "win-win" negotiation?
    - How did you feel during the "win-win" negotiation?
    - What are the advantages of win-win negotiation?
    - What are the disadvantages of win-win negotiation?
    - Which kind of negotiation have you experienced most frequently?

- Which negotiation do you prefer? For what reasons?
- How can you apply the learnings from this experience in your own life? (Twenty minutes.)

10. The facilitator distributes a copy of the Assignment Flexibility Case Study Sheet to each participant and goes over the information on the sheet. (Five minutes.)
11. The facilitator initiates a group discussion of participants' responses to the Case Study Sheet and what they have learned about assignment flexibility. (Ten minutes.)

Variations

- For a shorter activity, the facilitator can use only the win-win negotiation instructions and in processing ask participants how this type of negotiation compares to what they have experienced previously.
- This activity can be used with an issue other than assignment flexibility.
- A larger group can be accommodated if negotiators are chosen for the win-win negotiation segment.

Submitted by John E. Oliver.

John E. Oliver, Ph.D., is professor and head of the department of management and information systems at Valdosta State University. He has managerial and consulting experience in financial institutions, manufacturing plants, professional firms, and government organizations. His articles, cases, and experiential learning activities have appeared in several management texts and journals, including the Academy of Management Journal, Personnel Journal, International Journal of Management, *and the* Annuals.

ASSIGNMENT FLEXIBILITY THEORY SHEET

Assignment flexibility (AF) is the practice of assigning work to individuals in job classifications or unions that traditionally have not performed that work in the past (that is, work that traditionally has been assigned to another union or job classification). For example, production workers who are members of one union may be called on to perform minor maintenance and repair duties that traditionally have been performed by electricians or mechanics who are members of a different union. Likewise, maintenance mechanics and electricians may be asked to help production personnel in a crisis. Assignments under AF usually are classified according to who is helping whom, for example:

- Production helping production;
- Production helping maintenance;
- Maintenance helping production; and
- Maintenance helping maintenance.

Historically in the United States, labor unions have striven to keep "their work" from being performed by workers, managers, or others who were not union members. They also have been reluctant to perform work that "belonged" to other unions. When assignment flexibility is negotiated into a union contract/labor agreement, management is given the right to ask workers who are not busy or who are performing less critical tasks to be reassigned to more critical jobs that eliminate bottlenecks and keep production flowing smoothly. Thus, assignment flexibility theoretically allows management to ask workers to perform some duties that cross traditional union lines or job classifications in order to effect better utilization of human resources so that personnel costs are reduced and productivity (output per hour) is enhanced. These goals are important as firms face increased foreign and domestic competition.

Sometimes a part of the productivity gains from AF are passed on to workers through "gainsharing" plans. In addition, as productivity increases, the firm can charge less for its products, thereby increasing its competitive position. Increased sales may lead to expansion and the creation of new jobs. In this way, both the firm and the unions benefit. Increases in the firm's competitive position also make the workers' jobs more secure. As job security and the creation of new jobs are goals of the union, it is believed that all parties can gain from the implementation of AF.

In implementing AF, firms and unions have found that decisions to reassign workers must be made jointly by the supervisor and the workers involved. In each case, the following questions must be answered "yes" by the supervisor and worker to ensure safe and efficient working conditions:

1. Can it be done safely by this worker?
2. Does the person have the knowledge, skills, and ability to do the job?

3. Are the tools and time available?

4. Is it consistent with the contract language?

5. Does it make sense?

Only when the answer to all five questions is "yes" should a flexible assignment be made.

For AF to work, both worker and supervisor must participate in an open, honest, and cooperative way. When this is done, AF works well. Nevertheless, it should be recognized that implementing AF often is a drastic change from the traditional adversarial approach that unions and businesses have used in relating to each other. Change of this magnitude is never easy to implement and may be resisted by every facet of the organization.

ASSIGNMENT FLEXIBILITY UNION ROLE SHEET

All members of your subgroup are members of the same labor union. A few months ago the union negotiated a labor agreement with the employing company in which it was agreed that "assignment flexibility" (AF) would be implemented. In return for agreeing to implement AF, the company agreed to start a gainsharing plan in which union members receive incentive pay for any increases in productivity. Productivity is defined as output per worker.

Assignment flexibility means that members of one job classification may be asked to perform work ordinarily assigned to another job classification. The company believes that AF will result in better utilization of the existing work force so that productivity will increase and the company's competitive position in world markets will be enhanced, thereby increasing job security, which is a major concern of the union.

Traditionally, the union has fought to maintain job classifications so that senior workers perform tasks requiring more skill and junior workers perform tasks requiring less skill. Assignment flexibility will change that arrangement, and the union has some concerns about this.

First, the union wants to ensure worker safety. The union does not want its members to risk injury by performing jobs they do not know how to do safely. In this regard, the union would like to ensure that workers are not given tasks for which they do not have tools and time available, or for which they have not been trained.

Second, the union would like to preserve seniority rights as much as possible. In fact, the union would like to preserve job classifications or distinctions except when workers are assisting others. The union wants to be sure that assignments do not violate other provisions in the existing labor agreement, including overtime rights, salaries, and so forth.

The union also is interested in long-term job security, which means not *losing* any jobs due to AF. In addition, the union wants its members to be able to take pride in their jobs, be satisfied in their work, and know what is expected of them. The union is very concerned with maintaining harmony in the work force. The union would like for AF to be applied uniformly by all supervisors and for management to listen to workers' concerns and address problems promptly. "We shouldn't do things that don't make sense," the union president said, "but we said we'd do assignment flexibility and we have to find ways to do it sensibly." In fact, the union does not want assignment flexibility, but it is specified in the labor-management contract.

ASSIGNMENT FLEXIBILITY MANAGEMENT ROLE SHEET

All members of your subgroup are managers in the employing company. A few months ago, the company negotiated a labor agreement with the union in which it was agreed that "assignment flexibility" (AF) would be implemented. In return for the union's agreement to implement AF, the company agreed to start a gainsharing plan in which union members receive incentive pay for any increases in productivity. Productivity is defined as output per worker.

Assignment flexibility means that members of one job classification may be asked to perform work ordinarily assigned to another job classification. The company believes that AF will result in better utilization of the existing work force so that productivity will increase and the company's competitive position in world markets will be enhanced, thereby increasing job security, which is a major concern of the union.

Traditionally, the union has fought to maintain job classifications so that senior workers perform tasks requiring more skill and junior workers perform tasks requiring less skill. Assignment flexibility will change that arrangement, and the company has some concerns about this.

First, the company wants to ensure safety. The company does not want workers to risk injury by performing jobs they do not know how to do safely. In this regard, management will not train workers to do jobs they don't already know. However, supervisors will ask workers to assist one another, to do minor maintenance or repair work within their abilities, to do jobs below their classifications that they have done in the past, to use any tools for which they have the skills, or to do virtually any jobs the workers can perform safely. Workers will be asked to perform other jobs only when their own jobs are caught up or not in operation. In addition, the company will not lay off workers as a result of AF.

The company expects AF not to eliminate present job classifications, seniority, or job security. The company's main interest is to increase productivity by better utilization of the existing work force. By moving workers to eliminate bottlenecks, the company hopes to cut costs.

The company is also concerned about quality and does not want to do anything that might lower quality. Harmony in the work force and fair treatment of workers are important, but managers must also satisfy higher management and the stockholders. Down deep, the company wants unlimited assignment flexibility.

ASSIGNMENT FLEXIBILITY "HARDBALL" INSTRUCTIONS SHEET

Definition of Hardball Negotiation: Negotiation is a process wherein two or more parties with a conflict of interest meet voluntarily to divide resources or to resolve intangible issues. It is a sequential process involving demands or proposals, evaluation of the demands or proposals, and concessions. Following are the principles of hardball negotiation:

1. Opponents will not negotiate unless you can help them or hurt them.
2. Get all the information you can before negotiations begin.
3. Disguise your true interests.
4. Shoot high. Demand more than you are willing to settle for.
5. Listen carefully to the demands of the other side.
6. Develop trade-off strategies. What are you willing to give up in order to gain something more important?
7. Never give up anything without getting something in return.
8. Do not trust the other side. Double-check anything its representatives tell you.
9. Be willing to walk away from the negotiations.
10. There is no requirement for honesty, but you may have to face your adversary again later.
11. Have a "bottom line" or fallback position below which you will not budge.
12. Do not be too greedy.
13. Promises lead to solutions. Threats lead to deadlocks.
14. Some sources of power in bargaining include the following:
    - The other side's belief that you are honest;
    - Having more time than the other side has;
    - Having more information than the other side has;
    - Having more bargaining expertise than the other side has;
    - Being persistent;
    - Being patient;
    - Being willing to take a risk;
    - Having control of the resources needed by the other side;
    - Viewing bargaining as a game;
    - Convincing the other side that you care; and
    - Knowing when to be assertive.

Keeping these principles in mind, develop your negotiating strategy, including the following:

- A position statement;
- A list of initial demands;
- A corresponding list of acceptable bottom lines; and
- A list of possible trade-offs.

Then select a negotiator and prepare him or her to represent your subgroup.

ASSIGNMENT FLEXIBILITY "HARDBALL" WORK SHEET

Position Statement:

Initial Demands:

Minimum Acceptable Bottom Lines:

Trade-Offs:

ASSIGNMENT FLEXIBILITY "WIN-WIN" INSTRUCTIONS SHEET

Definition of Win-Win Negotiation: Negotiation is a process in which two or more parties seek to decide an issue jointly so that both come out better than they would without negotiating.

1. The *best* negotiation is one in which:
   - Both parties maximize their payoffs.
   - The joint decision is better than what either party could produce alone.
   - The parties are likely to comply with the agreement.
   - The relationship between the parties is enhanced.
   - The negotiation costs minimum time, money, and stress.

2. The *worst* negotiation is one in which:
   - Neither party gets what it wants.
   - No agreement is reached.
   - Agreement is reached, but the solution is not very good.
   - The parties are likely not to comply with the agreement.
   - The relationship between the parties is damaged.
   - The costs of the negotiation in terms of time, money, or stress are too high.

Steps

Keeping the characteristics of a "best" negotiation in mind, your subgroup should complete the following steps using the Win-Win Work Sheet:

1. Write a brief statement of the issue. One or two words will do.

2. Write a brief statement of your subgroup's position on the issue.

3. List all your subgroup's interests that underlie your position on the issue. Brainstorm: do not judge ideas; list all suggestions; dig deep; be open; be honest; divulge all your feelings.

4. Create a BATNA (Best Alternative to a Negotiated Agreement). Your BATNA is what you will do if you cannot get an acceptable number of your interests met in the negotiation. Most BATNAs have costs attached (for example, quit, strike, go back to college, start my own business). A BATNA keeps you from accepting a solution you should reject. Psychologically, you need a BATNA before you begin negotiating. It works better than saying, "I'll negotiate first; then if I don't get what I want, I'll decide what to do." Your BATNA is your alternative to any outcome of the negotiation. It becomes your standard for whether or not to accept the negotiated settlement. Therefore, choose your BATNA carefully. You may choose to disclose

your BATNA to the other side in the negotiations if doing so will help. You may choose not to disclose your BATNA if it is not very attractive to you.

5. Read the remainder of this instruction sheet and discuss the ideas within your subgroup.

What To Expect in the Negotiations

You are now ready to enter the negotiations. When you meet with the other subgroup, the facilitator will guide you in what to do.

During the negotiation, the facilitator will ask each subgroup to define the issue and will post the answers on the flip chart. Each subgroup will be asked for a position statement, which also will be written on the flip chart. Then each subgroup will be asked to explain its interests. You should make sure that the other side really understands your interests. Ask its members to paraphrase your interests after you have stated them.

When all interests of both sides are listed and understood, the participants will be asked to generate options that address the interests of both sides. When all available options are listed, the facilitator will ask if there are any options or combinations of options that satisfy an acceptable number of the interests of both sides. If so, an agreement is reached. If not, the facilitator will ask if there are objective standards that can be brought into the discussion in order to make an acceptable, rational decision.

If the final solution is not acceptable, or if one cannot be reached, either side may withdraw from the negotiations either temporarily or permanently, or exercise its BATNA.

1. What if the other side resorts to hardball tactics?
   - If they attack you or your ideas, do not defend or counterattack.
   - Refuse to react.
   - Use your energy to explore interests and options.
   - Ask what they would do if they were in your shoes.
   - Ask questions. Do not make statements.
   - Take no stand. Offer no target.
   - Channel the other side's attack toward the problem.
   - Assume that the other side is frustrated with the problem, not with you.
   - Stay cool, calm, and focused on the problem.

2. Overcome obstacles to creating options:
   - Do not judge options prematurely. One that is unacceptable alone may later be combined with another to create an attractive package.
   - Do not look for one single answer.
   - Accept the other side's problem as your problem.

- Do not limit your ideas to what is available now. Perhaps the total payoff can be increased.
- Do not focus on your own bottom line. Seek new information that changes the situation or generates new alternatives.
- Do not "anchor" the discussion by talking about numbers (costs, wages, and so on) prematurely.

3. Assumptions of win-win negotiation:
   - Both of us can have our needs met.
   - We should help each other win.
   - Together we can create better solutions.
   - Objective standards can be found for good decision making.
   - We can improve our relationship through honest negotiation.
   - Both negotiators are good people.
   - We can cooperate with each other.
   - Both negotiators are primarily interested in filling our own needs. That's O.K.
   - Perhaps we do not understand each other. Talking will help.
   - If we really listen to each other, we will both learn the other's real needs.

ASSIGNMENT FLEXIBILITY "WIN-WIN" WORK SHEET

Issue:

Your Position:

Your Interests:

Options:

Our Standards (what we have done in the past):

Standards from Outside (what others do):

BATNA:

ASSIGNMENT FLEXIBILITY CASE-STUDY SHEET

This issue was negotiated by a real committee of four managers and four union presidents with the author facilitating. The following outcome resulted:

Company Interests
- Safety
- Costs
- Productivity
- Long-term job security
- Quality
- Harmony with
  work force,
  higher management,
  others
- Fairness to all
- Compliance with contract

Union Interests
- Safety
- Seniority
- Consistent with agreement
- Long-term job security
- Harmony in work force
- Self-satisfaction
- Pride
- Trust
- Keep job distinctions except to assist other employees

Options

(Things we can do to protect *all* above interests)

- Maintain job distinctions except to assist others
- Supervisor training
- Employee meeting/training to discuss interests, etc.
- Continued committee involvement
- Comply with contract
- Protect trust, pride, harmony, employee satisfaction, etc.
- Address problems promptly
- Hear special concerns
- Follow these success criteria: safety, common sense, knowledge, skills and abilities, tools and time, cost-effectiveness, consistency with agreement

A consensus was reached that the committee was ready to design an implementation plan that includes training for supervisors (and perhaps other key people), employee meetings, a system of evaluation, and a process for supervisors to use to ensure that assignment flexibility (AF) is implemented in a manner consistent with the criteria developed.

517. HATS "R" US: LEARNING ABOUT ORGANIZATIONAL CULTURES

Goals

- To introduce the participants to four general types of organizational culture.
- To provide the participants with an opportunity to identify the culture of their own organization.
- To offer the participants an opportunity to explore their personal alignment or misalignment with their organization's culture.

Group Size

Four subgroups of four to six participants each. This activity is intended to be used with participants who are all employed by the same organization, although it can easily be altered to be used with a group of participants who represent different organizations.

Time Required

Approximately two hours and thirty to forty-five minutes.

Materials

- Four to six copies of each of the four culture sheets (a different sheet for each subgroup; a copy for each subgroup member).
- A copy of the theory sheet for each participant.
- A copy of the discussion sheet for each participant.
- A newsprint flip chart for each subgroup.
- Several different colors of felt-tipped markers for each subgroup.
- A pencil for each subgroup.
- A clipboard or other portable writing surface for each subgroup.
- A newsprint flip chart and a felt-tipped marker for the facilitator's use.
- Masking tape for posting newsprint.

Physical Setting

A large room in which the subgroups can work without disturbing one another. Movable chairs should be provided. Also, plenty of wall space should be available for posting newsprint.

Process

1. The facilitator assembles four subgroups of four to six participants each, gives each subgroup a newsprint flip chart and several felt-tipped markers, and makes the following comments:

    "During the upcoming activity you will be experiencing the dynamics of organizational culture. Each subgroup represents a company that is in the business of producing hats. You and your fellow subgroup members will be given a handout describing the type of organizational culture that exists in your hat company. Using the information in that handout, you will do three things: (1) Draw *a newsprint picture of a hat that you think that culture would produce;* (2) determine your culture's *goals for marketing the hat* that you drew and list these goals on newsprint; and (3) devise *an action plan that the culture could use to market the hat* and list the highlights of this plan on newsprint. All of these assignments—creating the picture of the hat, determining marketing goals, and devising an action plan for marketing—must be consistent with the cultural description that you will be given. After all subgroups have finished all three tasks, the subgroups will take turns presenting their hats, their marketing goals, and their action plans to the total group."

    As the facilitator explains the three tasks, he or she writes them on newsprint and posts the newsprint prominently.

2. The facilitator answers questions about the task and then distributes the culture sheets, giving the members of each subgroup a different sheet and asking them to read their sheets. After announcing that the subgroups have thirty minutes, the facilitator instructs the subgroups to begin. While the participants are working, the facilitator remains available to clarify and assist as necessary. (Forty minutes.)

3. After thirty minutes the facilitator asks the subgroups to stop their work and to take turns presenting their hats, their marketing goals, and their marketing action plans—*without revealing the cultures they are representing.* Each subgroup is instructed to post their newsprint drawing and lists and to leave these items posted after the presentation. (Twenty minutes.)

4. The facilitator distributes copies of the theory sheet, asks the participants to read this sheet, and then leads a discussion by asking the following questions:

    - Which hat belongs to which culture? What do the hats, the marketing goals, and the marketing action plans tell you about the organizational cultures involved?
    - How did you find yourself behaving while you were working with your subgroup? How was your work affected by the nature of the organizational culture that you were dealing with? How did that culture appear to affect other members of your subgroup?

- How did you feel about the culture that your subgroup dealt with? Which characteristics of the culture appealed to you? Which were not appealing?

    As the participants identify which hat belongs to which culture, the facilitator writes the culture names on the respective newsprint sheets. (Twenty to thirty minutes.)

5. The facilitator asks the participants to reassemble into their subgroups and gives each participant a copy of the discussion sheet. In addition, each subgroup is given a pencil and a clipboard or other portable writing surface (for the recorder's use). Each subgroup is instructed to discuss answers to the questions on the handout and to select one member to record answers and to report them later to the total group. (Thirty minutes.)

6. The facilitator reconvenes the total group and asks the subgroup recorders to take turns sharing the subgroup answers to the questions on the discussion sheet. As the recorders report, the facilitator writes salient points on two separate sheets of posted newsprint, one with the heading "The Organization's Culture" and the other with the heading "Alignment/Misalignment." (Twenty minutes.)

7. The facilitator leads a concluding discussion by asking these questions:
    - Which organizational cultures seem to be most represented by this group? What does that information suggest?
    - What purposes does an organizational culture serve for its members? For its customers or clients?
    - How might you and your organization be affected if you feel *aligned* with the organizational culture? How might you and your organization be affected if you feel *misaligned* with the culture?
    - How can you use what you have learned to help you and the company succeed in the future?

Variations

- This activity may be used as an introduction to strategic planning or developing a mission statement.
- Materials may be provided so that the subgroups can actually produce the hats.
- While completing the three tasks, the participants may be instructed to behave as members of their assigned cultures would behave. A manager may be designated for each subgroup and asked to function in the way that a manager from that culture would.
- During step 2, after some time has elapsed, one member of each subgroup may be asked to switch to a different subgroup. It is particularly effective to have someone from The Tough Guy, Macho Culture (culture sheet 1) switch

with someone from The Process Culture (culture sheet 4) and to have someone from The Work Hard/Play Hard culture (culture sheet 2) switch with someone from The Bet-Your-Company Culture (culture sheet 3). The processing should deal with the experiences of those who switched subgroups.

Submitted by Catherine J. Nagy.

Catherine J. Nagy *is a training and development manager for the Francis Scott Key Medical Center in Baltimore, Maryland. She has fifteen years of experience in designing and conducting supervisory, management, and customer-service training. She has held various training positions in the hotel and healthcare industries and has particular expertise in managing a one-person training department. In addition, she serves as the vice president of the Maryland Chapter of the American Society for Training and Development.*

HATS "R" US CULTURE SHEET 1[1]

Characteristics
- High risk, quick feedback (one year or less)
- Life and death/high financial stakes
- Intense pressure and frantic pace
- "All or nothing" environment

Values
- Risk taking and speed
- Motto: "Find a mountain and climb it"
- Survival of the fittest

Heroes and Survivors
- Gamblers, outlaws, and temperamental stars
- Aggressive, tough individualists
- People who are quick with ideas and decisions and need instant feedback

Rituals
- Superstitious rituals, lucky charms
- Tough internal competition; scoring points off one another
- Greetings to customers, clients, etc.: Appointments kept waiting a long time; receptionist hardly notices

Strengths and Weaknesses
- + Ability to work quickly and get the job done
- + Quick return and high financial rewards
- − Short-sightedness; no learning from mistakes
- − Lack of long-term investment, persistence, and endurance
- − Members who tend to be emotionally immature
- − High turnover; employees who are "slow bloomers" may not be successful in the short term

---

[1] Adapted from *Corporate Cultures: The Rites and Rituals of Corporate Life* by T.E. Deal and A.A. Kennedy, 1982, Reading, MA: Addison-Wesley.

HATS "R" US CULTURE SHEET 2[1]

Characteristics
- Low risk, quick feedback
- High level of activity, initiative, and persistence
- Fun and action

Values
- Customers and their needs
- Motto: "Find a need and fill it"
- High volume, low margin; losing one sale will not make or break an employee or the company

Heroes and Survivors
- Team players
- Those who are young, energetic, friendly, and good with people

Rituals
- Sales rallies, beer busts, contests, conventions, company songs, the sales pitch
- Greetings to customers, clients, etc.: Personal greeting at the door with a slap on the back and a cup of coffee

Strengths and Weaknesses
- + Speed and quantity
- + Ability to get a lot done and provide the mass-produced goods that consumers want
- + Short cycle time allows wrong decisions to be corrected quickly
- − High volumes, not high quality
- − Lack of thoughtful planning and attention
- − Quick fixes rather than long-term solutions
- − Employees who are more loyal to sales than to the company
- − Large turnover in salespeople if they are discouraged by low sales volumes

---

[1] Adapted from *Corporate Cultures: The Rites and Rituals of Corporate Life* by T.E. Deal and A.A. Kennedy, 1982, Reading, MA: Addison-Wesley.

HATS "R" US CULTURE SHEET 3[1]

Characteristics
- High risk, slow feedback
- High stakes: The entire company's future can be at risk as a result of one or two bad decisions
- Persistent pressure despite long product cycles
- Careful consideration before acting

Values
- Investing in the future
- Giving good ideas the opportunity to succeed
- Showing respect for authority and technical competence
- Making the right decision; checking and double-checking

Heroes and Survivors
- People with strong character and self-confidence to sustain them through the long haul
- People who are self-directed, strong willed, emotionally mature
- People who do not easily change their minds after making decisions
- People who can withstand long-term ambiguity with little or no feedback
- People who persevere until big projects become reality

Rituals
- Lengthy business meetings with seating according to rank
- Detailed discussions at meetings, but only by senior members
- Top-down decision making after considering input from all group members
- Shared knowledge; mentoring
- Very formal and polite behavior
- Frequent references to company history
- Greetings to customers, clients, etc.: Sign-in procedure, badges

Strengths and Weaknesses
- + Long-term perspective on careers, products, and profits
- + Innovative, high-quality, breakthrough products
- − Slow movement; vulnerability to short-term developments

---

[1] Adapted from *Corporate Cultures: The Rites and Rituals of Corporate Life* by T.E. Deal and A.A. Kennedy, 1982, Reading, MA: Addison-Wesley.

HATS "R" US CULTURE SHEET 4[1]

Characteristics
- Low risk, slow feedback
- Low financial stakes; no single transaction will affect an employee or the company
- Virtually no feedback to employees about their effectiveness unless they are blamed for something
- Protective, cautious; "cover-yourself" mentality; detailed memos for everything, copied to everyone
- Out of touch with external environment due to lack of feedback

Values
- Technical perfection
- Meticulous attention to correct process and details
- Focus on how the work is done rather than what work is done

Heroes and Survivors
- People who protect the integrity of the system to a greater extent than they protect their own
- People who follow procedures without questioning their relevance
- People who are neat, complete, accurate, orderly, punctual, and attentive to detail
- People who function as heroes (the jobs to which people are posted may turn them into heroes)

Rituals
- Long, rambling meetings focused on process, not content
- Asking questions that no one can answer
- Writing and discussing memos
- Attention to titles, rank, formalities
- Tightly structured hierarchical systems and processes
- Greetings to customers, clients, etc.: Sign-in procedure, badges

Strengths and Weaknesses
- + Putting "order into work that needs to be predictable"
- − Bureaucratic red tape

---

[1] Adapted from *Corporate Cultures: The Rites and Rituals of Corporate Life* by T.E. Deal and A.A. Kennedy, 1982, Reading, MA: Addison-Wesley.

HATS "R" US ORGANIZATIONAL-CULTURE THEORY SHEET

What Is Organizational Culture?

An organization's culture is the pattern of values and behaviors acquired and shared by its members. These patterns tend to persist over time, despite changes in the organization's membership. Values are common beliefs, attitudes, concerns, and goals that members share at a deep, invisible, emotional level. Group members manifest their beliefs through visible behaviors and practices such as formal and informal structures, reward systems, communication and decision-making processes, and internal and external relationships. Rites and rituals perpetuate the norms of group behavior associated with success. Individual members who personify organizational beliefs and values typically become heroes and role models.

The following material delineates the main characteristics of the four types of organizational culture identified by Deal and Kennedy (1982).

The Tough Guy, Macho Culture

Characteristics
- High risk, quick feedback (one year or less)
- Life and death/high financial stakes
- Intense pressure and frantic pace
- "All or nothing" environment

Values
- Risk taking and speed
- Motto: "Find a mountain and climb it"
- Survival of the fittest

Heroes and Survivors
- Gamblers, outlaws, and temperamental stars
- Aggressive, tough individualists
- People who are quick with ideas and decisions and need instant feedback

Rituals
- Superstitious rituals, lucky charms
- Tough internal competition; scoring points off one another
- Greetings to customers, clients, etc.: Appointments kept waiting a long time; receptionist hardly notices

Strengths and Weaknesses
- + Ability to work quickly and get the job done
- + Quick return and high financial rewards
- – Short-sightedness; no learning from mistakes
- – Lack of long-term investment, persistence, and endurance
- – Members who tend to be emotionally immature
- – High turnover; employees who are "slow bloomers" may not be successful in the short term

The Work Hard/Play Hard Culture

Characteristics
- Low risk, quick feedback
- High level of activity, initiative, and persistence
- Fun and action

Values
- Customers and their needs
- Motto: "Find a need and fill it"
- High volume, low margin; losing one sale will not make or break an employee or the company

Heroes and Survivors
- Team players
- Those who are young, energetic, friendly, and good with people

Rituals
- Sales rallies, beer busts, contests, conventions, company songs, the sales pitch
- Greetings to customers, clients, etc.: Personal greeting at the door with a slap on the back and a cup of coffee

Strengths and Weaknesses
- + Speed and quantity
- + Ability to get a lot done and provide the mass-produced goods that consumers want
- + Short cycle time allows wrong decisions to be corrected quickly
- – High volumes, not high quality
- – Lack of thoughtful planning and attention

- – Quick fixes rather than long-term solutions
- – Employees who are more loyal to sales than to the company
- – Large turnover in salespeople if they are discouraged by low sales volumes

The Bet-Your-Company Culture

Characteristics
- High risk, slow feedback
- High stakes: The entire company's future can be at risk as a result of one or two bad decisions
- Persistent pressure despite long product cycles
- Careful consideration before acting

Values
- Investing in the future
- Giving good ideas the opportunity to succeed
- Showing respect for authority and technical competence
- Making the right decision; checking and double-checking

Heroes and Survivors
- People with strong character and self-confidence to sustain them through the long haul
- People who are self-directed, strong willed, emotionally mature
- People who do not easily change their minds after making decisions
- People who can withstand long-term ambiguity with little or no feedback
- People who persevere until big projects become reality

Rituals
- Lengthy business meetings with seating according to rank
- Detailed discussions at meetings, but only by senior members
- Top-down decision making after considering input from all group members
- Shared knowledge; mentoring
- Very formal and polite behavior
- Frequent references to company history
- Greetings to customers, clients, etc.: Sign-in procedure, badges

Strengths and Weaknesses
- + Long-term perspective on careers, products, and profits

- + Innovative, high-quality, breakthrough products
- − Slow movement; vulnerability to short-term developments

The Process Culture

Characteristics
- Low risk, slow feedback
- Low financial stakes; no single transaction will affect an employee or the company
- Virtually no feedback to employees about their effectiveness unless they are blamed for something
- Protective, cautious; "cover-yourself" mentality; detailed memos for everything, copied to everyone
- Out of touch with external environment due to lack of feedback

Values
- Technical perfection
- Meticulous attention to correct process and details
- Focus on how the work is done rather than what work is done

Heroes and Survivors
- People who protect the integrity of the system to a greater extent than they protect their own
- People who follow procedures without questioning their relevance
- People who are neat, complete, accurate, orderly, punctual, and attentive to detail
- People who function as heroes (the jobs to which people are posted may turn them into heroes)

Rituals
- Long, rambling meetings focused on process, not content
- Asking questions that no one can answer
- Writing and discussing memos
- Attention to titles, rank, formalities
- Tightly structured hierarchical systems and processes
- Greetings to customers, clients, etc.: Sign-in procedure, badges

Strengths and Weaknesses
- + Putting "order into work that needs to be predictable"
- − Bureaucratic red tape

How Culture Is Shaped

Leadership at all levels can and should actively influence organizational culture. Deal and Kennedy (1982) emphasize that leaders within an organization need to know when to promote the existing culture and when to step outside it. For example, leaders need to invest time in creating and participating in rituals that reinforce the culture: celebrations, ceremonies, role modeling, setting social standards, orienting newcomers, and fine-tuning management processes. When normal, routine business problems arise, leaders in a Tough Guy, Macho Culture may reinforce the culture's strengths by backing the stars, whereas in a Bet-Your-Company Culture they may reinforce strengths by ensuring that all bases are covered.

Kotter and Heskett (1992) recommend that leaders behave consistently with the organization's adaptive values. Leaders need to hire, promote, and train individuals who share those same values. They also must embrace behaviors and practices that reinforce the company's adaptive values and fit its business strategies.

However, leaders may need to step outside the culture when the external business environment changes, when the company's performance becomes mediocre or worse, or when an ethical issue is at stake. Under these circumstances managers may deliberately announce practices that are in direct opposition to cultural norms, after which they need to provide the leadership needed to foster these new practices within the organization. For example, leaders may require teamwork from the Tough Guy, Macho Culture and quick responses from the Bet-Your-Company Culture.

Leaders also need to know how to work with subcultures within the main culture, such as the sales division or the finance department, to get things done. An important leadership task is balancing and reconciling legitimate differences and fostering tolerance, understanding, and appreciation of the unique strengths and values that each subculture adds to the company.

At a time when empowerment is an increasingly potent concept, it is important to note that the responsibility of appropriately maintaining or changing a company's culture does not rest solely with management. Although management initiates maintenance or change, all employees must have the necessary commitment to the organization and personal flexibility to follow management's lead.

References

Deal, T.E., & Kennedy, A.A. (1982). *Corporate cultures: The rites and rituals of corporate life.* Reading, MA: Addison-Wesley.

Kotter, J.P., & Heskett, J.L. (1992). *Corporate culture and performance.* New York: The Free Press.

HATS "R" US DISCUSSION SHEET

1. What culture does your own company (your real employer) represent?

2. What are your company's cultural values?

3. What are its strengths? What are its weaknesses?

4. What does the culture imply about the way people are expected to behave in your company?

5. In what ways do you feel aligned with your company's culture? In what ways do you feel misaligned with the culture?

518. PARSLEY, GARLIC, GINGER, PEPPER: INTRODUCTIONS[1]

Goals
- To introduce the participants to one another.
- To develop an atmosphere conducive to group interaction.

Group Size
Up to thirty participants.

Time Required
Forty-five minutes to one hour.

Materials
- A copy of the Parsley, Garlic, Ginger, Pepper Characteristics Sheets A, B, C, and D for each participant.
- A pencil and a clipboard or other portable writing surface for each participant.
- Signs made in advance to designate corners of the room as "Parsley," "Garlic," "Ginger," and "Pepper."
- Masking tape for posting signs.

Physical Setting
A room large enough for subgroups to interact without disturbing one another. Movable chairs should be provided.

Process
1. The facilitator briefly discusses the goals of the activity, establishing the expectation that the activity will be both useful and fun.
2. The facilitator distributes pencils, portable writing surfaces, and copies of the Parsley, Garlic, Ginger, Pepper Characteristics Sheets A, B, C, and D. Each participant is instructed to choose the one seasoning he or she most identifies with. (Five minutes.)

---

[1] This activity is based on *Find Your Seasoning, Find Yourself,* by Robert Hickey and Kathleen Hughes, Washington, DC: Acropolis Books, 1984.

3. While the participants are reading, the facilitator labels each corner of the room with a sign indicating one of the seasonings.

4. The participants are instructed to move to the area of the room designated for the seasoning they chose and to form subgroups. It is not important that each type be represented; if no one chooses a particular type, the activity continues without it. (Five minutes.)

5. The facilitator instructs each subgroup to prepare a brief (two to three minute) introduction for itself based on questions like the following:
   - What would be our strengths in a team?
   - What would be our areas for growth?
   - How would we act in a conflict situation?
   - How would we act when there is a problem to be solved?
   - How would we act as a participant in a training event?
   - How would we act as a manager of human resource development?
   - How would we act on a blind date?
   - In what ways do we complement the other seasonings?

   (Ten to fifteen minutes.)

6. Each subgroup introduces its members in terms of the preceding questions or others of their choice. (Ten to fifteen minutes.)

7. The facilitator leads a discussion of how participants can be sensitive to one another during the training. The danger of stereotyping one another is also pointed out. The facilitator elicits discussion using questions such as the following:
   - How did you react to being instructed to place yourself in a group based on certain characteristics?
   - What were your reactions to others in your group during the activity? When making and hearing introductions?
   - What did you learn about being in a homogeneous group?
   - What did you learn about introducing yourself to others? What did you learn about how introductions contribute to setting the atmosphere? How will this help you to be more sensitive to your fellow participants?
   - What implications do these learnings have for you back on the job?

   (Fifteen to twenty minutes.)

Variations
- The facilitator may bring in parsley, garlic, ginger, and pepper for the participants to sample to decide which subgroup to join or for subgroups to use in their descriptions of themselves.

- The activity can be used as an introduction to diversity.
- The activity can be used a part of a team-building effort.

Submitted by Marian K. Prokop.

Marian K. Prokop *is a senior editor for Pfeiffer & Company in San Diego, California. She previously worked as a writer/trainer for migrant education programs in New York and California. Ms. Prokop has coauthored two books:* Pfeiffer's Official Frequent Flyer Guide *(1989) and* Migrant Students at the Secondary Level: Issues and Opportunities for Change *(1985). She has been a frequent contributor to the* Annuals, *and her latest book,* Managing to Be Green: An Environmental Primer, *was published by Pfeiffer & Company in 1993.*

PARSLEY, GARLIC, GINGER, PEPPER CHARACTERISTICS SHEET A

Parsleys Like:
Dwight and Mamie Eisenhower
Good cheddar
French impressionists
Disneyland
Oklahoma!

Famous Parsleys:
Doris Day
Pat Boone
Mary Martin
Art Linkletter
Annette Funicello
Frankie Avalon
Jane Pauley
Perry Como
Marilyn Monroe
Troy Donahue

Key Traits of Parsleys:
Crisp
Fresh
Tender and traditional

What Parsleys Do:
Drive station wagons
Own garden tools
Make good brownies
Play Christmas carols on the electric organ
Have an ice cream freezer

Parsley Careers:
Librarian
Antique-reproduction furniture maker
Keypunch operator
Dump truck operator
Roofer
Home economics teacher
Carpenter
Tool-and-die maker
Crafts worker
Zoological-park animal feeder

PARSLEY, GARLIC, GINGER, PEPPER CHARACTERISTICS SHEET B

Garlics Like:
Zane Grey and Louis L'Amour
Baked beans
Sports trivia
Square dancing and polkas
Touch football

Famous Garlics:
Dolly Parton
Marlon Brando
Ann-Margret
Harry Belafonte
Tina Turner
John Wayne
Beverly Sills
Omar Sharif
Maria Callas
Rudolf Valentino

Key Traits of Garlics:
Ripe
Generous
Reeking of life

What Garlics Do:
Keep your children, pets, or relatives overnight
Have party snacks and beverages always ready for action
Smoke and overeat without guilt
Leave the tops off wine bottles, rubber cement, and nail polish
Never clean out a drawer or throw anything away

Garlic Careers:
Cosmetologist
Rehabilitation counselor
Bank cashier
Massage therapist
House parent
Shoe salesclerk
Missionary
Newspaper reporter
Orderly
Health-services administrator

PARSLEY, GARLIC, GINGER, PEPPER CHARACTERISTICS SHEET C

Gingers Like:
Alistair Cooke and Jackie Onassis
Crisp vegetables
Oil paintings
Psychotherapy
Fresh linen

Famous Gingers:
Audrey Hepburn
Humphrey Bogart
Joanne Woodward
Laurence Olivier
Katharine Hepburn
Andy Warhol
Joan Crawford
Truman Capote
Glenda Jackson
Frank Sinatra

Key Traits of Gingers:
Mysterious
Caustic
Subtle

What Gingers Do:
Like old culture, old paintings, old furniture
Always have four types of mustard on hand
Edit their conversations before they speak
Name their pets after characters in literature
Serve as excellent sources for resolving questions of etiquette

Ginger Careers:
Archaeologist
Electrocardiograph technician
Interior decorator
Political commentator
Welder
Art gallery curator
Bookbinder
Air-traffic controller
Food chemist
Chamber music choral director

PARSLEY, GARLIC, GINGER, PEPPER CHARACTERISTICS SHEET D

Peppers Like:
Fred Astaire and Ginger Rogers
Hot crab in a chafing dish
Folk art
The Greek Islands
Swan Lake

Famous Peppers:
Lauren Bacall
Groucho Marx
Zsa Zsa Gabor
Cary Grant
Judy Garland
Mickey Rooney
Lena Horne
Gene Kelly
Shirley MacLaine
Phineas T. Barnum

Key Traits of Peppers:
Fiery
Sensuous
Dramatic

What Peppers Do:
Are constantly in motion
Seek out applause
Wear conspicuous jewelry
Drive late-model, expensive cars
Give their children family names, but never call them by their given names

Pepper Careers:
Broadway star
Government spokesperson
Funeral director
Heart transplant surgeon
TV star
Talk show host
Festival organizer
University president
Monarch
Public relations specialist

519. DISABILITY AWARENESS: PROVIDING EQUAL OPPORTUNITIES IN THE TRAINING ENVIRONMENT

Goals

- To raise the participants' awareness of the need to provide equal access to training opportunities for persons with disabilities.
- To allow the participants to experience the potential frustrations that persons with disabilities may encounter in an environment or activity that does not accommodate them.
- To provide a model activity for use in disability-awareness training.

Group Size

Up to thirty participants. This activity is designed for use with practicing and prospective HRD trainers as participants.

Time Required

One hour and fifteen minutes to one hour and thirty minutes. Additional time is required to prepare the room for the activity (see Physical Setting).

Materials

- One red and one blue felt-tipped marker for each participant.
- One sheet of name-tent paper for each participant. Name-tent paper is $8\frac{1}{2}"$ x 11" white paper with a horizontal line one-third of the way down the page and a second horizontal line two-thirds of the way down the page (Figure 1). Folding the page at these lines creates a triangle-shaped name tent (Figure 2).

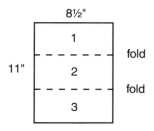

Figure 1. Name-Tent Paper

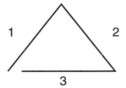

Figure 2. Name Tent

- A white, stick-on name tag for each participant, designated as follows:
  - One-fourth should have the words "Sight Impaired";
  - One-fourth should have the words "Mobility Impaired";
  - One-fourth should have the words "Physically Impaired";
  - One-fourth should have the words "Hearing Impaired"; and
- For one-fourth of the participants: Pieces of nylon string cut to lengths of 44" with the ends tied together to form a loop (see Figure 3).

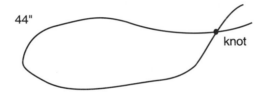

Figure 3. String Loops

- For one-fourth of the participants: Pairs of foam earplugs.
- For one-fourth of the participants: Posterboard strips cut 3" x 9" to be used as eye coverings. Each eye covering should have two 18" pieces of cotton string attached in a manner that allows the strips to be tied around a participant's head to cover his or her eyes (see Figure 4). Additionally, the eye coverings should be constructed so that one-half have no eye-holes and one-half have one eye-hole.

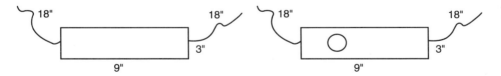

Figure 4. Eye Coverings

- For one-fourth of the participants: a roll of 1" or 2" paper surgical tape and a pair of scissors.
- A copy of the Disability Awareness Background Sheet for each participant.
- A paper name tent for each table, half of which have the number "1" written on both sides and half of which have the number "2" written on both sides.
- A newsprint flip chart and felt-tipped markers.
- Masking tape for posting newsprint.

Physical Setting

A large room with half of the tables and chairs on the left side of the room and half of the tables and chairs on the right side of the room. The tables on the left side of the room are labeled with the paper name tents with the number "1" written on both sides, and the tables on the right side of the room are labeled with the paper name tents with the number "2" written on both sides. Each table should be set up as follows:

- Sheets of white paper with horizontal lines in the center of the table, one sheet for each available chair.
- A red marker and a blue marker set at each chair.
- A stick-on labeled name tag placed at each chair, along with its corresponding training aid:
  - "Sight Impaired": either a solid eye cover or one with one eye hole;
  - "Hearing Impaired": a pair of earplugs;
  - "Mobility Impaired": a string loop; and
  - "Physically Impaired": a roll of surgical tape and a pair of scissors.

Process

1. The facilitator announces the goals of the activity and tells the participants that each has been assigned a disability, as indicated on the name tag at his or her place. Each participant is to take the name tag and to wear it throughout the activity or until told to remove it. (Five minutes.)

2. The facilitator tells the participants that, to get the full impact from the activity, they will simulate the disabilities assigned to them. The facilitator tells the participants that they will also find training aids at their places and that each participant is to use a training aid as follows:
   - Each participant whose name tag says "Sight Impaired" is to wear a poster board eye cover (i.e., tie the eye covering around his or her head so that the eyes are covered). If the eye covering has a hole, it should be placed over the participant's weakest eye (usually the one opposite the writing hand).

- Each participant whose name tag says "Hearing Impaired" is to put a foam earplug firmly into each ear.
- Each participant whose name tag says "Mobility Impaired" is to place a string loop on the floor and step through it with both feet so that it forms a circle surrounding both feet at the ankles. These participants should also be told to keep their feet approximately shoulder-width apart in order to keep the string from falling down.
- Each participant whose name tag says "Physically Impaired" should extend the fingers of each hand, with each thumb straight along the forefinger. A fellow participant should then use some of the surgical tape to tape the fingers and thumb of each hand together so that both hands are immobilized.

(Ten minutes.)

3. The facilitator announces that, when dealing with one another throughout this activity, the participants should respond on the basis of the disabilities indicated on the name tags worn by other participants. Assistance may be rendered to other participants during the activity. At this point, if the facilitator is using a microphone, he or she should turn it off. Otherwise, the facilitator should lower his or her voice for the remainder of the activity so that participants with ear plugs will have difficulty hearing the instructions. (Five minutes.)

4. Once all participants have their "disability" training aids in place, the facilitator tells the participants to stand and pick up all their personal belongings. The facilitator then tells the participants that they will have five minutes to move to the other side of the room and be reseated. In other words, those at tables with "1" name tents are to move to tables with "2" name tents, and vice versa. During this time, the facilitator remains alert to participants who need assistance; after allowing time for other participants to provide help, the facilitator assists the participants who need help and who are not receiving it. (Ten minutes.)

5. Once all participants are reseated, the facilitator informs them that they are now going to perform a simple task often experienced in a training or meeting environment. The facilitator instructs participants as follows:

"Everyone sitting at a table with a name tent bearing the number "1" will use the blue marker, and everyone at a table numbered "2" will use the red marker. In the center of each table is a stack of blank sheets of paper with lines drawn on them; each participant is to take one sheet." (Five to ten minutes.)

6. Next, the facilitator instructs each participant to use the appropriate marker to print his or her name in the center (between the two lines) of the page. Then, each participant is instructed to fold his or her sheet at the lines, thus turning the paper into a triangle-shaped name tent resembling

the numbered name tent on the table (Figure 5). Again, during this time, the facilitator remains alert to participants who need assistance; after allowing time for other participants to provide help, the facilitator assists the participants who need help and who are not receiving it. (Five to ten minutes.)

7. When all participants have accomplished the task, they are instructed to remove their training aids. The facilitator again begins to use the microphone or speak in a normal voice. (Five minutes.)

8. The facilitator leads a discussion of the experience by asking questions such as the following:
   - How did you feel about trying to follow the instructions while disabled? (The facilitator may create a list of the participants' feelings on the newsprint.)
   - How did you try to assist others in completing the task? How did you request assistance from others?
   - How many of you have asked people in training sessions to perform similar tasks such as moving, writing their names, assembling objects, etc.?
   - For those of you who have asked people to perform such tasks, what difficulties, if any, did each of you perceive during that activity?
   - What could I have done, as a facilitator, to reduce frustrations or difficulties in the activity we just concluded?

   (Fifteen minutes.)

9. Each participant is given a copy of the Disability Awareness Background Sheet and is asked to read it. (Five minutes.)

10. The facilitator then initiates a concluding discussion, listing the participants' responses on newsprint, based on the following questions:
    - What have you learned about how disabilities may affect training? How was your awareness raised?
    - What kinds of things can we do in general to make assignments and activities easier to people who have disabilities?
    - What can each of you do in your particular work and other environments to apply your learnings from this experience?

    (Ten to fifteen minutes.)

Variations

- The activity or task that participants perform once they relocate can be changed to fit the training topic or environment in which it is performed.

- Other training aids may be used by having participants:
  - Utilize wheelchairs or crutches to simulate a mobility impairment;
  - Wear mittens or socks on their hands to simulate a physical disability;
  - Wear sunglasses with petroleum jelly smeared on the lenses to simulate a sight impairment; or
  - Wrap poster board or other stiff material around their legs so that they cannot bend their knees, thus simulating a mobility impairment.
- After step 10, the participants can form subgroups and design a training activity that meets the guidelines outlined on the Disability Awareness Background Sheet.
- After step 10, each participant can use the guidelines on the Disability Awareness Background Sheet to redesign a training activity that he or she uses frequently and then share the results with the group.

Submitted by Robert William (Bob) Lucas.

Robert William (Bob) Lucas *is the Training Manager at the National Headquarters of the American Automobile Association in Heathrow, Florida. For the past twenty years, he has conducted training in profit, nonprofit, military, government, consulting, and volunteer environments. His areas of expertise include management training, interpersonal communication, adult learning, customer service, and employee development. Mr. Lucas has served on the boards of directors of ASTD in Florida and in Washington, D.C., on a product-advisory committee for the American Management Association, and on the Curriculum Review Board of Orlando College. He also is an adjunct faculty member at several colleges in the Orlando area. His recent publications include two books,* Coaching Skills: A Guide for Supervisors *and* Effective Interpersonal Relationships.

DISABILITY AWARENESS BACKGROUND SHEET

Many trainers and presenters use a variety of materials, activities, and techniques to teach and reinforce key concepts. In the past, however, few have given thought to the accessibility of the program or its contents to participants with disabilities.

Prior to January, 1992, failing to ensure that all people could access training locations, materials, and content meant a potential loss of participants with disabilities. In 1992, a new dimension was added. Under Title III of the Americans with Disabilities Act (ADA), organizations that offer public services must make them accessible to the disabled or face potential legal action. Under Title I of the ADA, on July 26, 1992, all organizations with twenty-five or more employees are required to make training and all other employee-development opportunities accessible to employees with disabilities. Organizations with fifteen or more employees come under the same guidelines on July 26, 1994.

"Accessible" means providing the means and opportunity for a person with a disability to access a program. The term "reasonable accommodation" is used in the text of the ADA to indicate that, within certain guidelines, you are expected to assist persons with disabilities in attaining access. These guidelines vary by organization and are subject to interpretation by the courts.

The penalties for failure to comply are potentially stiff: up to $50,000 for the first incident and up to $100,000 for subsequent violations. These fines are probably far more costly than modifying a training activity or selecting a training site to make it accessible to the disabled.

Some simple accommodations include the following:

- Soliciting special learning, environmental, or dietary needs of participants on program registration forms;
- Selecting a training site that is accessible, both inside and out, to all participants;
- Directing people to required seats as they arrive in order to reduce the need to move later;
- Providing prepared name badges and/or preassembled name tents, or preparing name tents for the participants when they register;
- Allowing participants more time to relocate, if moving is an essential part of the program;
- Using a microphone or speaking louder when giving instructions, to allow hearing-impaired participants to hear better;
- Disseminating notices or instructions in a variety of formats (e.g., overhead transparencies or other visual aids, written, tape recorded, voice mail, computerized E-mail) to ensure that all people have access to the information;

- Designing room layouts with accessibility for people with sight or mobility impairments;
- Selecting activities in which all participants can take part;
- Developing and using training aids that enhance the learning opportunities for all participants; and
- Stressing that for cohesiveness, networking, team building, time saving, or whatever, it is all right for participants to assist one other.

Complying with the ADA is not difficult and can go a long way in developing your reputation and that of your organization as caring and concerned. Providing accessibility for the disabled is no longer just good business, it is the law.

520. THE EMPLOYMENT CASE: EXPLORING ORGANIZATIONAL VALUE CONFLICTS

Goals

- To offer the participants an opportunity to examine, identify, and clarify their personal and professional values.
- To encourage the participants to explore the relationship between personal values and organizational values.
- To offer the participants an opportunity to influence and be influenced by one another in a value-based group decision-making task.
- To demonstrate how values affect organizational decision making.
- To reinforce the importance of making legal hiring decisions (by eliminating prejudice in hiring).

Group Size

Two to five subgroups of five to eight members each.

Time Required

One hour and twenty to thirty minutes.

Materials

- A copy of The Employment Case Background Sheet for each participant.
- A copy of The Employment Case Individual Ranking Sheet for each participant.
- A copy of The Employment Case Group Ranking Sheet for each subgroup.
- A copy of The Employment Case Discussion Sheet for each participant.
- A pencil for each participant.
- A clipboard or other portable writing surface for each participant.

Physical Setting

A room large enough so that each subgroup can work in a circular configuration and without disturbing the other subgroups. Movable chairs should be provided.

Process

1. After announcing the goals of the activity, the facilitator distributes copies of the background sheet, copies of the individual ranking sheet, pencils, and clipboards or other portable writing surfaces.
2. The participants are instructed to read the background sheet and then to complete the individual ranking sheet. (Fifteen minutes.)
3. The facilitator forms subgroups of five to eight members each, trying as much as possible to include a mix of genders and races in each subgroup. Each participant is given a copy of the group ranking sheet.
4. Each subgroup is instructed to act as the company's executive committee; to come to a group consensus ranking of the candidates, if possible; and to fill out the group ranking sheets if consensus is achieved. (Twenty-five minutes.)
5. After twenty-five minutes the facilitator calls time, reconvenes the total group, and asks these questions:
   - What differences did you see between your personal and professional values? What differences did you see between your personal values and the organization's values? How did those differences affect the ranking choices you made?
   - What similarities and differences in rankings did you see among the members of your subgroup?
   - What issues were most important to your subgroup?
   - What conflicts came up? How did you deal with those conflicts?

   (Fifteen minutes.)
6. The facilitator distributes copies of The Employment Case Theory Sheet, asks the participants to read this sheet, and then leads a discussion based on the following questions:
   - What have you learned about values that affect decision making in organizations? What examples can you cite from your own organizational experience?
   - What legal issues are involved in organizational hiring decisions?
   - What are some ways to deal effectively with value conflicts in organizational settings?
   - What have you learned about values and decision making that you can apply to your own organizational life?

Variations

- If the participants represent a single organization, the characteristics of candidates may be changed to more closely fit an organizational profile.

- The case may be used as an introduction to in-depth training on affirmative action or current hiring legislation.
- The subgroups may be given the same list of candidates but different company values. Differences in ranking and conflicts may then be related to differing company philosophies.

Submitted by Joann Keyton.

Joann Keyton, Ph.D., is an assistant professor of group and organizational communication in the Theatre and Communication Arts Department of Memphis State University in Tennessee. She consults with local and national companies and state and local governments. In addition, she provides training for chambers of commerce and civic organizations. She specializes in organizational groups, sexual harassment and flirting within organizations, mentoring, and employment discrimination. Professor Keyton also serves on the editorial board of Small Group Research.

THE EMPLOYMENT CASE BACKGROUND SHEET

Your company's public relations officer recently resigned, and in the wake of that resignation the company decided that this was a good time to upgrade the position to that of public relations director. The person hired for this position is to be responsible for directing all internal and external communication as well as dealing with the public and the media. You are a member of the executive committee, which is charged with selecting the best candidate for this new position. Your company values good internal relations, promoting from within to maintain a "family atmosphere," and maintaining quality versus rapid growth.

Like the other executive-committee members, you consider public relations to be an essential organizational function. Also, the person hired for this new position will be a fellow committee member, which means that you will be spending a great deal of time working closely with him or her in guiding the organization toward its future. Consequently, you are very concerned with putting the right person in the job.

Before the public relations officer resigned, she interviewed candidates for the job and narrowed the choices to the following five. You and your fellow committee members will make your choice from these five. Here are the outgoing officer's notes on the five candidates:

Tonya Russell is a black female who lives in another city. She is married, and her husband will relocate with her. Tonya has a Master's degree in public relations, is sharp in appearance, and has excellent interpersonal skills. However, her practical experience is limited. She has made it clear that she would expect the company to help her husband find employment after relocating.

Bill Chambers is a white male with a great personality. His résumé is full of success stories in a variety of endeavors, but he lacks solid public-relations credentials. Bill expects a salary 30 percent higher than the top of the range that the company has budgeted for this position.

Jane Phillips is a white female from another city. She is confined to a wheelchair. Jane is in great demand in the field of public relations; in fact, it is surprising that she applied for this position. Apparently, she wants to relocate to this city. Jane's references attest to the fact that she is extremely talented at public relations, but rumor has it that she is very difficult to work with. Hiring Jane would bring prestige and visibility to the company and would help it move from regional to national prominence.

Scott Vittelli is a white male who is currently employed in the company's Personnel Department, where the public-relations activity has been based previously. He has worked for the company for ten years and knows it inside and out. He could be immediately productive on the job. However, several secretaries say that Scott has the reputation of making inappropriate sexual advances toward his female colleagues.

Lin Chung is an Oriental male who was recommended by the semi-retired founder of the company, who serves as mentor to most of the members of the executive committee. Lin is married to the founder's daughter, who recently was diagnosed with a serious and often-fatal form of cancer. Previously Lin was the sales manager for a large national company, but he lost that job in a corporate merger. The company founder believes that Lin is capable of handling the new public-relations position.

THE EMPLOYMENT CASE INDIVIDUAL RANKING SHEET

Instructions: Rank order the candidates from 1 (your first choice) to 5 (your last choice). In each case write a brief rationale for your ranking.

Candidate	Rank	Rationale
Tonya Russell	_____	
Bill Chambers	_____	
Jane Phillips	_____	
Scott Vittelli	_____	
Lin Chung	_____	

THE EMPLOYMENT CASE GROUP RANKING SHEET

Instructions: After the members of your group have reached agreement, rank order the candidates from 1 (the group's first choice) to 5 (the group's last choice). In each case write a brief rationale for the group's ranking.

Candidate	Rank	Rationale
Tonya Russell	_____	
Bill Chambers	_____	
Jane Phillips	_____	
Scott Vittelli	_____	
Lin Chung	_____	

THE EMPLOYMENT CASE THEORY SHEET

Each of us sees the world through a screen composed of background and experience. We are drawn to certain ideas, people, and behaviors because of positive experiences associated with them; similarly, we withdraw from other ideas, people, and behaviors because of negative experiences associated with them, because of a lack of understanding, or because of the fear and skepticism that arise from inexperience.

We may like to think that we are free from prejudice or the effects of stereotyping, but the truth is that it is virtually impossible not to be influenced by our backgrounds. People's learned stereotypes and prejudices are evident in all kinds of settings, including the workplace. All of us are more inclined to collaborate with certain people, to praise certain people, to hire certain people, and to promote certain people—based at least partially on our personal likes and dislikes.

Often our personal and professional judgment will be at war with each other. For instance, I may admire the quality and timeliness of one coworker's monthly sales reports but feel uncertain about how to position myself when I talk to her because she is confined to a wheelchair. I may admire another coworker's confidence as he takes charge of complicated projects but dislike collaborating with him because he insists on doing things his way. I may admire another coworker's ability to deliver an effective presentation and still feel uneasy around that coworker because someone with the same ethnic background bullied me when I was eight years old. It may even be that my favorite colleague at work—the person to whom I am most naturally drawn—spends so much time at the coffee machine that I wonder how she avoids being fired. Day in and day out, our likes and dislikes come into play, often clouding our judgment.

To correct the negative effects of stereotyping, we need to become aware of our screens—how we are likely to interpret information because of the ways in which we perceive the world. Once we are aware, we can choose to change our impressions—to learn more about ideas, people, and behaviors so that we can eliminate our fears and broaden the information base on which we make judgments. Ultimately we can focus the majority of our attention at the workplace on the merits of people's work rather than on personal characteristics.

Another important issue is that in any hiring situation, the Equal Employment Opportunity Commission (EEOC) in the U.S. has clearly defined what criteria can be used in hiring decisions. The same is true of similar agencies in other countries. For example, hiring decisions based on race, gender, ethnic background, religious preferences, or even health conditions may be illegal. The bottom line is that all hiring decisions should be made on the basis of the job requirements and the job description.

INTRODUCTION TO THE INVENTORIES, QUESTIONNAIRES, AND SURVEYS SECTION

The contents of the Inventories, Questionnaires, and Surveys section are provided for training and development purposes. These instruments are not intended for in-depth personal growth, psychodiagnostic, or therapeutic work. Instead, they are intended for use in training groups; for demonstration purposes; to generate data for training or organization development sessions; and for other group applications in which the trainer, consultant, or facilitator helps respondents to use the data generated by an instrument for achieving some form of progress.

Most people have difficulty in describing another person in nonpejorative terms, especially if that person's behavior has had adverse effects. One of the principal benefits of using instrumentation in human resource development (HRD) is that instruments typically provide respondents with new, relatively neutral words to use in describing others. With such a new vocabulary, one can begin to describe another person's behavior as demonstrating "strong inclusion needs" or "low monetary commitment" rather than using more subjective and emotionally laden terms that inhibit rather than enhance communication.

In addition to helping respondents to identify behavior, the comparison of scores from an instrument provides respondents with a convenient and comparatively safe way to exchange interpersonal feedback. The involvement with their own scores helps respondents to understand the theory on which the instrument is based—a typical reason for using an instrument in training. Therefore, there are strong, positive reasons for using instruments in training and development work.

The trainer, consultant, or facilitator must recognize that the scores obtained by individuals on any instrument are the results of their answers to a series of questions at one point in time and that those scores should not be treated with reverence. Such responses typically change over time, for a variety of reasons. The individual's interpretation of a single question the next time may affect his or her answer; a variety of experiences may change the person's self-perception; and so on. Professionals in HRD are encouraged to use instruments simply as one additional means of obtaining data about individuals, with all the risks and potential payoffs that any other data source would yield.

There are three instruments in this year's *Annual*. "Value-System Instrument" stimulates personal reflection about values, needs, wants, and beliefs and generates discussion in groups about the conscious or unconscious ways in which these factors influence behavior. This instrument is best used as an awareness tool to promote teamwork, cooperation, and creativity through an understanding of one's own and others' values.

In "Studying Organizational Ethos," the author defines organizational ethos in terms of core values. He identifies the following as core values for organization development: openness, confrontation, trust, authenticity, proaction, autonomy, collaboration, and experimentation. The instrument measures ethos by examining these eight values. As a result of completing the inventory, respondents can identify weak aspects of ethos in an organization and begin planning the improvement of those aspects.

"Organizational-Type Inventory" is based on the book *Unstable at the Top: Inside the Troubled Organization,* which describes five patterns that result from problem personalities in top management: the dramatic organization, the suspicious organization, the detached organization, the depressive organization, and the compulsive organization. The instrument identifies the patterns that exist in an organization; it is intended to serve as an action-research tool rather than as a rigorous data-gathering instrument. After completing the inventory, respondents are encouraged to discuss the patterns that they identify and to begin action planning to increase individual and organizational use of healthy, positive patterns.

Each instrument includes the theory necessary for understanding, presenting, and using it. All interpretive information, scales or inventory forms, and scoring sheets are also provided for each instrument. Pfeiffer & Company publishes all of the reliability and validity data contributed by the authors of instruments; if readers want additional information on reliability and validity, they are encouraged to contact instrument authors directly. (Authors' addresses and telephone numbers appear in the Contributors list that follows the Presentation and Discussion Resources section.)

VALUE-SYSTEM INSTRUMENT

Michele Stimac

VALUES AND DIVERSITY

Shifting demographics have increased concern about how to manage and value diversity in organizations and in society in general. We are compelled to examine human resource policies and procedures, educational methodologies and practices, equal access, affirmative action, and cultural sensitivity (Morrison, 1992). In the 1970s, in the aftermath of the Watergate scandal, value clarification (Harmin, et al., 1973; Kirschenbaum, 1977) became an important activity, and now concern for values diversity as a spinoff of the larger diversity issue has returned to challenge organizations. As Jamieson and O'Mara (1991) point out:

> Today's workforce is characterized by a mix of values. Some employees will primarily value their home and family life, others their career. Some will value loyalty to their company, others loyalty to their profession, and still others loyalty to themselves. Sometimes men and women will share identical values; at other times their values will differ. Often, what people may have been lacking, such as money, respect, or control, will be most highly valued. Values may change with significant life experiences or simply with age. (p. 27)

It is important for the workplace, for institutions of higher education, and for training organizations to develop ways for individuals and groups to ask significant questions about their value systems in order to determine how diverse groups and individuals can live, work, govern, and develop social structures together.

Bennis (1989, p. 126) advances four tests for those interested in becoming leaders; the third is: "...knowing what your values and priorities are, knowing what the values and priorities of your organization are, and measuring the difference between the two." In his book *The 7 Habits of Highly Effective People*, Covey (1990) suggests that:

> Each of us has many, many maps in our head, which can be divided into two main categories: maps of *the way things are,* or *realities,* and maps of *the way things should be,* or *values.* We seldom question their accuracy; we're usually even unaware that we have them. (p. 24)

Gardner (1990, p. 113) offers the opinion that "If leaders cannot find in their constituencies any base of shared values, principled leadership becomes nearly impossible."

In examining the lives of seventy-seven women who span three generations and who include a group of influential individuals in the women's movement, Astin and Leland (1991) discovered that "clarity of values" was especially important in establishing the women as leaders. Gilligan (1982), in her research on the differences between the ways in which women and men think and solve problems, has shown that women often display values different from those of men, but the styles of leadership that emanate from their values are not less appropriate than those of men.

Frankl (1959), speaking from his own experience in a holocaust camp, states emphatically that human beings are able to live and even die for the sake of their ideals and values.

Examining one's own values, in conjunction with the diverse individuals and groups that surround us, is essential. Teamwork, cooperation, and creativity are more likely to occur when the members of organizations understand their own and their coworkers' values.

THE VALUE-SYSTEM INSTRUMENT

The Value-System Instrument has a twofold purpose: to stimulate personal reflection about *values, needs, wants,* and *beliefs* and to generate discussion in groups about the conscious or unconscious ways in which these influence behavior. Although values, needs, wants, and beliefs are distinct, they are existentially inseparable. It is for this reason that they are integrated into a composite system in the instrument.

The instrument is not normed; it has no scoring method. Its purpose is not to promote certain values and denounce others. Rather, its primary purpose is to generate reflection and discussion about values represented by the diversity of individuals in organizations. It is up to individuals and the organizations in which they function to determine the effects that their values have on either themselves or their organizational systems and to determine what individual or organizational changes need to be made to develop individual and collective cooperation, vision, mission, and goals.

The instrument also can be used in institutions of higher learning in which individuals are being trained as educational leaders or in counseling settings in which individuals are led to explore their values for the purpose of personal growth.

The instrument can be administered in its entirety or in part. Participants can be asked to complete the entire instrument, following the directions in both Step I and Step II, or they can be asked to focus only on certain segments selected by a facilitator who has specific instructional purposes in mind. Those who wish to examine values that appear to impact the workplace, for instance, may prefer to focus on segments such as race/ethnicity, gender, education, age/disability, career/profession/job, and personal fulfillment/wellness. Personal growth facilitators may wish to focus on segments such as marriage/single life, sex, family, etc. Educators may wish to direct their peers' attention to attitudes toward those whom they serve as well as toward those with whom they work.

Sample Use of the Value-System Instrument

There is always risk in describing ways to use an instrument. Readers can lock onto these descriptions as rigidly representing the only appropriate ways to use it. It is presumptuous to assume that any description of group process will fit any situation perfectly. However, this section will offer a sample of how to use the instrument, trusting that it will be perceived as only a hypothetical sample to be adapted appropriately to the situations in which users find themselves.

Three brief scenarios are presented to identify examples of settings in which the instrument might be used. The scenarios are followed by an outline of group process that can be used in working with the instrument. The process is designed with Scenario One in mind. Those who find the other two scenarios closer to their actual situations are encouraged to adapt the process described or to design their own.

Scenario One

The setting is a workplace in which leaders are concerned about maximizing the organization's human resources through effective teamwork. These leaders are pleased that they have achieved some measure of racial, ethnic, and gender diversity in their organization. Now they realize that it is important that the employees in each work unit work together cooperatively as a group and, at the same time, feel free to be individually creative. They decide that providing employees with an opportunity to focus on what they value as individuals and what this means in terms of organizational values, mission, and goals is important. They engage facilitators of group work to conduct this exploration, knowing that issues of diversity are sensitive and that dialogue about them needs to be led by individuals with the proper expertise.

Scenario Two

The setting is a college/university class on leadership attended by adult students who seek an advanced degree in management/leadership. The professor decides that it is important for future leaders to understand their value systems because their values will influence the visions they bring to the workplace, the ways in which they facilitate corporate vision, how they define organizational mission, and how they behave with colleagues. The professor's objective is to get the students who come from various work settings to examine their own values and to discuss how they believe these values influence their behaviors in their organizations.

Scenario Three

The setting is a group counseling one. The counselor has determined that understanding one's values is necessary for personal growth and development. The individuals in the group represent a modest cross-section of society in background, age, gender, and ethnicity. They are more homogenous than heterogeneous. The counselor decides to use a value instrument with the group.

Description of Group Process Related to Scenario One

Time Frame

A block of three hours is scheduled for work on values in each organizational unit (fifteen to twenty-five individuals).

Climate Setting and Clarification of Terms

(Twenty to thirty minutes.) The facilitators establish an open and accepting climate to reduce tension and raise trust. They make sure that everyone is introduced and physically comfortable. They explain at the beginning of the session what values are and the importance they play in personal and professional lives.

According to Rokeach (1979, p. 5), a value system "is an enduring organization of beliefs concerning preferable modes of conduct or end-states of existence along a continuum of relative importance." In other words, values are the "ends" and "means" that we prefer and choose. Rokeach's definition of a value system and Raths, Harmin, and Simon's (1966) criteria for value establishment can be presented to participants for consideration as they complete the instrument. These authors believe that for something to be classified as a value, it has to satisfy several criteria. Persons who "value something" must do the following:

1. Choose freely, choose from alternatives, and choose after thoughtful consideration of consequences;
2. Cherish and affirm what they consider a value; and
3. Repeat actions based on what they value.

Raths et al. believe that if we cannot openly declare a "value," that which we believe to be a value is probably not really a value at all, but only a "value indicator." Value indicators may be easier to change.

Although not everyone may agree that these are criteria for values, they serve as an underpinning for Step II of the Value-System Instrument.

Administration of the Instrument

(Twenty to thirty minutes.) When climate setting is complete and terms are understood, the participants are given twenty to thirty minutes to complete the Value-System Instrument. They are encouraged to work rapidly through Step I. They may take more time with Step II, but their first reactions to the items in Step I are probably the most honest.

In order to allow participants more time to complete the instrument, the facilitators may distribute it prior to the group session and suggest that the participants take it home, where they can spend as much time as they wish completing it. Regardless of where or when the participants complete the instrument, they should be encouraged to respond quickly and spontaneously to the items and then to reflect later on their responses as preparation for the group discussion.

Small-Group Discussion

(Sixty to ninety minutes.) In the group setting, subgroups of four or five members each should be created. If the subgroups are too large, members are less inclined to share their values, needs, wants, and beliefs. Membership in the subgroups can be assigned randomly or can be self-selected; subgroups can be created with some *purposeful diversity mix* in mind.

It is important that participants be advised to share only as much as they wish; the purpose of the instrument is to provoke thinking and honest discussion of the influences in participants' lives but not to do so in a threatening way. On the other hand, facilitators should stress the importance of sharing thoughts. Human beings learn in several ways: by reading, writing, listening, reflecting, and also by talking. When we can articulate what we think, we often discover for the first time what we really believe.

It is obvious from the comprehensiveness of the values instrument that one hour of discussion will not exhaust the issues it generates. Users of the instrument can extend the length of time devoted to the discussion of issues by arranging several meeting times with the same group of participants. Not every value issue needs to be discussed in a single sitting. Participants can learn a great deal from having taken the instrument and reflected on it privately. In the group, they may choose to discuss the issues that are most significant to them and most relevant to the organization and the objectives of the group session. In Scenario One, issues of diversity are an objective. It is up to leaders of the group process to guide the group to reach this objective.

As the subgroups work, the facilitators move from group to group, taking note of what is and what is not being discussed. With this information, they develop questions related to issues they believe the groups need to address. After one-half hour to forty-five minutes of discussion, the facilitators may wish to have the subgroups break and regroup after the facilitators have displayed on a flip chart, overhead projector, or marker board the issues that the groups should consider discussing.

Sample questions that might be displayed are the following:

- Specifically, how do certain values, needs, wants, or beliefs influence your lives: the goals you have set for yourself, your decisions, your behaviors in the organization? (The more specific participants can be, the better.)
- What impact do you think certain of your values have on your coworkers, supervisors, or those whom you supervise?
- What are the great motivators in your value system?
- What in your value system do you see as a force that will contribute to your working as a team member? What do you see as standing in the way of your working as a team member?
- What in your value system will help you to cooperate with others? What will keep you from cooperating with others?
- Can you keep the values you have and be creative in this organization?
- Who are the individuals you might list as persons you would *not* want to share your values with? Why? (Name these only if you are comfortable doing so.)
- Do you want to change any of your responses on the instrument? Which ones? Why?
- Are you interested in changing certain values? How? Why?
- What must you and your organization do to accommodate and maximize acceptance of the diversity of values that exist in the individuals in the organization? Is it possible to do so?
- What happens in the workplace composed of diverse individuals when one or more persons do not like to be with individuals from diverse ethnic backgrounds and races?
- What effect can negative attitudes toward the opposite gender, toward disability, or toward nontraditional sexual orientation have on people's ability to work together? What can we do if such attitudes exist either in ourselves or others?

Facilitators should think through their objectives for the session and develop appropriate questions, which may or may not be similar to the ones above. Facilitators may wish to distribute the questions to participants at the very beginning of the small-group discussion.

Large-Group Discussion and Work

(Thirty to sixty minutes.) When facilitators believe that sufficient time has been devoted to small-group discussion and that critical issues have been examined in the subgroups, the larger group of participants is reassembled. The chief focus of the large group (the organizational work unit) is to debrief what happened in the subgroup discussions, to examine the data generated from those discussions, and to assess where the group as a unit should go from here.

As subgroups are asked to debrief their processes, outcomes should be recorded on flip chart, marker board, or other visual aid so that the entire group can see and work with it.

If the group is comfortable enough to strive for specificity and concreteness, the facilitators should guide the group in that direction. It is, after all, in concreteness that behavior can really be explained and that the impetus to change and grow can develop. Questions such as the following might be posed:

- How satisfied is the group with itself in terms of being a cooperative, productive unit?
- How much more work needs to be done to create cohesive teamwork? What specific work needs to be done? What issues need to be addressed?
- If training is needed, what kind of training is needed? Who should take the lead in providing it?
- What does the larger organization need to do to maximize the work unit's potential?

If facilitators perceive that participants in the large group are uncomfortable and that moving forward in the larger group would be counterproductive, they may deduce that more subgroup work needs to be done. In this case, a follow-up process should be designed to facilitate this work. Rushing through activities for the sake of activity is nonproductive.

Creating learning organizations, as promoted by Senge (1990), can serve as a model for organizational facilitators who attempt to lead individuals to engage in creative dialogue. If units within organizations learn to really communicate, listening takes on a deeper meaning so that trust is built and complex, subtle issues can be uncovered and problems solved collegially. Facilitators who believe in the idea of learning organizations can attempt to guide the large group to communicate and create new ground on which to build solid teamwork. If the subgroup discussions have been thorough and forthright in dealing with value issues, and if the large group is willing to forge new learning, facilitators can help the participants to peel off the veneer of superficial teamwork and develop a truly collaborative work ethic. Facilitators must always, however, take their cue from the observations they make during the small-group discussions and from the tone they detect in the large group to determine the level of learning they should push for.

As indicated earlier, the process outlined above is designed for the situation described in Scenario One. Users of the instrument and facilitators of group process need to be attentive to their unique situations and use their own judgment in devising a process that is tailored to their needs.

As with any learning instrument, the Value-System Instrument should never be used to coerce, chasten, inhibit, or threaten individuals or groups.

REFERENCES

Astin, H.S., & Leland, C. (1991). *Women of influence, women of vision.* San Francisco: Jossey-Bass.

Bennis, W. (1989). *On becoming a leader.* Reading, MA: Addison-Wesley.

Covey, S.R. (1990). *The 7 habits of highly effective people.* New York: Simon & Schuster.

Frankl, V.E. (1984). *Man's search for meaning.* New York: Simon & Schuster.

Gardner, J.W. (1990). *On leadership.* New York: The Free Press.

Gilligan, C. (1982). *In a different voice.* Cambridge, MA: Harvard University Press.

Harmin, M., Kirschenbaum, H., & Simon, S.B. (1973). *Clarifying values through subject matter.* Minneapolis, MN: Winston Press.

Jamieson, D. & O'Mara, J. (1991). *Managing workforce 2000.* San Francisco: Jossey-Bass.

Kirschenbaum, H. (1977). *Advanced value clarification.* San Diego, CA: Pfeiffer & Company.

Morrison, A.M. (1993). *The new leaders: Guidelines on leadership diversity in America.* San Francisco: Jossey-Bass.

Raths, L.E., Harmin, M., & Simon, S.B. (1966). *Values and teaching.* Columbus, OH: Charles E. Merrill.

Rokeach, M. (1979). *Understanding human values: Individual and societal.* New York: The Free Press.

Senge, P.M. (1990). *The fifth discipline.* New York: Currency and Doubleday.

Michele Stimac, Ph.D., *is a professor at Pepperdine University, Graduate School of Education and Psychology. A member of the original team that created Pepperdine's doctoral program in Institutional Management, Dr. Stimac teaches courses in leadership and management of human resources and serves as chairperson for doctoral dissertations. She has published articles in the areas of leadership, career development, peace education, conflict management, and consensus building.*

VALUE-SYSTEM INSTRUMENT

Michele Stimac

Step I

Instructions: Consider each of the items below. Decide which belong in your "value system"—the ones that identify or describe a *value, need, want,* or *belief* of yours. Place an "S" on the line before those items.

In a few instances, you may not accept an item as a part of your own value system but you may believe that it is acceptable for others to do so. Place an "O" before those items.

Before items that you neither accept as part of your own system nor believe others should accept, place an "N."

If you are undecided about any items, place a "U" before those.

Only one letter should appear before each item. It is assumed that if you accept an item as part of your own system, you think it is acceptable for others to do so. In responding to each item, try to be as honest as you can.

Scoring Key:

S = a value, need, want, or belief in my own value system
O = a value, need, want or belief acceptable for others but not for myself
N = a value, need, want, or belief not acceptable for myself or others
U = undecided

Step II

Instructions:

1. After you have completed Step I, go back through the items and reflect on how you marked each one. Place an "X" in the parentheses ( ) after any item that you wish you could have marked differently. In other words, identify those items with which you are personally dissatisfied and would like to change.

2. Finally, underline those items that you would be unwilling to share with others. Identify the persons with whom you would not want to share them and write those persons' names in the margin space next to the items.

> Scoring Key:
>
> S = a value, need, want, or belief in my own value system
> O = a value, need, want, or belief acceptable for others but not for myself
> N = a value, need, want, or belief not acceptable for myself or others
> U = undecided

RACE/ETHNICITY

_____	races are equal	( )
_____	ethnic groups are equal	( )
_____	intermarriage (racial)	( )
_____	intermarriage (ethnic)	( )
_____	willingness to socialize with other races	( )
_____	desire to socialize with other races	( )
_____	willingness to socialize only with certain races	( )
_____	desire to socialize only with certain races	( )
_____	willingness to work with other races	( )
_____	desire to work with other races	( )
_____	willingness to socialize with other ethnic groups	( )
_____	desire to socialize with other ethnic groups	( )
_____	preference for company of own race	( )
_____	preference for company of own ethnic group	( )
_____	preference for socializing with only certain ethnic groups	( )
_____	refusal to work with some ethnic groups	( )
_____	willingness to work with any ethnic group	( )
_____	desire to work with any ethnic group	( )
_____	unwillingness to intermingle with other races	( )
_____	unwillingness to intermingle with other ethnic groups	( )
_____	own ethnic group is superior to others	( )
_____	own race is superior to others	( )
_____	other races are superior to own	( )
_____	other ethnic groups are superior to own	( )

> Scoring Key:
>
> S = a value, need, want, or belief in my own value system
> O = a value, need, want, or belief acceptable for others but not for myself
> N = a value, need, want, or belief not acceptable for myself or others
> U = undecided

GENDER

_____	male and female genders are equal	( )
_____	own gender is superior to the other	( )
_____	control by only males is unjust	( )
_____	control by only females is unjust	( )
_____	partnership between genders in all matters is right and just	( )
_____	the woman's place is in the home	( )
_____	men and women should share domestic responsibilities	( )
_____	men should share the nurturing of children	( )
_____	traditional male and female roles can be reversed	( )

DISABILITY

_____	persons with disabilities have the same rights as those without disabilities	( )
_____	persons with disabilities should have equal access to opportunities	( )
_____	willingness to work with persons with disabilities	( )
_____	desire to work with persons with disabilities	( )
_____	desire to socialize with persons with disabilities	( )

AGE

_____	old age is to be feared	( )
_____	old age is the better part of life	( )
_____	aged people are physically unattractive	( )
_____	aged people are generally useless	( )
_____	aged people are generally as beautiful in spirit as young people	( )
_____	desire to socialize with aged persons	( )
_____	ability to relate well with aged persons	( )
_____	wisdom and age go hand in hand	( )

The 1994 Annual: Developing Human Resources

> Scoring Key:
>
> S = a value, need, want, or belief in my own value system
> O = a value, need, want, or belief acceptable for others but not for myself
> N = a value, need, want, or belief not acceptable for myself or others
> U = undecided

CAREER/PROFESSION/JOB

_____ having a career is more important than being married ( )

_____ having a job is more important than building a career ( )

_____ having a career or profession is more important than developing friends ( )

_____ a career/profession or job is more important than family ( )

_____ having leisure time is more important than building a career ( )

_____ a service-oriented career (job) is more important than a career (job) that only produces goods ( )

EDUCATION

_____ pursuing education for personal growth ( )

_____ pursuing education for professional promotion ( )

_____ pursuing education for monetary gain ( )

_____ pursuing education for aesthetic reasons ( )

_____ pursuing education for joy of discovery ( )

_____ pursuing education for competence ( )

_____ pursuing education for status ( )

_____ pursuing education for power ( )

_____ not wishing to pursue education ( )

_____ education is unnecessary ( )

_____ education is generally irrelevant in the work world ( )

_____ a person cannot get ahead in life without education ( )

_____ life without an education is only partially fulfilled ( )

> Scoring Key:
>
> S = a value, need, want, or belief in my own value system
> O = a value, need, want, or belief acceptable for others but not for myself
> N = a value, need, want, or belief not acceptable for myself or others
> U = undecided

PHYSICAL FITNESS/WELLNESS

_____ being physically fit is important ( )
_____ exercising regularly is important ( )
_____ pleasure that comes from eating and drinking is more important than being physically fit ( )
_____ eating the right foods is important ( )
_____ moderation in drinking alcoholic beverages is important ( )
_____ drinking alcoholic beverages in any amount is unacceptable ( )
_____ drugs of any kind (other than prescription) are destructive to an individual ( )
_____ prescription drugs should be avoided if at all possible ( )
_____ prescription drugs can be used without concern ( )
_____ drugs of any kind can be used liberally ( )

AESTHETICS

_____ beautiful surroundings ( )
_____ the arts ( )
_____ sports are more important than the arts ( )
_____ life is incomplete if lived in unattractive surroundings ( )
_____ beauty is unnecessary ( )
_____ art is worthless ( )

URBAN/RURAL LIVING

_____ preference for living in the city ( )
_____ preference for living in the suburbs ( )
_____ preference for living in a small town ( )
_____ hating the city but not being able to live without it ( )
_____ preference for rural living ( )

> Scoring Key:
>
> S = a value, need, want, or belief in my own value system
> O = a value, need, want, or belief acceptable for others but not for myself
> N = a value, need, want, or belief not acceptable for myself or others
> U = undecided

MATERIAL POSSESSIONS

_____	money is very important	( )
_____	when making decisions, I almost always consider whether or not I will gain money as a result	( )
_____	money is of little importance when making decisions	( )
_____	a person can live contentedly with little money	( )
_____	refusing a marriage partner who has very little money	( )
_____	getting and keeping money is a top priority	( )
_____	getting and spending money is a top priority	( )
_____	having material possessions	( )
_____	possessions must be expensive	( )
_____	quality of possessions is more important than quantity	( )
_____	possessions are unimportant	( )
_____	relationships are preferable to possessions	( )
_____	love is preferable to possessions	( )
_____	wearing expensive clothing is essential to feeling good about oneself	( )
_____	having an expensive car is important	( )
_____	having an expensive home is important	( )
_____	owning a home is important	( )
_____	not wanting to own a home	( )

Scoring Key:
S = a value, need, want, or belief in my own value system
O = a value, need, want, or belief acceptable for others but not for myself
N = a value, need, want, or belief not acceptable for myself or others
U = undecided

MARRIAGE/SINGLE LIFE

_____ marriage before 22 years of age ( )
_____ marriage between 22 years and 30 years of age ( )
_____ marriage after 30 years of age ( )
_____ no marriage ( )
_____ divorce if partners want it ( )
_____ no divorce ( )
_____ living with a member of the opposite sex outside of marriage ( )
_____ commitment without marriage ( )
_____ marriage to a man (woman) fifteen or more years older ( )
_____ marriage to a woman (man) ten or more years younger ( )

SEX

_____ sex only in marriage ( )
_____ extramarital sex ( )
_____ homosexuality ( )
_____ bisexuality ( )
_____ sex only for procreation ( )
_____ sex without commitment ( )
_____ abortion at will of woman ( )
_____ abortion at will of man ( )
_____ abortion only at will of both man and woman ( )
_____ therapeutic abortion only ( )
_____ abortion only in case of rape or incest ( )
_____ abortion never ( )
_____ in vitro fertilization ( )
_____ birth control ( )

> Scoring Key:
>
> S = a value, need, want, or belief in my own value system
> O = a value, need, want, or belief acceptable for others but not for myself
> N = a value, need, want, or belief not acceptable for myself or others
> U = undecided

PERSONAL FULFILLMENT

- _____ being personally fulfilled is more important than making money ( )
- _____ being personally fulfilled is more important than having status ( )
- _____ being personally fulfilled is more important than owning possessions ( )
- _____ a satisfying career is personally fulfilling ( )
- _____ a home life is necessary to be personally fulfilled ( )
- _____ a spouse is necessary to be personally fulfilled ( )
- _____ children are necessary to be personally fulfilled ( )

FAMILY

- _____ traditional concept of family essential to health of society ( )
- _____ concept of family must be redefined ( )
- _____ wanting to have children ( )
- _____ children are essential to family ( )
- _____ wanting only one child ( )
- _____ not wanting to have children ( )
- _____ wanting two children ( )
- _____ wanting more than two children ( )
- _____ wanting a child without marriage ( )
- _____ spouse is most significant other ( )
- _____ mothers are more significant than fathers ( )
- _____ fathers are more significant than mothers ( )
- _____ mothers and fathers are equally significant ( )
- _____ siblings are more significant than parents ( )

Scoring Key:

S = a value, need, want, or belief in my own value system
O = a value, need, want, or belief acceptable for others but not for myself
N = a value, need, want, or belief not acceptable for myself or others
U = undecided

OTHERS

_____	preferring the company of others to being alone	( )
_____	having many significant others	( )
_____	having a few significant others	( )
_____	needing a great deal of time alone	( )
_____	others bring comfort most of the time	( )
_____	others bring pain most of the time	( )
_____	occasionally liking to be alone	( )
_____	not ever liking to be alone	( )
_____	"taking or leaving" others	( )

GOD

_____	there is a God	( )
_____	maybe there is a God	( )
_____	belonging to an organized religion is important	(_)
_____	being privately "religious" is better than belonging to organized religion	( )
_____	being spiritual is more important than being religious	( )
_____	there is hell and punishment after death	( )
_____	there is life in heaven after death	( )
_____	there is nothing after life	( )
_____	having a personal relationship with God is important	( )
_____	God is "the Other," greater than humans, but impersonal	( )
_____	marriage only to someone of the same faith	( )
_____	own religion is only way to God	( )
_____	there are many ways to God	( )

Scoring Key:
S = a value, need, want, or belief in my own value system
O = a value, need, want, or belief acceptable for others but not for myself
N = a value, need, want, or belief not acceptable for myself or others
U = undecided

DEATH

_____ death is to be feared ( )
_____ talking about death is not frightening ( )
_____ death ends all; there is nothing after death ( )
_____ death begins a new life ( )
_____ frequent thinking about death ( )
_____ ability/willingness to imagine oneself dying ( )
_____ death is remote ( )
_____ people are reincarnated ( )

ECOLOGY

_____ concern for the earth and atmosphere is more important than personal convenience ( )
_____ the earth is here for humankind's use, however humans wish to use it ( )
_____ technological advances are more important than preservation of the environment ( )
_____ human progress is more important than preservation of the environment ( )
_____ human progress is measured in terms of conquering the universe ( )
_____ human progress is measured by living in harmony with the earth and with other humans ( )

> Scoring Key:
>
> S = a value, need, want, or belief in my own value system
> O = a value, need, want, or belief acceptable for others but not for myself
> N = a value, need, want, or belief not acceptable for myself or others
> U = undecided

PEACE/WAR

_____ humankind has outgrown war; war is outmoded ( )
_____ there is no such thing as a just war ( )
_____ peace cannot be attained without justice ( )
_____ war will always be necessary as long as humans inhabit the earth ( )
_____ peace is the absence of conflict ( )
_____ peace is that situation in which conflict is resolved through discussion, negotiation, or law ( )
_____ the media foster violence ( )
_____ as long as humans exist, there will be violence ( )
_____ violence is abhorrent ( )
_____ humans can vanquish violence ( )

POLITICS

_____ politics as a career ( )
_____ avoiding discussing politics whenever possible ( )
_____ disliking politics ( )
_____ one cannot be in politics and have a sense of peace ( )
_____ one has to participate in politics to have a sense of peace ( )
_____ keeping informed about politics ( )
_____ politics is fascinating ( )
_____ politics "makes the world go 'round" ( )
_____ being barely knowledgeable about politics ( )
_____ being knowledgeable about politics ( )
_____ total disinterest in politics ( )
_____ politics and morality are incompatible ( )

If you are finishing Step I, refer to page 141 for directions for Step II.

STUDYING ORGANIZATIONAL ETHOS: THE OCTAPACE PROFILE[1]

Udai Pareek

THE NEED FOR TAXONOMICAL CLARITY

Studies of organizational culture use different terminology, and the same terms are used with different meanings. There is a need to clarify terms and to create common understanding of their use. Brief definitions of some often-used terms are offered here as a precursor to using these terms for further study.

Words used in the context of organizational culture include ethics, values, beliefs, attitudes, norms, ethos, climate, environment, and culture. Ethics refers to normative aspects—what is socially desirable. Values, beliefs, attitudes, and norms are interrelated. Interactions between beliefs and values result in attitude formation (beliefs x values = attitudes) and then produce norms. When these become "institutionalized" (accumulated and integrated), the result is social phenomena.

Culture-related concepts also can be seen as multilevel concepts. At the core (first level) are the values, which give a distinct identity to a group. This is the *ethos* of the group. The *Random House Dictionary* defines ethos as "the fundamental character or spirit of a culture...dominant assumptions of a people or period."

The second-level concept is that of climate, which can be defined as the perceived attributes of an organization and its subsystems as reflected in the way it deals with its members, groups, and issues. The emphasis is on *perceived attributes* and the working of the subsystems.

The third-level concept relates to the effects of the climate. The *Random House Dictionary* defines atmosphere as a "distinct quality" and environment as "...affecting the existence or development of someone or something." The concept of *atmosphere* can be proposed as one related to the effect of climate.

The fourth-level concept is that of culture, the cumulative beliefs, values, and assumptions that underlie transactions with nature and important phenomena, as reflected in artifacts, rituals, and so on. Culture is reflected in the means that are adopted to deal with basic phenomena.

---

[1] Expanded, with permission, from a preliminary note published in *HRD Newsletter*, October-December 1992, pp. 4-7, 16.

These concepts need elaboration and discussion. The author has developed four instruments to measure them: ethos (OCTAPACE Profile), climate (MAO-C), atmosphere (MAO-A), and culture (Organizational Survey). The instrument on ethos is shared here. Interested readers can obtain information on the other instruments from the reference list at the end of this article.

ORGANIZATIONAL ETHOS AND VALUES

As already suggested, organizational ethos can be defined in terms of core values. The author suggests seven organizational values: openness, confrontation, trust, authenticity, proaction, autonomy, and collaboration (Pareek, 1975) as the core values for organization development. The initial instrument was used extensively in OD and HRD (Rao & Abraham, 1990), and another value was added, that of experimentation.[2] In addition to being an acronym for the values, "octapace" is a meaningful term, indicating eight (octa) steps (pace) to create functional ethos. The following definitions may help to clarify the values:

1. **O**penness: Spontaneous expression of feelings and thoughts and receiving feedback and information without defensiveness;
2. **C**onfrontation: Facing—not shying away from—problems; deeper analysis of interpersonal problems; taking on challenges;
3. **T**rust: Maintaining confidentiality of information shared by others and not misusing it; a sense of assurance that others will help when needed and will honor mutual obligations and commitments;
4. **A**uthenticity: Congruence between what one feels, says, and does; owning one's actions and mistakes; unreserved sharing of feelings;
5. **P**roaction: Initiative; preplanning and preventive action; calculating payoffs before taking action;
6. **A**utonomy: Using and giving freedom to plan and act in one's own sphere; respecting and encouraging individual and role autonomy;
7. **C**ollaboration: Giving help to, and asking for help from, others; team spirit; working together (individuals and groups) to solve problems; and
8. **E**xperimentation: Using and encouraging innovative approaches to solve problems; using feedback for improving; taking a fresh look at things; encouraging creativity.

---

[2] Somnath Chattopadhyay suggested this value. He also prepared a long questionnaire to measure the eight OCTAPACE values.

THE OCTAPACE PROFILE

The OCTAPACE Profile has been developed to measure organizational ethos in terms of the eight values listed previously. The instrument contains three items that measure values and two items that measure beliefs on each of the eight dimensions, with a total of forty items. Respondents rate their organizations on eight aspects, using a five-point scale. The scores range from 5 to 20 on each aspect.

Reliability and Validity

Split-half reliability of the OCTAPACE Profile on a sample of 135 college/university teachers was found to be .81 (Mathur, 1991).

To discover the internal consistency of the instrument, each of the forty items was correlated with the total score for a group of 102 managers from three steel plants. Out of forty, twenty-seven items had correlations significant at the .001 level, four at the .01 level, and two (numbers 19 and 35) at the .05 level. Six items (numbers 12, 22, 25, 31, 36, and 40) had zero correlation, and one (14) had negative but nonsignificant correlation with the total score. Five items with zero and negative correlations are on the aspects of openness (25), authenticity (12), autonomy (14, 22), collaboration (23), and experimenting (40). It is interesting to note that all these items are among the eleven items that are worded negatively. On the whole, item-total correlations provide satisfactory results.

To test the effect of social desirability on the items, analysis of kurtosis and skewness was carried out on all forty items, eight aspects, and the total OCTAPACE Profile on a sample of 102 managers from three steel plants. Only two items (numbers 15 and 26) had higher kurtosis, the first item being leptokurtic and the second platikurtic. Confrontation and collaboration also were leptokurtic. Skewing was satisfactory except for items 29, 33, and 34, all of which were negatively skewed. On the whole, the indices were acceptable.

Validity was indirectly tested by comparing the scores from three departments ranked by two judges for their effectiveness. The rankings of the judges, independently done, agreed with one another. Tests showed no differences between the first- and second-ranked departments or between the second- and third-ranked departments. However, there were significant differences between the first- and third-ranked departments, the former having higher means than the latter on the following aspects: confrontation (significant at the .01 level), collaboration (.04 level), proaction (.048 level), and openness (.10 level). Validity needs to be further tested and established.

The mean values of seven groups are provided in Table 1. Based on mean and standard deviation (SD) values, tentative norms were obtained, and these are shown in Table 2.

Table 1. Mean Values of the OCTAPACE Profile

	College/University Teachers	General Managers	Managers in Steel Plants			Construction Managers	Dairy Co-Op Managers	
	T n=135	M n=55	S1 n=42	S2 n=35	S3 n=25	C1 n=35	D1 n=29	D2 n=85
O	14.5	15.8	14.4	15.2	13.6	11.4	13.4	15.0
C	13.2	15.0	14.0	14.2	12.0	13.8	14.8	14.9
T	13.2	14.8	13.6	13.8	13.1	11.2	13.2	14.5
A	12.6	13.1	12.5	12.8	12.4	11.2	11.5	14.2
P	13.6	14.4	15.0	16.6	13.7	13.0	13.4	15.4
A	12.3	14.0	13.8	14.9	13.9	12.7	12.7	12.3
C	14.4	14.9	14.9	15.0	13.4	13.0	15.7	13.9
E	13.8	14.0	13.7	14.7	12.6	12.4	12.4	13.6

Table 2. Tentative Norms for the OCTAPACE Profile

	:	Low	:	High
1. Openness	:	13	:	17
2. Confrontation	:	10	:	16
3. Trust	:	10	:	16
4. Authenticity	:	10	:	14
5. Proaction	:	12	:	18
6. Autonomy	:	11	:	16
7. Collaboration	:	13	:	17
8. Experimenting	:	11	:	16

CORRELATES OF ORGANIZATIONAL ETHOS

To study the correlates of ethos, OCTAPACE Profile scores were correlated with internality (internal locus of control) at the individual level and with motivational climate and organizational learning at the organizational level.

Internality was measured by a scale developed for use in organizations (Pareek, 1992). It measures internality, externality (others), and externality (chance). Correlations were found for two groups (N = 39 and N = 35, respectively). In one group (N = 39), externality (chance) did not have significant correlations with any aspect of ethos. Regarding internality, all aspects except authenticity had positive correlations significant at the .01 level. In the other group (N = 35), there were three positive correlations, significant at the .05 level (for confrontation, authenticity, and experimenting). Externality (others) was negatively correlated (significant at the .01 level) for five aspects; proaction, autonomy, and collaboration did not have significant correlations. It can be concluded that OCTAPACE ethos reinforces internality among managers, or that managers who score high on internality perceive the ethos in a positive way.

Regarding organizational variables, motivational climate was measured by the MAO-C (Pareek, 1989). This instrument assesses organizational climate in terms of six motives, three positively correlated to organizational functioning (achievement, expert power, and extension) and three negatively correlated (control, affiliation, and dependency). In one group of thirty-five managers, achievement climate was positively correlated (.05 level of significance) with openness. Extension climate (concern for others and larger cause) had positive correlations (significant at the .01 level) with all aspects except autonomy and collaboration. Control climate had negative correlations (at the .05 level of significance) with openness and confrontation. No other correlation was significant. It can be concluded that extension climate seems both to contribute to and be promoted by OCTAPACE ethos.

Organizational learning (OL) mechanisms were assessed by means of the Organizational Learning Diagnostics (OLD) (Pareek, 1988). This instrument helps to diagnose organizational learning during the three phases of change (innovation, implementation, and stabilization) and five OL mechanisms (experimenting and flexibility, mutuality and teamwork, contingency and incremental planning, temporary system, and competence building). Of all the correlations between the OCTAPACE Profile and the OLD, the most significant aspect was trust, which had five positive correlations (.01 level of significance) with two phases (implementation and stabilization) and three mechanisms (teamwork, contingency planning, and temporary systems). The implementation phase had four significant correlations (all significant at the .01 level) with openness, confrontation, trust, and proaction. It can be concluded that although trust promotes organizational learning, OCTAPACE ethos is especially important at the stage of implementation of change.

In conclusion, internal locus of control and OCTAPACE ethos reinforce each other. OCTAPACE ethos promotes and is reinforced by extension climate; trust promotes organizational learning, whereas OCTAPACE ethos is critical mainly in the implementation phase. These findings are tentative and need further exploration.

SCORING AND INTERPRETATION

Based on the tentative norms (Table 2), scores shown under the column labeled "Low" or scores below these show weak aspects of the ethos in the organization. These can then be used for action planning to improve organizational ethos, as suggested in the next section. New norms can be evolved by finding mean scores of each aspect of ethos for a large sample, and using one-half standard deviation, "low scores" can be fixed (mean *minus* $\frac{1}{2}$ SD).

Use of the Instrument

This instrument can be used by HRD professionals and OD consultants to improve organizational ethos and to increase openness, creativity, and collaboration. The following uses have been tried in some organizations:

1. After they have responded to the instrument, the participants are given definitions of the eight values of organizational ethos. They may then work in small groups to prepare a profile of their organizational ethos in terms of "low," "medium," or "high." While this is being done, the instrument is being scored. The profile of the organization derived from the scoring of the participants' responses to the instrument then is distributed to the groups, and the members discuss how the two profiles match or differ and why.

2. The "weak" aspects of the organizational profile are used for action planning. Each weak value is assigned to a small group that prepares four lists: indicators of the weakness of that value in their organization, outcome of the weak aspect (its cost to the organization), forces that promote that value in the organization, and forces that make the value weak. These findings are then discussed in the larger group.

3. Then small groups regroup to prepare action plans—specific action steps to improve a specific value of ethos (ways of promoting positive forces and, more importantly, of reducing or eliminating the negative forces).

4. After four to six months, the group reviews the progress of implementation of the action plans and improvement in organizational ethos and notes indicators of improvement or deterioration.

5. The instrument can be completed for the total organization (O), or a specific unit (U), and/or the "ideal" ethos (I) one would like to have in the organization. Differences in the mean values of the eight aspects of ethos (O, U, and I) then can be calculated.

6. Small groups can be assigned to work on the differences. The difference in mean values for the organization and the unit may show if the respondents perceive the ethos of the total organization (macro ethos) as "better" than that of the unit (micro ethos), or vice versa. There also may be differences in specific dimensions. For example, in a multilocational manufacturing company, mean scores of micro ethos were higher than those for macro ethos, although the difference was significant only on one value (confrontation), indicating that the company was seen as avoiding basic issues. This information became a useful lead for discussing implications and possible action to be taken.

7. Indices of "fit" also can be derived, between desired or ideal ethos and the perceived ethos. This can be done by averaging the difference between I (ideal) and O (macro ethos), and between I and U (micro ethos). In the case of the manufacturing company, for example, it was

found that there was a good fit on autonomy for both the macro and micro ethos. For both micro and macro ethos, there was the least fit on confrontation and proaction, followed by openness, trust, and collaboration. The need to work on increasing the fit (and reducing dissatisfaction) on these values was recognized. This could be done by small-group work, analysis, action planning, and making the plans a strategy for improving ethos.

REFERENCES

Mathur, S. (1991). *A study of some psychological and organization correlates of role stress in college and university teachers.* Unpublished master's thesis in psychology, University of Udaipur.

Pareek, U. (1975). The concept and the process of organization development. *Indian Journal of Social Work, 36*(2), 109-125.

Pareek, U. (1988). Organizational learning diagnostics (OLD): Assessing and developing organizational learning. In J.W. Pfeiffer & L.D. Goodstein (Eds.), *The 1988 annual: Developing human resources* (pp. 125-135). San Diego, CA: Pfeiffer & Company.

Pareek, U. (1989). Motivational analysis of organizations—climate (MAO-C). In J.W. Pfeiffer & L.D. Goodstein (Eds.), *The 1989 annual: Developing human resources* (pp. 161-178). San Diego, CA: Pfeiffer & Company.

Pareek, U. (1992). Locus of control inventory. In J.W. Pfeiffer (Ed.), *The 1992 annual: Developing human resources* (pp. 135-148). San Diego, CA: Pfeiffer & Company.

Rao, T.V., & Abraham, E. (1990). HRD climate survey. In J.W. Pfeiffer (Ed.), *The 1990 annual: Developing human resources* (pp. 143-151). San Diego, CA: Pfeiffer & Company.

Udai Pareek, Ph.D., *is the chairman of the Institute of Development Studies, Jaipur, India, and of the Jaipur HRD Research Foundation. In addition, he is the chairman of the Scientific Advisory Committee of the Indian Institute of Health Management Research and an adjunct professor of health policy and administration at the University of North Carolina at Chapel Hill. He consults with organizations in the areas of training and organization development. He is on the editorial boards of several international professional journals and is a member of the Advisory Group for Pfeiffer & Company's* Theories and Models in Applied Behavioral Science.

OCTAPACE PROFILE

Udai Pareek

Name: _____ Job title: _____

Organization: _____ Date: _____

This instrument will help you to look at some values and beliefs of your organization. Below are statements that indicate some organizational values. If these are values of top management, they generally will be shared in an organization. Read each statement and indicate in the blank to the left of the statement how much the spirit contained in the statement is valued in *your* organization. Please be candid in answering.

Instructions: Use the following key for your responses:

        4 = Very highly valued in the organization
        3 = Valued in the organization
        2 = Given rather low value in the organization
        1 = Not valued in the organization

_____ 1. Free interaction among employees, each respecting the feelings, competence, and judgment of others

_____ 2. Facing problems, not shying away from them

_____ 3. Offering moral support and help to employees and colleagues in crisis

_____ 4. Congruity between feelings and expressed behavior

_____ 5. Preventive action on most matters

_____ 6. Employees' taking independent action relating to their jobs

_____ 7. Teamwork and team spirit

_____ 8. Employees' trying out innovative ways of solving problems

_____ 9. Genuine sharing of information, feelings, and thoughts in meetings

_____ 10. Going deeper rather than doing surface-level analysis of interpersonal problems

_____ 11. Interpersonal contact and support among employees

4 = Very highly valued in the organization
3 = Valued in the organization
2 = Given rather low value in the organization
1 = Not valued in the organization

_____12. Tactfulness, cleverness, and even a little manipulation to get things done

_____13. Superiors' encouraging their subordinates to think about their development and take action in that direction

_____14. Close supervision and direction of employees regarding action

_____15. Accepting and appreciating help offered by others

_____16. Encouraging employees to take a fresh look at how things are done

_____17. Free discussion and communication between superiors and subordinates

_____18. Facing challenges inherent in the work situation

_____19. Confiding in superiors without fear that they will misuse the trust

_____20. "Owning" mistakes made

_____21. Considering both positive and negative aspects before taking action

_____22. Obeying and checking with superiors rather than acting on one's own

_____23. Performing immediate tasks rather than being concerned about larger organizational goals

_____24. Making genuine attempts to change behavior on the basis of feedback received

Instructions: Use the following key for the remainder of your responses:

4 = This belief is very widely shared in the organization
3 = This belief is fairly well shared in the organization
2 = Only some people in the organization share this belief
1 = Few or no people in the organization share this belief

_____25. Effective managers suppress their feelings.

_____26. Pass the buck tactfully when there is a problem.

_____27. Trust begets trust.

4 = This belief is very widely shared in the organization
3 = This belief is fairly well shared in the organization
2 = Only some people in the organization share this belief
1 = Few or no people in the organization share this belief

_____28. Telling a polite lie is preferable to telling the unpleasant truth.

_____29. Prevention is better than cure.

_____30. Freedom for employees breeds lack of discipline.

_____31. Emphasis on teamwork dilutes individual accountability.

_____32. Thinking and doing new things tones up organizational vitality.

_____33. Free and candid communication between various levels helps in solving problems.

_____34. Surfacing problems is not enough; we should find the solutions.

_____35. When the situation is urgent and has to be dealt with, you have to fend for yourself.

_____36. People are what they seem to be.

_____37. A stitch in time saves nine.

_____38. A good way to motivate employees is to give them autonomy to plan their work.

_____39. Employee involvement in developing the organization's mission and goals contributes to productivity.

_____40. In today's competitive situation, consolidation and stability are more important than experimentation.

OCTAPACE PROFILE SHEET

Instructions: The OCTAPACE Profile assesses eight aspects of organizational culture. Each aspect is listed below, along with the items related to it. For each aspect, add the ratings you assigned to the item numbers indicated. ***Important:*** **For each item with an asterisk, you must convert your rating as follows: 1 becomes 4, 2 becomes 3, 3 becomes 2, and 4 becomes 1.**

Openness

Items 1 _____
9 _____
17 _____
25* _____
33 _____
Total _____

Proaction

Items 5 _____
13 _____
21 _____
29 _____
37 _____
Total _____

Confrontation

Items 2 _____
10 _____
18 _____
26* _____
34 _____
Total _____

Autonomy

Items 6 _____
14* _____
22* _____
30* _____
38 _____
Total _____

Trust

Items 3 _____
11 _____
19 _____
27 _____
35* _____
Total _____

Collaboration

Items 7 _____
15 _____
23* _____
31* _____
39 _____
Total _____

Authenticity

Items 4 _____
12* _____
20 _____
28* _____
36 _____
Total _____

Experimentation

Items 8 _____
16 _____
24 _____
32 _____
40* _____
Total _____

OCTAPACE INTERPRETATION SHEET

Ethos can be defined as the underlying spirit or character of the beliefs, customs, or practices of an entity or a group. At the base of ethos are core values. The seven values of organizational ethos are **O**penness, **C**onfrontation, **T**rust, **A**uthenticity, **P**roaction, **A**utonomy, **C**ollaboration, and **E**xperimentation. In addition to being an acronym for these values, OCTAPACE is a meaningful term, indicating eight (octa) steps (pace) to create functional ethos. The following definitions may help to clarify the values.

1. **O**penness: Spontaneous expression of feelings and thoughts and sharing of these without defensiveness.
2. **C**onfrontation: Facing—not shying away from—problems; deeper analysis of interpersonal problems; taking on challenges.
3. **T**rust: Maintaining confidentiality of information shared by others and not misusing it; a sense of assurance that others will help when needed and will honor mutual obligations and commitments.
4. **A**uthenticity: Congruence between what one feels, says, and does; owning one's actions and mistakes; unreserved sharing of feelings.
5. **P**roaction: Initiative; preplanning and preventive action; calculating payoffs before taking action.
6. **A**utonomy: Using and giving freedom to plan and act in one's own sphere; respecting and encouraging individual and role autonomy.
7. **C**ollaboration: Giving help to, and asking for help from, others; team spirit; working together (individuals and groups) to solve problems.
8. **E**xperimentation: Using and encouraging innovative approaches to solve problems; using feedback for improving; taking a fresh look at things; encouraging creativity.

Norms for the OCTAPACE Profile

	Low	High
1. Openness	13	17
2. Confrontation	10	16
3. Trust	10	16
4. Authenticity	10	14
5. Proaction	12	18
6. Autonomy	11	16
7. Collaboration	13	17
8. Experimentation	11	16
Based on studies of the OCTAPACE Profile so far, these are the high- and low-scoring norms.		

High scores indicate strong belief in the values and, thus, a strong organizational ethos. Low scores show weak aspects of the ethos in the organization. If the average or mean score for your organization is low, the questions on the profile can be used as the basis for action planning to improve organizational ethos and to increase openness, creativity, and collaboration. Remember that items 12, 14, 22, 23, 25, 26, 28, 30, 31, 35, and 40 are scored backward, that is, the items on the profile reflect a low organizational ethos, not a high one.

ORGANIZATIONAL-TYPE INVENTORY

Manfred F.R. Kets de Vries, Danny Miller, and Gaylord Reagan

Organizations mirror the styles of their chief executive officers. Strategies, structures, and cultures all bear the imprint of executives' personalities. In some cases top managers (and their organizations) are composed, open, engaged, stimulating, and thoughtful. In other cases, top managers (and their organizations) are dramatic, suspicious, detached, depressive, or compulsive. Executives can produce organizations that boast tremendous success, such as IBM or 3M or Hewlett-Packard; or, given the existence of certain vulnerabilities and biases, executives can gravely damage their organizations. The first step in avoiding or combating a problem in executive-management style is to confirm its presence by identifying the type of organization that the executive has built.

THE INVENTORY

Theoretical Framework

In the book *Unstable at the Top: Inside the Troubled Organization,* Kets de Vries and Miller (1987) describe five patterns that result from problem personalities in top management:

1. The dramatic organization;
2. The suspicious organization;
3. The detached organization;
4. The depressive organization; and
5. The compulsive organization.

These patterns can produce disastrous consequences for their host organizations. Kets de Vries and Miller (1987) contend that by identifying an organization's dominant pattern, one can either avoid these consequences or detect and overcome them:

> Too often the problems in unsuccessful organizations come about because...top executives get stuck in a specific scenario...from which they are unable to disentangle themselves.... Obsessions motivate a need to control; fears breed suspicion; dramatic behaviors lead to grandiosity. The executives hold fast to archaic, unhealthy, counterproductive activities that once proved effective or pleasant for them, but that no longer seem to be working. The result is a general

ossifying of the organization.... When this happens, it can all but completely cancel out the company's effectiveness. (pp. 195-196)

Kets de Vries and Miller (1987, p. 199) caution readers that only a "disposition toward self-discovery and exploration can provide organizations with insight into their counterproductive behaviors. And only in this way can a new, effective configuration evolve, one in which the individual pieces complement each other, one that is in tune with the market." Finally, they write (1987, p. xiv) that this framework applies "...mainly where decision-making power and initiative reside largely in the chief executive. But in healthy organizations, and where power is dispersed...there tend to be fewer extremes, less uniformity in culture, structure, and strategy, and as a result, fewer problems."

Reliability and Validity

The Organizational-Type Inventory is designed for use as an action-research tool rather than as a rigorous data-gathering instrument. Applied in this manner, the inventory has demonstrated a high level of face validity when used with audiences ranging from executive managers to nonmanagement personnel.

Administration

The following suggestions will help facilitators to administer the inventory:

1. Before respondents begin completing the inventory, discuss the five organizational patterns identified by Kets de Vries and Miller.
2. Distribute copies of the Organizational-Type Inventory, and read the instructions aloud as the respondents follow. Resolve any questions at this time.
3. Urge respondents to avoid overanalyzing their choices. For each item, each respondent should record an initial impression by checking either the "Yes" box or the "No" box, indicating his or her response to each question in each of the five pattern categories. Then each respondent should circle the number indicating his or her reaction to the attribute described in each question.
4. Ask respondents to wait to score their instruments until all respondents have finished.
5. After scoring their inventories and discussing the resulting scores, respondents should prepare brief answers to Steps 2 through 5 on the interpretation sheet. These answers provide a useful entry point to the processing of the inventory.

Scoring

Each respondent should be given a copy of the Organizational-Type Inventory Scoring Sheet. Using the scoring sheet, respondents should first record the number of "Yes" choices they made within each of the five pattern categories. Then they should record their "No" choices in a similar manner. Finally, respondents should record the total of their "Reaction" choices for each of the pattern categories.

The pattern(s) with the most "Yes" choices best describes the respondent's organization as the respondent perceives it. Specifically, if a respondent checked half or more of the "Yes" boxes within a pattern, that person is probably working in that type of organization. However, if a pattern receives only one or two "Yes" choices, the respondent is probably not working in that type of organization.

"Reaction" scores are used to determine the kind of organization that respondents should seek out or avoid. A low reaction score for a given pattern suggests that the pattern is regarded favorably by the respondent. Conversely, a higher score suggests that the respondent regards the pattern unfavorably.

Respondents may find it easier to interpret their reaction scores if they first convert those scores into numeric averages for each pattern. Averages nearer "1" suggest a favorable reaction, whereas averages nearer "3" indicate an unfavorable reaction.

Interpretation and Processing

When respondents finish scoring their inventories, the facilitator should distribute copies of the interpretation sheet. The interpretation sheet contains brief descriptions of each of Kets de Vries and Miller's five patterns. The descriptions provide information about the characteristics, strengths, weaknesses, and needs of each pattern and offer brief prescriptions for overcoming problems associated with the patterns. While reading this information, respondents should remember that organizations (and individuals) generally do not fall into a single pattern. It is normal for organizations (and individuals) to be hybrids.

Some groups find it useful to prepare a large copy of the scoring sheet on newsprint. In this case the facilitator polls individual respondents about the "Yes"/"No" and reaction scores that they assigned to each of the five patterns. The shared results then form the basis for a group discussion.

The brief answers that respondents wrote for Steps 2 through 5 on the interpretation sheet should also be discussed at this point. The facilitator should allow sufficient time to cover this information, as it provides respondents with an opportunity to apply Kets de Vries and Miller's model to their organization. Special attention should also be devoted to discussing the effects of the organizational weaknesses described in the interpretation sheet and to identifying ways to mitigate those effects. This is a good opportunity for respondents to begin forming a group action plan.

While respondents process the results of their inventories, it is important for the facilitator to encourage them to view their collective results in a positive manner. Once respondents identify their organization in one or more of the five patterns, there is an understandable tendency for the ensuing discussion to become somewhat negative. Respondents should be aware of Kets de Vries and Miller's (1987, p. 196) admonition that all organizations share elements of several of the styles, "...each of which tends to become more pronounced under varying circumstances. There is cause for concern only if one style takes over and consistently dominates all aspects of an organization's life." In addition, the authors point out that it is possible for organizations to influence the personalities of top managers. For example, failing organizations can depress previously successful executives. Also, Kets de Vries and Miller note that it is possible for the weaknesses of one pattern to be canceled out by the strengths of another pattern.

Uses of the Inventory

The Organizational-Type Inventory is designed to accomplish the following objectives:

1. To identify the presence (or absence) of the five patterns within respondent organizations;
2. To encourage discussion of the impact of identified patterns on respondent organizations;
3. To initiate discussions about the appropriateness of respondent pattern preferences within the context of an organization's short- and long-term viability;
4. To help differentiate respondent preferences for the five patterns; and
5. To stimulate planning designed to increase individual and organizational-group use of healthy, positive patterns.

REFERENCE AND SELECTED BIBLIOGRAPHY

Kets de Vries, M.F.R. (1980). *Organizational paradoxes: Clinical approaches to management.* London: Tavistock.

Kets de Vries, M.F.R. (Ed.) (1984). *The irrational executive.* New York: International Universities Press.

Kets de Vries, M.F.R., & Miller, D. (1984). *The neurotic organization.* San Francisco: Jossey-Bass.

Kets de Vries, M.F.R., & Miller, D. (1987). *Unstable at the top: Inside the troubled organization.* New York: New American Library.

Miller, D., & Friesen, P.H. (1984). *Organizations: A quantum view.* Englewood Cliffs, NJ: Prentice-Hall.

Zahznik, A., & Kets de Vries, M.F.R. (1985). *Power and the corporate mind* (rev. ed.) Chicago: Bonus Books.

Manfred F.R. Kets de Vries, D.B.A., holds the Raoul de Vitry d'Avaucourt Chair of Human Resource Management at the European Institute of Business Administration (INSEAD) in France. He holds doctoral degrees from the University of Amsterdam and the Harvard Business School. He is also a practicing psychoanalyst and has held professorships at McGill University and the Harvard Business School. He has published nine books, including Unstable at the Top: Inside the Troubled Organization *(with coauthor Danny Miller), and more than ninety scientific papers; presently he is preparing two more books. He is a consultant on organizational design/transformation and strategic human resource management and has done executive-development work with such companies as Volvo and Shell.*

Danny Miller is a research professor of management strategy and organizational theory at the Ecole des Hautes Commerciales of the University of Montreal and a visiting professor at the Faculty of Management, McGill University. He consults internationally with a variety of organizations in the area of strategic change. His recent books are The Icarus Paradox *and* Unstable at the Top: Inside the Troubled Organization. *His research focuses on organizational change, the effects of leadership, and organizational simplicity.*

Gaylord Reagan, Ph.D., is an independent consultant specializing in total quality management, management training, and organization development. In addition to operating his own company and serving as an adjunct instructor at four universities, he has been a director of training and management development, manager of employee education and development, human resource manager, and internal consultant for organization development. His professional memberships include the American Management Association, Academy of Management, and the Society for Human Resource Management.

ORGANIZATIONAL-TYPE INVENTORY[1]

Manfred F.R. Kets de Vries, Danny Miller, and Gaylord Reagan

Instructions: For each of the numbered items in patterns A to E below, check "Yes" or "No"; then refer to the following three-point scale and circle the number that indicates your reaction to that condition (or the lack of that condition).

1 = Favorable
2 = Neutral
3 = Unfavorable

	Yes	No	Reaction
Pattern A			
1. Is power within your organization highly centralized in the hands of the chief executive?	☐	☐	1 2 3
2. Is there a very strong organizational culture in which everyone at the managerial level sees things in essentially the same way?	☐	☐	1 2 3
3. Is the chief executive "put on a pedestal" by many employees?	☐	☐	1 2 3
4. Is there suppression of dissent and contrary opinions by getting rid of or ignoring "rebels?"	☐	☐	1 2 3
5. Does the chief executive seem overburdened with work because he or she tries to do everything himself or herself?	☐	☐	1 2 3
6. Are there many grandiose and risky ventures that deplete organizational resources?	☐	☐	1 2 3
7. Does the chief executive make decisions rapidly and without consulting other people?	☐	☐	1 2 3
8. Is the organization rapidly diversifying, introducing many new products or services, or expanding geographically in a way that depletes organizational resources?	☐	☐	1 2 3
9. Does the chief executive appear to be vain or egotistical?	☐	☐	1 2 3

---

[1] This instrument is based on *Unstable at the Top: Inside the Troubled Organization* by Manfred F.R. Kets de Vries and Danny Miller, 1987, New York: New American Library.

1 = Favorable
2 = Neutral
3 = Unfavorable

	Yes	No	Reaction

10. Are sycophants the main ones being promoted?   ☐ ☐   1 2 3
11. Does most information flow down rather than up the hierarchy?   ☐ ☐   1 2 3
12. Does the strategy of the organization reside mainly inside the chief executive's mind?   ☐ ☐   1 2 3
13. Are growth and expansion pursued seemingly for their own sake?   ☐ ☐   1 2 3

Pattern B

1. Is there an atmosphere of suspicion and distrust in the organization?   ☐ ☐   1 2 3
2. Do managers blame external "enemies" (regulators, government, competitors) for the organization's problems?   ☐ ☐   1 2 3
3. Is there a strong emphasis on management information systems to identify inadequacies and assign blame?   ☐ ☐   1 2 3
4. Are there organizational "spies" who inform top managers about what is happening at lower levels?   ☐ ☐   1 2 3
5. Is organizational loyalty a big factor in assessing personnel performance?   ☐ ☐   1 2 3
6. Does the chief executive have a "siege mentality," constantly defending against perceived external attacks?   ☐ ☐   1 2 3
7. Is the organization's strategy focused more on copying other organizations than on trying new, unique approaches?   ☐ ☐   1 2 3
8. Is there much secrecy regarding performance information, salaries, decisions, etc.?   ☐ ☐   1 2 3
9. Does the organization's strategy vacillate too much according to external conditions?   ☐ ☐   1 2 3

1 = Favorable
2 = Neutral
3 = Unfavorable

	Yes	No	Reaction
10. Is there excessive risk avoidance in the organization?	☐	☐	1 2 3
11. Is the organization too unfocused?	☐	☐	1 2 3

Pattern C

1. Is the organization badly split, with much disagreement among the various functional areas or divisions? ☐ ☐ 1 2 3
2. Does political infighting occur very often? ☐ ☐ 1 2 3
3. Is the chief executive somewhat reclusive, refraining from personal contact and preferring to communicate by memo? ☐ ☐ 1 2 3
4. Is there a "leadership vacuum" in the organization? ☐ ☐ 1 2 3
5. Do decisions get delayed for long periods of time because of squabbling? ☐ ☐ 1 2 3
6. Do the personal ambitions of managers take dramatic precedence over broader organizational goals? ☐ ☐ 1 2 3
7. Are strategies badly fragmented, vacillating between one approach and another according to which senior manager is favored by the chief executive? ☐ ☐ 1 2 3
8. Is the chief executive too busy with outside matters to pay much attention to the organization and its business? ☐ ☐ 1 2 3
9. Do very few decisions emanate from the top of the organization as things just drift along? ☐ ☐ 1 2 3
10. Is it difficult to perceive what the chief executive really wants? ☐ ☐ 1 2 3

                        1 = Favorable
                        2 = Neutral
                        3 = Unfavorable

	Yes	No	Reaction

Pattern D

1. Is there a feeling of helplessness to influence events on the part of the chief executive or the key top managers? □ □ 1 2 3

2. Has the organization stagnated while other, similar organizations have advanced? □ □ 1 2 3

3. Are the organization's products or services antiquated? □ □ 1 2 3

4. Is there very little "scanning" of the organization's environment? □ □ 1 2 3

5. Are work facilities poor and inefficient? □ □ 1 2 3

6. Are the organization's strategies very narrow and resistant to change? □ □ 1 2 3

7. Is there a lack of action, an atmosphere of "decision paralysis"? □ □ 1 2 3

8. Do many young, aggressive managers leave the organization because of the stifling climate and the lack of opportunity for advancement? □ □ 1 2 3

9. Is there extreme conservatism when it comes to making capital expenditures? □ □ 1 2 3

10. Do bureaucratic rules set long ago replace communication and deliberation in decision making? □ □ 1 2 3

Pattern E

1. Is the organization very bureaucratic, filled with red tape, regulations, formal policies and procedures, and the like? □ □ 1 2 3

2. Is there a tendency for precedents to decide issues more than analysis or discussion? □ □ 1 2 3

3. Has strategy remained essentially unchanged for many years? □ □ 1 2 3

The 1994 Annual: Developing Human Resources

1 = Favorable
2 = Neutral
3 = Unfavorable

	Yes	No	Reaction
4. Is the organization slow to adapt to trends in the marketplace?	☐	☐	1 2 3
5. Does the chief executive hoard power?	☐	☐	1 2 3
6. Is the chief executive overly concerned with one or two elements of strategy (efficiency, productivity, quality, costs) to the exclusion of most others?	☐	☐	1 2 3
7. Did a former chief executive leave a strategic legacy that is held to be sacrosanct by current managers?	☐	☐	1 2 3
8. Are strategies very precisely articulated, down to the last detail?	☐	☐	1 2 3
9. Do information systems provide too much "hard" and too little "soft" data on customer reactions, trends, etc.?	☐	☐	1 2 3
10. Does the chief executive prefer subordinates who follow directives very precisely and refrain from arguing?	☐	☐	1 2 3
11. Is there a great emphasis on position and status?	☐	☐	1 2 3

ORGANIZATIONAL-TYPE INVENTORY SCORING SHEET

1. Count the number of "Yes" checks for each pattern, and enter each total below.
2. Count the number of "No" checks for each pattern, and enter each total below.
3. Add the numbers circled under "Reaction" for each pattern, and enter each total below.

Name of Pattern	Number of "Yes" Checks	Number of "No" Checks	Reaction Total
Pattern A: "The Dramatic Organization"			
Pattern B: "The Suspicious Organization"			
Pattern C: "The Detached Organization"			
Pattern D: "The Depressive Organization"			
Pattern E: "The Compulsive Organization"			

ORGANIZATIONAL-TYPE INVENTORY INTERPRETATION SHEET[1]

Step 1

Determine which pattern collected the most "Yes" responses. If you checked only one or two "Yes" boxes within a pattern, you probably *are not working* in that type of organization. However, if you checked half or more "Yes" boxes within a pattern, you probably *are working* in that type of organization.

→ *Pattern A: "The Dramatic Organization"*

Characteristics

- Has strong leader who is idealized by subordinates
- Has leader who is the primary catalyst for subordinates' morale and initiatives
- Exhibits very centralized policy making (in hands of impulsive, hyperactive leader)

Strengths

- Can create momentum needed to take organization through start-up phase
- Has ability to rebound after failures and to continue moving forward
- Comes up with ideas to revitalize the organization

Weaknesses

- Lacks a consistent strategy
- Sometimes lacks necessary controls
- Tends to avoid consulting with, or getting feedback from, lower levels

Needs

- Distribute authority—empowerment, delegation
- Codify a clear strategy
- Establish a clear hierarchy
- Provide controls and coordination
- Scan the organization's environment

---

[1] The content of this interpretation sheet is based on *Unstable at the Top: Inside the Troubled Organization* by Manfred F.R. Kets de Vries and Danny Miller, 1987, New York: New American Library.

- Scale down huge projects
- Review core business
- Sharpen focus—get rid of worthless propositions

Prescription
- Plant both feet firmly on the ground

→ Pattern B: "The Suspicious Organization"

Characteristics
- Has fight-or-flight culture
- Lacks trust—emphasis placed on intimidation and uniformity
- Is reactive, conservative, overly analytical, secretive

Strengths
- Shows good knowledge of events inside and outside the organization
- Avoids dependence on a single market segment/customer
- Provides positive opportunities for growth and diversification

Weaknesses
- Lacks a concerted and consistent management strategy; falls victim to "groupthink"
- Has reactive, piecemeal, contradictory, distrustful atmosphere
- Experiences high staff turnover because of insecurity and disenchantment

Needs
- Foster trust and break down communication barriers
- Establish a participative culture
- Break down "policing" systems
- Pursue strategic themes
- Create distinctive competencies

Prescription
- Develop a unified strategy and sense of mission

➻ *Pattern C: "The Detached Organization"*

Characteristics
- Lacks warmth and emotion
- Engages in jockeying for power—lots of conflict and insecurity
- Demonstrates strategic thinking dominated by indecisive, inconsistent, narrow perspectives

Strengths
- Has middle managers who play an active role
- Shares variety of points of view in formulating strategies
- Has individual managers who take initiative

Weaknesses
- Lacks leadership
- Exhibits inconsistent or vacillating strategy
- Decides issues by political negotiating rather than on the basis of facts

Needs
- Get a senior manager willing to provide active leadership
- Establish active coordinating committees
- Discourage parochial interests
- Reward overall organizational performance
- Pursue strategic themes
- Create distinctive competencies

Prescription
- Consider the whole

➻ *Pattern D: "The Depressive Organization"*

Characteristics
- Lacks initiative—lots of passivity and negativity
- Lacks motivation—leadership vacuum
- Drifts, with no sense of direction—inward focused

Strengths
- Generally enjoys an excellent reputation for past successes

Weaknesses
- Tends to live in the past, when things were good for the organization
- Focuses on supplying dying markets/customers/products/services
- Has apathetic and inactive senior management

Needs
- Seek new leadership that is focused on new markets/customers/products/services
- Prune unpromising or older ventures
- Obtain resources for organizational reorientation and renewal
- Find new opportunities in identified markets
- Scan the organization's environment

Prescription
- Challenge the status quo

→ *Pattern E: "The Compulsive Organization"*

Characteristics
- Is rigid, directed inward, insular
- Fosters submission, lack of creativity, and insecurity in subordinates
- Focuses on one aspect of a strategy (quality, efficiency, cost cutting); is unable to switch focus quickly

Strengths
- Possesses fine internal controls
- Has a tightly focused strategy
- Exhibits efficient operations

Weaknesses
- Is too attached to tradition
- Responds inflexibly and inappropriately to customer/market demands
- Stifles creativity and influence of middle managers

Needs

- Conduct creativity seminars
- Change selection practices
- Become open to suggestions from lower levels
- Scan markets for problems and opportunities
- Respond better to customer needs
- Get rid of bureaucratic structures

Prescription

- Wage a battle against control

Step 2

Write brief answers to each of the following ten questions. Use specific examples where possible. Do your answers to these questions help you to understand why you classified your organization within the pattern(s) you did? In the book *Unstable at the Top: Inside the Troubled Organization,* Kets de Vries and Miller point out that organizations falling into one or more of these patterns can be very unpleasant places to work and will be unlikely to change without extreme pressure from within to do so.

1. How would you describe your organization's environment?

2. What does your organization stand for? What are its goals?

3. What are your chief executive's "dreams"?

4. What aspects of your organization's functioning are important to its senior leaders? What makes them excited, angry, happy?

5. How are crises and "critical incidents" dealt with in your organization?

6. What kind of people do well in your organization?

7. What measures of performance are used in your organization? What are the criteria for rewards and punishment?

8. What are the criteria for selection, promotion, and termination in your organization?

9. What kind of organizational "war stories" and "rituals" exist in your organization? What are the "taboos"?

10. How would you describe your organization's structure?

Step 3

By totaling your reaction scores for each pattern, you can determine the kind of organization that is most comfortable for you. The higher your reaction score is for a given pattern, the more unfavorable that pattern appears to you. What do your scores suggest? Are you and your organization a "good fit"? Write your answers to these questions in the space that follows.

Step 4

Kets de Vries and Miller identify five "cultural blockades" to adaptation that influence the strength of an organization's culture as well as its resistance or receptivity to change. Which of these blockades exist in your organization, and what needs to be done to make sure that they produce positive results?

1. Adverse (or favorable) impact of senior leaders' legacy

2. Similarity (or dissimilarity) of views within groups whose membership is highly stable

3. Lack (or presence) of employee commitment to overall goals and procedures

4. Presence (or absence) of organizational conflict and distrust

5. Climate of stagnation (or change)

Step 5

Kets de Vries and Miller identify seven "organizational blockades" to adaptation that must be eliminated. Which of these blockades exist within your organization, and how can they be mitigated? For each blockade that you identify as applicable to your organization, use the space provided under the suggestion to jot down notes about steps you might be able to take.

Excessive Bureaucracy

- *Suggestion:* Identify and combat unnecessary rules, regulations, and procedures with the support of top management.

Inadequate Information Systems

- *Suggestion:* Question the relevance of reports, and ask whether the system truly enlightens the organization about emerging trends.

Uneven Distribution of Power

- *Suggestion:* Maintain constant vigilance and an awareness of the abuses of power.

Overexplicit Planning

- *Suggestion:* Constantly update plans, goals, objectives.

Overly Narrow Goals and Strategies

- *Suggestion:* Create alternative plans and contingency plans.

Reliance on Past Success

- *Suggestion:* Critically evaluate present strategy, information systems, power distribution, and so forth.

Limited Resource Availability

- *Suggestion:* Keep track of the flow of resources. Determine how many failures can be tolerated.

INTRODUCTION TO THE PRESENTATION AND DISCUSSION RESOURCES SECTION

This section brings together a variety of materials that would be useful to human resource development (HRD) practitioners in their personal and professional development. The Presentation and Discussion Resources section includes the contents that previously were found in the Lecturettes, Theory and Practice, Resources, and Professional Development sections of earlier *Annuals*. These materials provide information about issues that affect the rapidly developing field of HRD: the directions in which the field is heading; new technologies (and new uses of old technologies); the dilemmas experienced by HRD practitioners in their daily work; new areas for application; new processes, perspectives, outlooks, and theoretical developments; and attempts to integrate specific content areas.

Included in this section are articles that HRD practitioners can bring to the attention of management or use in a training session. Such articles often are useful in documenting or supporting a position or in explaining a complex or subtle point. In addition, these articles can help HRD professionals to "sell" a broader understanding of the HRD function to line managers, who often need documentation in order to modify their views or to support their emerging understanding.

This year's section consists of nine articles. The first is entitled "Danger—Diversity Training Ahead: Addressing the Myths of Diversity Training and Offering Alternatives." At a time when organizations worldwide are striving to value and manage diversity, this article begins by introducing and dispelling six myths about diversity training. After a discussion of how diversity changes the existing power structures, the author suggests alternate viewpoints of diversity.

The second article in the section, "Behavior Management Interventions: Getting the Most Out of Your Employee Assistance Program," addresses the identification and confrontation of workers who might benefit from employee assistance program (EAP) services. The article outlines a variety of approaches for motivating supervisors to take responsibility for identifying and confronting substance abuse in the workplace.

"Fostering the Effectiveness of Groups at Work," the third article in the section, highlights the importance of the group experience in organizations. The article begins with the premise that knowledge of group development and group dynamics can help supervisors and employees in working together effectively. Therefore, the authors outline the stages of group development in terms of the leader and member functions that are applicable at each stage.

The fourth article, "Using Mentoring for Professional Development," provides a perspective on facilitating a formal mentoring program and developing a culture for mentoring. In the process, it addresses how to identify mentors and prospective protégés, how to develop a learning culture for succession planning and employee development, and how to recognize the skills and characteristics that people need to learn.

"The Enneagram" describes nine different worldviews that affect many aspects of life, including how decisions are made, how conflict is resolved, what is valued, and how obstacles are overcome. The article applies the ideas of the Enneagram to the underlying assumptions and values of an organization; in this application, the Enneagram focuses attention on what really matters in the organization and makes clear the particular interventions that would improve the organization's functioning.

The sixth article, "Journey to Excellence: One Path to Total Quality Management," presents a model for the journey toward total quality. The six phases of this tested approach are as follows: orientation and self-assessment, preparation and learning, strategic quality planning, implementation, evaluation, and continuous improvement—which cycles back to strategic quality planning. In this way, the journey is one of continuous improvement toward total quality.

A theme is to a training program what a mission is to an organization. "Theme Development: Finally Getting Control of the Design Process" defines a theme as the unifying element that represents the purpose of the program. This article points out the importance of having a unifying theme for a training program; it offers descriptions of a theme's characteristics and functions through the use of specific examples.

"Evaluating the Effectiveness of Adult Education and Training Programs" is a comprehensive overview of current research on evaluation using Donald Kirkpatrick's model. The four levels of this model are as follows: Level 1: Reaction Evaluation; Level 2: Learning Evaluation; Level 3: Behavior Evaluation; and Level 4: Results Evaluation. The article offers guidelines for conducting each level of evaluation and points out the need for further research in the overall field of training evaluation.

The final article, "Why Job and Role Planning Is Critical to the Future," forecasts some important trends in the nature of work. Above all, the article underscores the fact that the ability to learn will make the difference in the future. People must become perpetual learners; in this context, job and role planning will become virtually perpetual processes that are integral to the management function itself.

As with every *Annual,* this volume covers a variety of topics; not every article will appeal to every reader. Nevertheless, the range of articles presented should encourage a good deal of thought-provoking, serious discussion about the present and the future of HRD.

DANGER—DIVERSITY TRAINING AHEAD: ADDRESSING THE MYTHS OF DIVERSITY TRAINING AND OFFERING ALTERNATIVES

Paula Grace

VALUING AND MANAGING DIVERSITY IN THE WORKPLACE

"Valuing diversity" and "managing diversity" are popular buzz words these days. If you ask ten people what they mean, you will get ten different answers. At least nine of those answers will derive from the premise that diversity has to do with the unique qualities that people of different races, genders, and ethnic heritages bring to the workplace. The common belief is that organizations will benefit from appreciating these unique qualities and from learning to accommodate the challenges that these unique qualities present.

In addition, the United States, like several other nations, has affirmative action programs that come into play in addressing the issue of diversity. Affirmative action has been successful in bringing more women and minorities into organizations, but it has not been successful in retaining them or in helping them to climb the organizational ladder.

As a result of the push to appreciate people's unique qualities and the need to go further than simply incorporating women and minorities into the organizational fold, the era of valuing diversity has begun. Thousands of organizations have jumped on the diversity-training bandwagon and embarked on the road to "valuing and managing diversity." Human resource managers, affirmative action officers, training directors, diversity task-force leaders, and other interested parties have begun to embrace "valuing diversity" as the newest hope for business.

The underlying logic is that if we could learn more about the different racial and ethnic groups with whom we work—as well as the differences between men and women—we could all get along better and be more productive in the process. Millions of dollars will be spent this year on diversity training based on this logic, yet there is no research data to support it. Before your organization contributes to this statistic, you should ask, "Why is my company investing in diversity training? To be able to 'value' diversity? What does that mean? To enable employees to understand one another better, to be able to get along together better? To improve morale? Or is the company simply joining the bandwagon because someone read the Hudson Institute's report *Workforce 2000: Work and Workers for the Twenty-First Century* (Johnston & Packer, 1987), and anticipates increasing diversity?"

THE MYTHS OF DIVERSITY TRAINING

Diversity is indeed of primary importance to the success of organizations in the 1990s, but not in the way that 95 percent of organizations approach the issue. With so much at stake, consultants, trainers, and managers would do well to explore the myths and facts surrounding this topic.

Myth 1: Diversity Is a Matter of Gender, Race, and Ethnicity

The problem with this myth is that in order to classify people by gender, race, or ethnicity, we automatically move into the dangerous position of describing them in terms of group norms. When we classify someone based on explicit variations such as gender or race, we tend to assign that person a set of behaviors, beliefs, concerns, strengths, and weaknesses based on gender or race. This skin-deep approach ignores the fact that we are all products of multiple groups of which we are members.

For example, for every woman who fits the group norm of being a woman, there are plenty of women who are outside that group norm. For every black who fits the group norm of being black, there are plenty of blacks who are outside that group norm. Although there are some characteristics that all women or all blacks share, these characteristics are far outweighed by the individual uniqueness that each person carries within him or her.

I have a hard time believing that Margaret Thatcher brought a special "female" perspective to government in Britain or that Clarence Thomas brings a special "black" perspective to the U.S. Supreme Court. If this were the case, one should be able to point to specific definitions of "female" and "black" that fully describe how these group perspectives were and are being demonstrated. The chances are that there is no reliable way of defining such perspectives.

By focusing exclusively on the outer, most obvious group affiliations, we devalue people's unique qualities (beliefs, values, skills, and so forth) as well as their less obvious group memberships (such as religion, politics, class, family, education). By defining diversity in terms of explicit group affiliations, we assemble people into large groups, which is exactly the opposite of what the term "diversity" is intended to reflect. True diversity lies in the unique differences between individual people. It is a result of not only group affiliations, but also interaction with the environment, successful survival strategies, and individual psychological and social orientations.

Just as I am uncomfortable being labeled a white female, because this label assumes a certain mind-set, belief structure, and set of challenges and concerns, you might be uncomfortable being labeled a black male or a Hispanic female or an Asian female or a white male, because any of these categorizations carries with it a set of connotations that has very little to do with who you are. Every time we define diversity in terms of gender, race, or ethnicity, we are robbing individual people of their unique contributions.

Myth 2: A Diverse Work Force Necessarily Produces Good Results

As mentioned previously, there is no evidence to support the myth that diversity—as defined by the explicit indicators of gender, race, or ethnicity—necessarily produces good results. According to Johnston and Packer (1987), the authors of the now-famous *Workforce 2000: Work and Workers for the Twenty-First Century*, we have no choice but to include more people of color, women, and ethnic minorities in the work force because there will be far more of them available to work in the U.S. than there will be white males by the end of this decade. Perhaps it is this portent of the future, coupled with moral and social imperatives, that has made the business community so conscious of diversity and so desirous of recruiting people of color, women, and ethnic minorities.

The problem is that including more people of color, women, and ethnic minorities in business does not automatically lead to enhanced business performance. An environment that respects and honors diverse viewpoints and values, on the other hand, does stand a better chance of producing good results than one that does not. For many years the research on group effectiveness has demonstrated that decision-making processes that encourage the expression of alternative views produce superior decisions. However, it is important to remember that diverse viewpoints and values do not arise exclusively from diversity in race, gender, or ethnicity.

One of my clients, for example, has a factory outside of Brussels, Belgium. All of the employees are white, Flemish-speaking males. On the surface it may appear that there is no diversity in this workforce, but the facts are otherwise. When you scratch the surface, you find a wide range of viewpoints and values, both about work and about life. The challenge for this client, as for any organization, is to create an environment in which this diversity is allowed to be expressed so that it can add to the overall mixture of options available to the organization.

Myth 3: Diversity Training Should Focus on Raising Awareness of Minority Groups and the Problems They Face

This myth is perhaps the most dangerous in that it exerts such influence on the majority of diversity-training programs being offered in organizations. Raising awareness about minority groups and their problems necessitates focusing on the group. But the research of the last forty years rejects the approach of heightening awareness of groups by discussing group differences (Allport, 1958; Brown & Turner, 1981; Dovidio & Gaertner, 1986; Sherif & Sherif, 1969; Stephan, 1985; Tajfel, 1982). Talking about our own group affiliations and how other groups are different from ours actually increases the boundaries between ourselves and others.

When we focus on group differences, our own perceptions of one another move from an interpersonal to an intergroup level. At the intergroup level, people tend to think of others as outsiders, categorizing all outsiders together into one faceless, indistinguishable mass. Interpersonal uniqueness, the true foundation of diversity, is buried by group stereotypes and unconscious prejudices. Talking about minority cultures or "experiencing" another group's culture may appear to cause positive changes in the short term. However, social-science research indicates that this approach will not break down barriers between people but will actually reinforce stereotypes and prejudices (Allport, 1958; Brown & Turner, 1981; Dovidio & Gaertner, 1986; Sherif & Sherif, 1969; Stephan, 1985; Tajfel, 1982).

Myth 4: Only People of Color, Women, or Minorities are Qualified To Do Diversity Training

As has already been mentioned, it is a mistake to assume that diversity is defined only by gender, race, or ethnicity because this assumption excludes deeper expressions of diversity. Also, if people of color, women, or minorities are the only people qualified to train in the area of diversity, then it must be true that these people are qualified to train *only* in that area—an absurdity. Perhaps Arthur Schlesinger, Jr. (1992) says it best:

> The doctrine that only blacks can teach and write black history leads inexorably to the doctrine that blacks can teach and write only black history as well as to inescapable corollaries: Chinese must be restricted to Chinese history, women to women's history, and so on. (p. 105)

An incident from the arena of acting highlights the negative impact of ascribing to this absurdity. Actors' Equity tried to prevent the British actor Jonathan Pryce from playing in New York the role he created in London in *Miss Saigon,* announcing that it could not condone "the casting of a Caucasian actor in the role of a Eurasian." Pryce responded that if this doctrine prevailed, "I'd be stuck playing Welshmen for the rest of my life." Actors' Equity did not, however, apply the same principle to the black actors Morgan Freeman and Denzel Washington, who were both acting in Shakespearean plays at that time in New York. *The Wall Street Journal* acidly suggested that, according to the principle invoked, not only whites but also the disabled should protest the casting of Denzel Washington as Richard III because Washington lacked a hunchback (Schlesinger, 1992).

There is yet another danger in ascribing to this absurd myth that only people of color, women, or minorities are qualified to train in the area of diversity: We might rob ourselves of much of the valuable research and debate on the topic of diversity, which is being carried on today by people who do not fit these narrow restrictions.

Myth 5: The White-Male Power Structure Needs To Be Overthrown

This myth may have elements of truth in it, but many people draw the wrong conclusion from it. It is certainly true that the existing power structure in most large organizations in the U.S. consists of white males. For moral, social, and (most compelling to the business community) financial reasons, this power structure needs to be changed.

The problem comes when we believe that the white-male power structure should be overthrown and replaced by one or more groups of people defined by gender, race, or ethnicity. This action would simply mean replacing one group with another group. Promoting people of color, women, and minorities into positions of power does not automatically cause the benefits of diversity to suddenly spring forth. We can all think of people we know or work with who are members of minority groups yet typify the cultural values of the current power structure, which in the U.S. is often white and male. Again, Margaret Thatcher and Clarence Thomas come to mind.

We should promote all people who have earned the right to promotion, regardless of race, gender, or ethnic heritage. But simply promoting people of color, women, and minorities does not ensure diversity in thought, behavior, or experience. The barriers to diversity in thought, behavior, or experience reside in the fundamental culture of the organization itself. An organization forms itself around common goals and quickly develops norms and values by which it simplifies and sustains its social existence; it forms a culture. This culture becomes a screen for membership and leadership. Regardless of race, gender, or ethnicity, many people can join and climb as long as they conform to the culture. The resulting organization is diverse in explicit ways, but is still inhospitable to differing views. Such an organization is not truly "valuing diversity." Valuing diversity and gaining the diversity advantage have to do with far more than explicit indicators. The sooner we understand this, the sooner we can stop abusing white males and "celebrating" our differences and, instead, start creating workplaces in which individual diversity makes profound, positive contributions to our organizations.

Myth 6: Diversity Is Affirmative Action for the Nineties

Legally mandated affirmative action programs were and are appropriate responses to hiring practices that exclude capable, competent people from receiving equal opportunities in education and employment. The goal of affirmative action is to bring women and minorities into organizations and allow them opportunities to move up the corporate ladder. To this end, special hiring concessions and training programs have been developed to help both the newly hired women and minorities and the people who will manage them.

The goal of most affirmative action programs is assimilation. According to Dr. Roosevelt Thomas (1991, p. 17), president/founder of the American Institute for Managing Diversity, "Affirmative action has been the chief, often the exclusive, strategy for including and assimilating minorities and women into the corporate world." When women and minorities do not "fit" into the corporate structure, managers usually offer special interventions to help "better equip" them to overcome obstacles to their assimilation.

The dilemma, however, appears to be balancing the assimilation objectives of affirmative action with the ability to capitalize on individual uniqueness, which is the objective of most diversity initiatives. "Because assimilating people want to fit in," Dr. Thomas (1991, p. 8) says, "they focus on doing the expected or accommodating the norm, on playing it safe. They avoid offering suggestions that would make them stand out." In other words, they suppress any innovative or creative ideas that are not part of the mainstream way of operating. Assimilation deliberately frustrates individual uniqueness.

Diversity initiatives, on the other hand, are designed to capitalize on the unique perspectives and experiences that every employee brings to the job. Seen in this light, diversity could become a strong benefit to the organization and a real aid to the aims of affirmative action. People could move up in the organization with less conformity and with a greater expression of the uniqueness through which they will contribute to accomplishing the organization's goals. Affirmative action programs have not been successful in fully enfranchising women and minorities in organizations because the organizations themselves have not been ready to receive them. Most organizations have not questioned the basic assumptions under which they operate, the very assumptions that produce the organizational cultures into which people are expected to assimilate.

It is not yet time to abandon affirmative action programs, but it is time to expand the perspective of what affirmative action is meant to accomplish. Diversity initiatives are not meant to replace affirmative action, but neither are they meant to enfranchise women and minorities exclusively. When properly instituted, diversity initiatives will enfranchise all employees, regardless of race, gender, or ethnicity.

POWER, COGNITIVE CONFLICT, AND SUPERORDINATE GOALS

Power

For most organizations, the tolerance of differences changes the way in which they use power. Formal authority has its ultimate source in the consent of the managed to the purpose for which the authority is used. This purpose is always related to how much authority is granted, to whom, and how it is used. The determination and continual reaffirmation of the organization's purpose is precisely where diversity of experience and perception has its greatest payoff.

"Why are we cooperating?" is the survival question of every organization. The best answer is the one that most appropriately prepares the organization to confront its changing environment of resources (including people), technologies, and markets. Diversity of knowledge and opinion is the only way to improve the organization's ability to answer its survival question.

But people who hold different opinions have historically been seen as disloyal, perhaps bordering on rebellious. Expressions of different values have been perceived by those in power as disapproval of their authority or disagreement with the stated purpose of the organization. People in positions of power often fear that people from different backgrounds will not be able to commit fully to the organization's purpose and, therefore, cannot be trusted to exercise authority appropriately. Only by recognizing that a diversity of perspectives is beneficial to organizations will authority be granted to people who express differing opinions.

The ability to create a culture in which diversity of knowledge and opinion is not just passively tolerated but is actively required is the key to organizational effectiveness. The preservation of diversity within the organization is the preservation of survival options. As the relationship between survival and diversity proves itself, as it currently is through competition in the global market and all large regional markets, organizations begin changing their expectations of how authority should be exercised. Instead of valuing conformity (including racial, gender, and ethnic similarity) in the people who are given managerial authority, organizations begin valuing those whose expertise and experience are genuinely different. But difference will not be the only criterion for success.

Cognitive Conflict

Those who bring diverse perceptions to the decision-making process in organizations must also have certain skills of expression and persistence. They will have to listen as much as they talk. They will have to demonstrate understanding of positions different from their own. They will have to patiently persist in the expression of their own views until they are satisfied that they have been understood. In short, they will be valued for their skill at cognitive conflict, that is, at engaging in the decision-making process without insisting on agreement or conformity.

How does an organization function when agreement and conformity are not requirements of participation? And how is organizational tolerance of differences related to agreement and conformity? As previously mentioned, studies on group effectiveness have demonstrated that decision-making processes that value cognitive conflict lead to superior decisions. In a cognitive-conflict mode, people are under no obligation to change their positions or come into agreement with other positions. They respect their own and one another's intellectual integrity. And regardless of their disagreements, they treat their colleagues with respect.

They are, however, under obligation to reach resolution. A resolution can be thought of as a temporary organizational rule. Managers commit to explaining and enforcing the rule until it proves itself no longer effective in serving the organization's goals. They do not need to pretend to "believe" in the rule, nor must they expect anyone else to. The rule is appreciated as a tool, not as a commandment engraved in stone. Such temporary rules are important in order for the organization to take action from day to day, but they also must be seen as forever imperfect and in need of continual improvement.

This behavior of managers is sometimes called "disagree and commit"—a necessary skill in the exercise of authority in organizations that value and preserve diversity. It is the essence of what is meant by power exercised with tolerance. One organization that I know has so deeply integrated this notion of "disagree and commit" that people who sit passively in meetings, who do not ask questions, or who refuse to challenge colleagues soon find themselves on the outside. Diversity of values, beliefs, opinions, and knowledge is so prized that the organization has made cognitive conflict and "disagree and commit" integral components in how it runs every meeting and how it makes every decision.

The results? This organization of over twenty thousand people is one of the most successful firms in its industry and leads the market in launching new products and maintaining market share. It has attracted and retained a wide assortment of people with differing values, experiences, and opinions, who also happen to represent a wide range of races and ethnic heritages as well as both genders.

And it is an organization in which the best contributors in the field want to work. All systems are set up to reward achievement. Achievement within the organizational structure, regardless of race, gender, or ethnicity, is valued above all else. The purposes of the organization are clear to all employees, and all employees can voice their opinions about those purposes. As those purposes are all related to remaining number one in their industry (and breaking into new, related areas), people find it easy to support them. This commonality of purpose provides the foundation for the variety of approaches, suggestions, and solutions that are introduced daily.

This organization has learned that when organizational purposes become mutual goals that are shared by the work force, the goals tend to supersede individual differences that might interfere with their achievement.

Superordinate Goals

In my work I refer to the concept of all-encompassing mutual goals as "superordinate goals." Superordinate goals serve a vital function in organizations. Working on superordinate goals is the most underutilized yet effective means of enabling people from different cultures, races, and genders to work together successfully while simultaneously reducing their levels of prejudice and stereotyping. Even if a group fails to achieve a superordinate goal, its members stand a good chance of viewing one another with less prejudice as a result of working together. And when different people are able to work together without the interference of prejudice or stereotyping, their participation and contributions will inevitably increase and will form the foundation from which a diversity of knowledge and opinions can be expressed. As already noted, a diversity of knowledge and opinions is the only way to improve an organization's ability to answer its survival question.

HOW TO PRESENT ALTERNATIVE VIEWPOINTS OF DIVERSITY

What To Watch for

There are many challenges to presenting alternative viewpoints. Here are just a few of the situations that you may encounter:

1. *Lack of support.* Although there is a lot of emphasis on training as the preferred method for addressing diversity in organizations, training sessions will not help unless senior management is committed to creating an environment that supports and values individual differences. Without such support, training holds no value.

2. *People who want to concentrate on groups instead of each individual person's uniqueness.* If you decide to approach diversity beyond race, gender, and ethnic heritage and try to emphasize each person's uniqueness, you will encounter some people who want to speak solely as representatives of their groups and want to talk to other participants solely as representatives of their respective groups. They will not be pleased with your approach.

3. *People who want shortcuts for dealing with those from different cultural backgrounds.* These people will expect you to provide tips for getting along with and working with certain kinds of people or groups.

4. *People who are not interested in learning about their own assumptions and values.* Even if you explain to these people that the only way to begin exploring interpersonal differences is by gaining an awareness of one's own assumptions and values, they will not see the benefit of self-knowledge. Instead, they will want to begin immediately applying a system or model of diversity to their work situations.

5. *Affirmative action officers and diversity-training managers who have no real power to effect change.* These people's sole responsibility is to implement diversity training. In their organizations, diversity initiatives fall into the domain of training, human resources, or affirmative action—not the domain of organizational or cultural change. Given the magnitude of the diversity problems that most organizations are facing, your efforts with these people may feel like shouting into a hurricane.

What To Emphasize

If you focus on the following three points, your efforts will remain headed in the right direction:

1. *Diversity cannot be defined simply by gender, race, or ethnic heritage.* It must include much deeper individual designations, such as basic assumptions and values, which can be shown to have a more direct impact on the organization.

2. *Organizations must be willing to tolerate beliefs, values, and styles of work that do not represent the status quo.* Only when diverse viewpoints are allowed to be constantly expressed and acted on will the organization benefit from diversity.

3. *Managing diversity is often a matter of uncovering opportunities for employees to work together on teams to achieve superordinate goals.*

Where To Begin

To assist your organization's diversity initiative, begin by asking some hard questions:

1. *Why is my organization interested in the issue of diversity?* If the answer to this question relates to affirmative action goals, you have some serious work ahead of you in separating diversity from affirmative action. If the answer relates to an initiative generated from the training, human resources, or affirmative action department, you have some serious work ahead of you in educating and enlisting the power brokers at the top of the organization. If the answer relates to enhanced business performance, then you are on your way.

2. *Is the diversity initiative being championed by someone at the top?* If the answer to this question is no, then you should consider finding such a champion and selling him or her on your diversity initiative before you commit time and money to the process.

3. *Does my organization have a long-term commitment to diversity?* A "long-term" commitment is at least five years. If the answer to this question is no, then be aware that the problem with any effort shorter than five years is that your short-term gains will fall apart over time. Managing diversity is a long-term process, not a year-long series of training programs. Short-term fixes not only do not work but also are detrimental to the organization's effectiveness.

4. *What opportunities exist to create superordinate goals that are compelling to the employees and beneficial to the organization?* Forget trying to inspire employees to achieve the goals outlined in the company mission statement. Although the mission statement represents a superordinate goal, for most employees it is just a sign in the lunchroom or a plaque on the wall.

Superordinate goals that are compelling to employees are projects that they have some control over, that they can monitor the results of, and that they know make a difference to the success of the organization. The art of creating superordinate goal structures lies in selecting the project, selecting the team members, and then facilitating the process so that the team members have a chance to work together without impediments. The superordinate goal cannot be artificially contrived; it must relate to the organization's effectiveness or performance.

Group members must be given latitude for expression and individual contribution. They should be rewarded for speaking up, for suggesting alternative solutions, and for challenging the status quo. They may need to be trained in cognitive conflict so that they have the skills and resources to tolerate conflict successfully.

Awareness of diversity (in the form of diverse views and values) can become an integrated part of all group facilitation. For example, diversity may constitute a regular item in a meeting checklist used to determine how well a group is functioning.

5. *Have I done my homework?* Become familiar with the trends in diversity training. Read some of the books and articles listed in the References and Bibliography section that follows. Know enough about diversity to dispute approaches that are unproved and could waste the organization's money. Your efforts will be worthwhile, because a diverse work force is the greatest asset that any organization has—but only if the people in the organization are able to appreciate and empower those who are different from themselves.

REFERENCES AND BIBLIOGRAPHY

Allport, G.W. (1958). *The nature of prejudice.* New York: Doubleday-Anchor.

Brown, R., & Turner, J.C. (1981). *Intergroup behavior.* Oxford, England: Blackwell.

Dovidio, J.F., & Gaertner, S.L. (1986). *Prejudice, discrimination, and racism.* New York: Academic Press.

Hamilton, D.L. (1979). A cognitive-attributional analysis of stereotyping. In L. Berkowitz (Ed.), *Advances in experimental social psychology* (Vol. 12). New York: Academic Press.

Johnston, W.B.., & Packer, A.E.. (1987). *Workforce 2000: Work and workers for the twenty-first century.* Indianapolis, IN: Hudson Institute.

Miles, R. (1989). *Racism.* London: Routledge.

Schlesinger, A.M. (1992). *The disuniting of America, reflections on a multicultural society.* New York: Norton.

Sherif, M., & Sherif, C.W. (1969). *Social psychology.* New York: Harper and Row.

Steele, S. (1990). *The content of our character.* New York: St. Martin's Press.

Stephan, W.G. (1985). Intergroup relations. In G. Lindzey & E. Aronson (Eds.), *The handbook of social psychology* (3rd ed., Vol. 2, pp. 599-658). New York: Random House.

Tajfel, H. (1982). *Social identity and intergroup relations.* Cambridge, England: Cambridge University Press.

Taylor, S.E., Fiske S.T., Etcoff, N., & Ruderman, A. (1978). The categorical and contextual bases of person memory and stereotyping. *Journal of Personality and Social Psychology, 36*(7), 778-793.

Thomas, R.R. (1991). *Beyond race and gender: Unleashing the power of your total work force by managing diversity.* New York: AMACOM.

Thomas, R.R. (1990). From affirmative action to affirming diversity. *Harvard Business Review, 68*(2), 107-117.

Worchel, S., & Austin, W. (1986). *Psychology of intergroup relations* (2nd ed.). Chicago: Nelson-Hall.

Paula Grace *is a consultant and trainer based in San Francisco, California. She has written a number of training designs and has conducted training on the topics of cultural diversity, international business, management development, and sales and marketing in North America, Europe, and Africa. As the director of training and human resource development for DHL Worldwide Express, she traveled throughout the world consulting with business managers and conducting training programs. She is on the faculty of the University of California, Berkeley Extension, where she teaches courses in training and human resource development.*

BEHAVIOR-MANAGEMENT INTERVENTIONS: GETTING THE MOST OUT OF YOUR EMPLOYEE ASSISTANCE PROGRAM

Robert T. Brill

THE PROBLEM OF SUBSTANCE ABUSE

The abuse of drugs and alcohol in the workplace is a very serious problem. The consequences of such behavior are evidenced in poor performance, increased absenteeism and turnover, unsafe working behaviors, and increased medical costs incurred by employers. The cost to the U.S. economy of substance abuse in the workplace was estimated at $57.9 billion in 1983 (Norman & Salyards, 1989) and it has risen since then. The pervasiveness of the problem is alarming; approximately 25 percent of the work force seems to be involved (Wrich, 1988). The problem exists in almost all types of jobs and at all levels; white and blue collar workers, management, and staff have been found to have substance-abuse problems. In addition to the negative consequences in the workplace, many spillover effects accompany substance abuse. Traffic accidents, deterioration of relationships and households, criminal activity, and the spread of the AIDS virus by intravenous drug users are just some of the negative social implications of substance abuse.

EMPLOYEE ASSISTANCE PROGRAMS

Employee assistance programs (EAPs) address a variety of problems encountered by employees; substance abuse is one of them. Others include marital problems, coping with tragedy, and general life stress. A combination of confronting the problem and providing treatment for the employee has been shown to obtain both an impressive success rate (65 to 80 percent) and a profitable savings for the organization (as much as $8 million) (Shain, Suurvali, & Boutilier, 1986). EAP personnel serve as experts and consultants for supervisors, managers, and union shop stewards. Roman (1989) identifies other benefits of EAPs, including minimized litigation through clearly stated policies; a common goal for management and labor; and enhanced public opinion by means of a constructive, rather than a punitive, approach to substance abuse. Companies that have been effective in reducing substance abuse are characterized by strategies that build an environment of trust, confidentiality in treatment, and guaranteed fairness in the workplace (Epp, 1988).

The function of EAPs is to provide counseling for the work force. EAPs provide systematic ways to deal with a wide array of personal issues. According to Roman and Blum (1985), the "core technology" of EAPs involves the following components:

1. The identification of employees' problems based on job performance;
2. Carefully developed and widely disseminated policies and procedures;
3. Appropriate use of constructive confrontation;
4. Links with community resources when necessary; and
5. Adherence to confidentiality regulations and avoidance of unnecessary referrals.

These five components make the EAP a unique system, one that requires a delicate balance of attention to the concerns of the employee, the work organization, and community resources (Sonnestuhl & Trice, 1986).

THE ROLE OF THE SUPERVISOR

Typically, the first and third components of the EAP technology fall on the shoulders of the supervisor. Workers often do not realize that they need counseling, and it becomes necessary for supervisors to encourage such workers to take advantage of the opportunity. Such encouragement sometimes evolves into a mandate, with the worker's continued employment based on his or her seeking help.

Unfortunately, several potential obstacles constrict the effectiveness of the supervisor within an EAP. For instance, without top-management support, union cooperation, employee acceptance, or an organizational culture that promotes sobriety, employees may feel inhibited about using the EAP, and it may be difficult for the supervisor to carry out his or her role in the process. Although it is often perceived as being difficult and aversive, the supervisory role is crucial in identifying "problem" employees and encouraging them to use the EAP.

APPLYING BEHAVIOR-MANAGEMENT STRATEGIES TO EAPS

The purpose of this paper is to integrate principles of applied behavioral analysis with the implementation of EAPs and their referral strategies in order to maximize the effectiveness and utilization of EAPs. Specifically, behavior-management strategies will be applied to two behaviors: *identification* and *confrontation* of workers who might benefit from the EAP services. Promotion and reinforcement of these behaviors are critical in the cases of employees who need help but who are in denial or blind to the ongoing consequences of their inability to manage the sources of their problems. To ensure even greater benefits from EAPs, it is realistic and prudent for companies to expect and encourage these two behaviors to be practiced by coworkers as well as by supervisors. Behavior-management strategies taken from Geller, Ludwig, Gilmore, and Berry's (1990) taxonomy will be used to discuss interventions for improving coworkers' and supervisors' ability and motivation to serve as change agents for workers who are experiencing quality-of-life problems.

Implementation of some of these strategies should greatly contribute to improving the utility of EAPs. To increase any desired behavior, change interventions should typically address two issues: An individual must first be *capable of performing the behavior* and also must be *motivated to carry it out*.

THE SUPERVISOR'S ABILITY TO IDENTIFY PROBLEMS

The first and foremost step in improving the effectiveness of the supervisory role within an EAP is a clear policy that is communicated by top management and that states:

- Its commitment to improving the employees' quality of life through implementation of the EAP; and
- Its encouragement and direction for supervisors concerning their EAP responsibility.

Direction refers to the explicit procedures that supervisors are to follow in identifying and confronting "problem" employees. This should include:

- Specific details regarding how often performance indices should be recorded (the format should be determined individually for each job);
- How to properly document a "noticeable decrement" in performance;
- How to maintain employee confidentiality;
- What procedure is to be followed in referring an employee to the EAP; and
- How to handle the initial confrontation.

In terms of the last point, the policy should emphasize approaching the employee in general terms (e.g., "Based on your recent performance, a problem seems to exist"), not in a presumptuous, accusative style (e.g., "Are you a substance abuser?" or "Do you have problems at home?").

The Job-Performance Model

The job-performance model, on which EAP referrals are based, relies on the identification of decrements in job performance. One problem with the policy guides discussed above is the ambiguity of the term "noticeable decrement" in performance. Such vague terminology can lead to confusion and inaction on the part of managers. To avoid such paralysis, the specific criteria for nonacceptable decreases in performance should be discussed and established at the supervisor-subordinate level. Such discussions are common at initial employment, when supervisors clarify their expectations concerning the minimal level of performance acceptable before termination. Unlike those dialogues, discussion of the level of performance at which counseling services should be considered as a resource is much less foreboding. It should be more pleasant and help oriented. This facilitates a more cooperative, less defensive dialogue about specific performance standards for relevant job dimensions. The type of performance-appraisal system, expected variability in job performance, and the criticalness of the job in terms of safety and profit are factors to be considered in these discussions. If necessary, the supervisor may wish to consult his or her superior for input, but such third-party involvement should be avoided if possible so as to maintain the confidentiality that most EAPs encourage.

Rater Training Programs

Research has demonstrated that many basic skills—both psychomotor and cognitive—relevant to job performance are impaired by most drugs. Therefore, confidence in the reliability and accuracy of the method used to measure performance is of the utmost importance. Wherever possible, objective measures such as attendance, customer grievances, and substandard production should be used. More often, employees will need to rely on supervisory ratings. Because of their subjective nature, valid performance ratings are a challenging endeavor. Supervisors need to be given ample opportunity to observe performance in order to ensure confidence and accuracy in the assessment of performance. Also, as Sonnestuhl and Trice (1986) suggest, a supportive top management must communicate its commitment to an EAP policy that incorporates the job-performance model and must clearly demonstrate how the necessary behaviors may be integrated into the supervisors' already existing job duties and responsibilities. Such direction and increased supervisor confidence and accuracy can be obtained by means of rater training programs (Hedge & Kavanagh, 1988).

Performance-appraisal research has refined and increased the effectiveness of rater training programs (Borman, 1991). One such program, frame-of-reference training, was developed on the basis of improved understanding of the rater's information-processing capabilities (Bernardin & Pence, 1980). The objective of this training strategy is to provide raters of the same job title with a common framework of standards (e.g., what are good and poor examples of performance) for each of the multiple work dimensions in that job. This is achieved by familiarization with the behavioral content relevant for each dimension; discussion of what constitutes different levels of performance; and practice and review, preferably with actual performance examples filmed or simulated.

Through consultation with EAP counselors, specific job behaviors that may be more susceptible to the effects of stress or substance abuse may be identified and integrated into the content of the training program. A good supplement to frame-of-reference training is the practice of diary keeping (DeNisi, Robbins, & Cafferty, 1989), in which supervisors record critical work incidents of both excellent and poor performance by workers. This information can assist the supervisor in the rating process and improve the quality, detail, and credibility of the documentation of a "noticeable" performance problem. This will not only be more convincing to the subordinate but should also provide the supervisor with greater confidence to initiate a referral.

These methods can be an effective step toward giving supervisors the ability to identify performance problems and can provide the additional benefit of more reliable and accurate appraisal ratings in general.

THE SUPERVISOR'S ABILITY TO CONFRONT

Once decreased performance is identified, a supervisor faces the difficulty of confronting the worker. This task is so unpleasant that supervisors have been known to inflate ratings in order to justify avoiding such confrontation (Kipnis, 1960; Latham, 1986). This demonstrates the importance of the appraisal issues discussed previously.

Training to improve constructive confrontation ability should employ actual demonstration supplemented by consensus-seeking practice and role playing. This type of training should begin with reiteration of the policy issues concerning top management's support, documentation of performance, the referral process, etc. This is followed by a demonstration of the constructive-confrontation phase of the referral, performed by professional trainers and/or EAP coordinators or counselors. Although the initial approach of a supervisor can be somewhat standardized (i.e., performance-based, nonaccusative), the nature of the employee's reaction can take a variety of forms, including defensiveness, denial, anger, and rationalizing. Therefore, multiple vignettes should be designed, demonstrated, and discussed for various subordinate rebuttals. These will afford the supervisors the opportunity to directly observe what is considered to be an effective constructive-confrontation strategy. The demonstration should be prefaced with the understanding that any discussion or questions (which should be encouraged) must be conducted within the framework of hypothetical, ideal, supervisory behaviors, not real or actual experiences, successes, or failures. This last point must be emphasized so as to maintain the confidentiality that should be protected at all costs.

Although direct observation has been shown to be an effective teaching tool, it is recommended that sessions be conducted so that supervisors can practice and refine their abilities in approaching workers. Similar training can be provided for employees, to introduce and promote constructive confrontation at the peer level.

MOTIVATING IDENTIFICATION AND CONFRONTATION EFFORTS

Communication

Once ability issues are addressed, identification and confrontation can be further promoted through many of the communication strategies suggested by Geller and colleagues (1990). In implementing the EAP, effort should be made to educate both workers and supervisors about the positive aspects of EAPs. This serves two purposes: 1) It informs employees who have problems about this means of obtaining help, and 2) it helps to diminish the perceptions of supervisors and coworkers that they are "ratting" on their fellow workers by identifying and confronting them. This perception can be replaced with a more appropriate understanding of "intervening to help" fellow employees.

In an organization in which performance tasks and safety require interdependence of workers, it is essential that workers be educated about the direct implications of tolerating substance abuse or other performance problems. These implications range from loss of production bonuses to serious injury or fatality. Sheridan (1987) describes an effective brochure that presents these points to the employees of the Union Pacific Railroad. Its efforts to promote a drug-free workplace often focus on the "silent majority" who do not abuse drugs or alcohol, but who suffer the consequences yet fail to intervene when they could provide a great service for other employees. To increase the impact of such informational tools, the relevant consequences or specific injuries for the particular jobs within the organization should be stressed (e.g., drowning for boat operators, electrocution for those who work with electricity, fractures and broken bones for jobs that involve moving large objects), rather than general consequences such as increased absenteeism, decreased production, and decreased safety.

Consensus-Seeking Activities

In addition to the education and training programs mentioned thus far, small groups of supervisors and employees can participate in consensus-seeking activities. The typical method of providing such practice is group decision making, in which participants and a facilitator come together with diverse expectations about an issue and leave with unanimity concerning the preferred response. This process often leads to increased group satisfaction and commitment to the issue or the course of action (Hegedus & Rasmussen, 1986).

In this context, the initial decision to be made should focus on the basic question of whether or not EAPs are worthwhile and what role should they play within the organization. The group begins discussing general issues such as the benefits of EAPs and the importance of a coworker's or supervisor's referral to help employees with problems. Discussion should move toward a consensus that would instill a greater sense of commitment on the part of individual employees and supervisors to become more adept at identification and confrontation behaviors. Consensus seeking is not an easy task, and great emphasis is put on the role of the facilitator. Many strategies for obtaining consensus and evaluating its impact have been developed. The potential commitment to improving the quality of life for employees through EAPs that could come from such exercises makes them a worthwhile endeavor.

The dialogue within the exercise can pinpoint supervisors' and employees' fears and break down many of the obstacles that prevent their intervening, such as their concern for the affected employee's job security, concern about how others will perceive them, lack of faith in the referral and counseling process, confidentiality concerns, and fear of interpersonal repercussions. When brought into the open and discussed, these fears and perceived obstacles often disappear.

Role Playing

Motivation interventions can build on the ability-training program discussed above. Effective supervisory techniques should be role played, and hesitant or skeptical supervisors should be asked to play the role of a troubled employee (perhaps a substance abuser). Role playing has been shown to be successful in changing people's attitudes and perceptions about an issue (McCombe & Stires, 1990). When directed by a facilitator who is skilled in using such techniques, role playing helps supervisors to understand the confusion and emotional struggles that "problem" employees are likely to feel. When they become sufficiently absorbed in the role, they actually experience some of the things the employee may be experiencing, such as a sense of lost control, frustration, and helplessness. Eventually the role player is "introduced" to and accepts the option of EAP counseling. Such powerful role-reversal experiences often elicit strong attitudinal changes. The objective is to help supervisors to understand that although their role is difficult, it is truly a helping role. Many trainers and counselors possess the qualifications to conduct role plays.

Written and Visual Activators

Another intervention strategy that can further promote an organizational culture conducive to improved quality of life through EAPs is a written or visual activator (Geller et al., 1990), a mechanism put into place to activate appropriate behaviors. For instance, a memorandum delineating the company's EAP policy serves as a written activator to motivate employees to use the EAP and supervisors to carry out their role. For visual activators, the policy's highlights could be posted. Symbols and images are very effective in motivating behaviors in an antecedent fashion. Union Pacific's program, Operation Red Block, frequently used the display of the railroad's bright red stop sign to communicate its message, a symbol that was clear in meaning and with which the workers could easily identify (Sheridan, 1987). Other activators that may be effective when posted include brief but profound statistics (e.g., percentage of workers injured, percentage helped by EAP) and scenarios depicting substance abusers, depressed individuals, and marital problems before and after EAP referral and counseling.

Success Stories

Success stories can be profiled by means of newsletters and bulletin boards, featuring narratives and pictures of actual supervisors and employees who benefited from the referral and counseling components of the EAP. In this way, individuals who have been helped by the system become intervention agents who demonstrate the benefits of the EAP to others. Of course, no workers who have benefited from the EAP should be coerced to permit such a feature. However, one may be surprised at how cooperative and helpful successfully treated workers become. Hypothetical narratives and name changes are optional strategies for this type of intervention.

Supervisory Pledges and Incentives

Additional suggestions include efforts at building commitment by having supervisors sign pledge cards that specifically state, "I will serve the needs of the EAP and my employees by identifying and confronting those whose performance noticeably decreases so as to encourage and support them in overcoming their problems."

Many activator interventions are geared toward the individual supervisor (e.g., incentives, disincentives) or use the motivating power of penalties and competition (Geller et al., 1990). Such approaches are not recommended in this context because the target behaviors, identification and confrontation, are not desirable unless the situation truly indicates a problem employee, and the situation will differ for each supervisor. However, within the policy statement and supervisor's job description, it should be pointed out that supervisors who fail to confront workers whose performance noticeably decreases are not completing their job duties, and this may be reflected in their own performance evaluations.

Goals and incentives for the supervisors as a group are recommended. In fact, a drug-free workplace should be a general goal that all supervisors internalize. More specific goals may be set by establishing certain levels of absenteeism and turnover that would be desirable to achieve relative to current levels. It is necessary to reiterate how important it is that supervisors perceive the EAP as an effective means of achieving improvements in absenteeism and turnover. In this regard, effective educational programs are critical. These goals can be assigned by top management, but preferably supervisors will reach consensus and set goal levels participatively. Upper management can tie group incentives to the realization of these goals. Similar goals and incentives can be extended to the work force in general.

As with the activators, it is recommended that negative consequences, such as penalties for failing to identify or confront "problem" workers, be avoided. Such interventions may have a boomerang effect and inhibit supervisors from accepting and being committed to the overall EAP philosophy. A common consequence would be for supervisors to inflate performance ratings in order to protect them from being "liable" or deserving of the penalty.

A more constructive and effective consequence is feedback at the group and individual level. Group feedback would involve continual updates of progress toward any goals that have been set, as well as reports at meetings of data concerning the effectiveness of the EAP (e.g., number of employees receiving help and results of confidential and anonymous surveys of employee satisfaction with the referral process and counseling). To ensure anonymity, these surveys could be distributed by the EAP staff with return envelopes addressed to the human resource department or some designated office that will tally the results. Individual feedback would involve assessment of strengths and weaknesses in a nonthreatening, one-on-one training setting that is conducive to discussing and reinforcing the effective aspects of the supervisor's behavior and correcting or improving the negative aspects. In other words, there should be no connection between the feedback and one's performance evaluation. Documented performance problems by supervisors would be concerned only with failure to confront, not with ineffective confrontation, as it is a developed skill. This feedback may be provided by the supervisor, a peer supervisor, an EAP staff member, or an EAP coordinator.

Many of these interventions are implemented and monitored by a designated EAP coordinator within the organization. In some cases, it is a full-time job; in other cases, it is one of the human resource manager's job responsibilities; and in still other cases, the responsibilities are delegated and rotated throughout the organization's management.

CONCLUSION

An EAP offers a multiple-intervention approach. Some employees seek help simply as a result of the education, marketing, and availability of the EAP. Others benefit from the preventive focus of the EAP's efforts and the organization's overall concern for quality of life. In general, a large number of workers receive substantial guidance and assistance from the EAP and from an organization that promotes a healthy work force.

However, many of the more serious problems of addiction, stress, and family turmoil are accompanied by strong denial on the part of the affected workers. They refuse to recognize the seriousness of their problems or are too egotistical to believe that they need help. These workers are the ones for whom the supervisory referral component of the EAP mission is so critical. Here the balance between supportive rehabilitation and mandated measures is crucial. The former should be emphasized, and the latter used as a last resort. It is a challenging balance for supervisors to maintain as they serve as change agents in identifying and confronting poorly performing subordinates in order to get them into a setting where they will be helped.

Organizations have been reluctant to encourage fellow workers to serve as intervention agents who share responsibility for identifying and confronting "problem" employees, despite the fact that they often have a direct interest in seeing that coworkers are helped when needed. Employees can be encouraged to extend the work of the supervisory role in a professional, caring manner. Organizations may never know the full impact that the EAP has on individual employees, or the number of employees who are helped by the EAP, but this should not downplay the necessity of fostering a culture of "sobriety" and "high quality of life" in which employees demonstrate a genuine concern for other workers, whether at the supervisory or peer level.

REFERENCES

Bernardin, H.J., & Pence, E. (1980). Effects of rater training: Creating new response sets and decreasing accuracy. *Journal of Applied Psychology, 66,* 458-463.

Borman, W.C. (1991). Job behavior, performance, and effectiveness. In M.D. Dunnette & L.M. Hough (Eds.), *Handbook of Industrial/Organizational Psychology* (Vol. 2, 2nd ed.). Palo Alto, CA: Consulting Psychologists Press.

DeNisi, A.S., Robbins, T., & Cafferty, T.P. (1989). Organization of information used for performance appraisals: Role of diary-keeping. *Journal of Applied Psychology, 74*(1), 124-129.

Epp, J. (1988). Substance abuse and the workplace: A federal perspective. *Worklife Report (Canada), 6,* 1-3.

Geller, E.S., Ludwig, T., Gilmore, M., & Berry, T. (1990). A taxonomy of behavior change techniques for community intervention. *The Community Psychologist, 23*(21), 4-6.

Hedge, J.W., & Kavanagh, M.J. (1988). Improving the accuracy of performance evaluations: Comparison of three methods of performance appraiser training. *Journal of Applied Psychology, 73,* 68-73.

Kipnis, D. (1960). Some determinants of supervisory esteem. *Personnel Psychology, 13,* 377-391.

Latham, G.P. (1986). Job performance and appraisal. In Cooper C. Robertson (Ed.), *Review of industrial/organizational psychology* (pp. 117-155). Chichester, England: Wiley.

Norman, J., & Salyards, S.D. (1989). An empirical evaluation of preemployment drug testing in the U.S. postal service: Interim report of findings. In S.W. Gust & J.M. Walsh (Eds.), *Drugs in the Workplace: Research and evaluation data.* (NIDA Research Monograph 91), pp. 219-226.

Roman, P.M. (1989). The use of EAP's in dealing with drug abuse in the workplace. In S.W. Gust & J.M. Walsh (Eds.), *Drugs in the Workplace: Research and evaluation data.* (NIDA Research Monograph 91), pp. 219-226.

Roman, P.M., & Blum, T.C. (1985). The core technology of employee assistance programs. *Journal of Studies on Alcohol, 42,* 244-272.

Shain, M., Suurvali, H., & Boutilier, M. (1986). *Healthier workers: Health promotion and employee assistance programs.* Lexington, MA: Lexington Books.

Sheridan, P.J. (1987). Operation red block signals stop to alcohol and drug abuse. *Occupational Hazards, 49,* 43-45.

Sonnestuhl, W.J., & Trice, H.M. (1986). *Strategies for employee assistance programs: The crucial balance.* (Key Issues Series No. 30). Ithaca, NY: ILR Press.

Wrich, J.T. (1988). Beyond testing: Coping with drugs in the workplace. *Harvard Business Review, 66,* 120-130.

Robert T. Brill, Ph.D., is a professor of industrial/organizational psychology in the Psychology Department of Moravian College in Bethlehem, Pennsylvania. His consulting experiences have involved development and validation of selection tests and implementation of performance-appraisal systems for several companies. He conducts research in the areas of performance appraisal, job complexity, and employee assistance programs. He serves on several human-resource committees in the Lehigh Valley and Philadelphia.

FOSTERING THE EFFECTIVENESS OF GROUPS AT WORK

Patrick J. Ward and Robert C. Preziosi

It is clear that the mandate for organizational leaders is changing. The tasks of controlling and directing are evolving into facilitating—including coaching, encouraging, listening, and teaching. At the same time the focus on total quality management (TQM) and continuous improvement have given rise to an increasing emphasis on the development of groups. Yet danger lurks down the road for organizations if they do not understand how groups develop and function and if they do not recognize and plan for the complexity involved in fostering the group experience. Management training must prepare organizational leaders for their responsibilities as facilitators of group development.

Historically, many managers have begun their careers as line workers who have shown aptitude and/or loyalty in production. These characteristics, however, have not always been accompanied by interpersonal skills; people's experiences as line workers do not generally make them aware of the complexities of forming and working with groups, nor do these experiences teach them the skills they need to facilitate groups successfully.

The success of groups in the workplace depends on training managers—as well as line workers—in how groups develop and what skills are required to use a group effectively. Success also depends on an organizational environment that encourages communication, the exchange of ideas, and the ability to be self-critical in the interest of improvement. Organizational members must be open to feedback regarding themselves and their work groups. Groups must be tied to the goals and purposes of the organization, and these connections need to be clear. The function of each group needs to be supported by top management. Finally, after being trained, both supervisors and nonsupervisory employees need to nurture communication skills. Group skills should become part of the criteria on which people's performance is evaluated. In fact, ideally, evaluation would be done with the group rather than the individual.

Instead, managers in the United States often have been trained to focus on numbers. They are usually evaluated according to whether they meet quotas and stay under budget. In other words, they are judged on their production, not their communication (D'Aprix, 1982). Consequently, in dealing with employees, they become more emotionally distant to maintain objectivity and to be "businesslike"; and this behavior is sometimes interpreted as lacking emotion. The interpersonal skills needed for effective group work are often overtly as well as covertly discouraged. Under such norms, it is difficult to cultivate the skills necessary to enhance communication, to foster effective group work, and to be open to feedback concerning the needs of the organization.

When faced with problems within the organization, first-line supervisors may feel pressured and defensive in protecting their interests and advancement. This is particularly true if they are not properly trained in problem solving, communication, and systems practices. Managers and supervisors who lack such training may revert to rigidly doing as they are told without questioning (Argyris, 1991). This form of "learned helplessness" creates frustration but at the same time absolves them of responsibility. The organization achieves a sense of predictability and "control," but at the expense of responsiveness and continuous improvement.

Finally, managers and supervisors succumb to attribution—attributing the causes of difficulty to others—while sensing that they have not been adequately prepared or supported. Thus, they may be blind to their own ineffectiveness and may lose contact with the overall goals of the organization. The primary focus of management—and, therefore, of the organization—ultimately becomes control in the interest of self-protection.

Without effective leadership, workers feel frustrated, ignored, and isolated. Lacking avenues of communication, they sublimate their anger and resentment, thus fostering resistance, sabotage, and passive-aggressive patterns.

To throw these groups together without appreciation for the complexity and power (both constructive and destructive) of the group process is a waste of time, money, and potential. If the proper organizational climate and support systems are not already in place, TQM, continuous improvement, and the use of groups should be postponed until training and team-building efforts can be completed.

THE IMPORTANCE OF THE GROUP EXPERIENCE IN ORGANIZATIONS

Groups can be a vital and important organizational tool. Gersick (1988) points out that "organizations largely consist of permanent and temporary groups," from work units, to project teams, to special committees or task forces. Beckhard (1972) suggests the following major purposes for using groups in the workplace:

- To set goals or priorities;
- To analyze work and assign responsibility and accountability;
- To examine the norms, both formal and informal, of the organization; and
- To examine the relationships of the people doing the work.

The potential of groups to assist their organizations is enormous. For example, organizations are increasingly using task groups to meet the challenges of legal requirements. Employee input into job analysis, for instance, helps organizations in the U.S. to comply with laws regarding Equal Employment Opportunity, Affirmative Action, and rights regarding "protected groups." Improper job analysis, along with lack of awareness of changing laws and regulations, can make an organization vulnerable to lawsuits and charges of noncompliance (Veres, Locklear, & Sims, 1990). Similarly, groups can be used to meet other challenges, such as those of employee testing. Managers can be encouraged to work with groups in monitoring compliance with legal mandates governing employment tests, aptitude tests for promotion and advancement, lie-detector and drug-screen tests for potential employees, and treatment of employees and applicants with disabilities.

Knowledge of group development and dynamics can assist supervisors and employees in exploiting the opportunities presented in these cooperative experiences. The use of groups can be extremely effective in an organization, not only in protecting it from legal problems but also in:

- Helping to infuse new ideas and attitudes into the culture;
- Encouraging employee participation and nurturing a sense of involvement and increased personal investment;
- Providing employees with new insights regarding their own and their groups' behaviors;
- Offering an alternative means for evaluating performance and evaluating the organization's abilities to support employee efforts;
- Providing an opportunity for employees to learn through observation and modeling, thereby increasing their own skill levels and contributing more to their groups and the organization as a whole;
- Representing a microcosm and providing indicators of how clients and customers may view the organization; and
- Teaching employees how to listen and communicate—how to check their perceptions and avoid misconceptions.

It is important to note that groups also can have devastating effects if they are managed poorly, thereby driving communication underground, creating negative agendas, and setting up divisive alliances. If groups are to be used effectively, organizations must help all employees to understand the development and the life cycle of a group. For managers, such training could ease the pressures of supervising and could teach the skills associated with successful facilitating; for nonmanagerial employees, this training could teach them to derive maximum benefit from the group experience.

Success in this endeavor requires the cooperation and participation of all levels in the organization. Group leadership is a skill that can be taught, but the learner must be patient and dedicated and must grow to understand and respect the group process. It is equally important that senior management understand and respect the group process and lend it their support. For optimal effectiveness in group work to occur, the organization must consider such work to be part of a comprehensive attempt to enhance communication. Group work is not a panacea; it is one tool among many for increasing effectiveness in meeting tactical and strategic challenges.

THE STAGES OF GROUP DEVELOPMENT

As every group is a collection of individuals, each experience is unique and requires special consideration. Despite the differences among groups, though, a certain developmental progression or life cycle can be expected. The stages of group life outlined in the remainder of this article—pregroup, initial, transition, working, final, and postgroup—are meant to suggest the complexity of the group experience. This information is intended to define and describe some of the dynamics that can be expected in working with a group. The discussion is presented in terms of the leadership functions and the member functions that are applicable in each stage. In addition, Table 1 identifies the key issues at each stage.

Table 1. Key Issues at Each Stage of Group Development

Stage	Leader Issues	Member Issues	Leader/Member Issues
Pregroup	Gaining commitment from top management	Developing enthusiasm for the group	Needs assessment; diagnosis
Initial	Training for participation in group	Committing to organizational needs	Group-process skill development
Transition	Encouraging autonomy of group members	Working through conflicts	Conflict resolution; mediation
Working	Helping group members to interpret behaviors; facilitating and encouraging	Supporting one another	Esteem-building behavior
Final	Reinforcing behavioral changes by asserting influence	Completing any unfinished business	Celebration of success
Postgroup	Making resources for change available	Monitoring group effectiveness	Measurement

Although all stages of group work are important, it is most important to focus on pregroup and postgroup activities. The other stages occur naturally, while those efforts before and after the group experience require concerted energy and special effort. When the leader and the members know what to expect at various stages, they can accomplish more, follow through better in group meetings, and increase their chances of putting energy and ideas to use.

In addition to the leadership functions listed below, it is also important that the leader maintain communication with top management and with other groups. The leader is the primary linkage between the group and the other parts of the organization.

Pregroup Stage

It is imperative that every group have a purpose, a clear reason for being. Today many groups are formed as quality-improvement teams or task groups whose job is to tackle certain problems. However, a group must work on its own *processes* as well as the *problems* that it is assigned. Also, the group must be empowered to offer solutions and suggestions; and, regardless of whether these solutions and suggestions are accepted and acted on, the organization must validate and respond to them.

In addition to a reason for being, a group must have specific goals that are both understood and supported by top management. The group members must be able to answer "yes" to a number of questions:

- Do the members of the group have the assurance that their findings and recommendations will be considered?
- Do they have established parameters under which to operate?
- Do they understand not only the problem that they are to address but also the organization's objectives in the identified area?
- Do they have a clear understanding of the organization's goals?
- Do they have the assurance of top management that their work is of more than just passing interest and is truly important?

Leadership Functions in the Pregroup Stage

- Developing a clearly written proposal for the formation of the group, outlining its purpose and goals.
- Conducting needs-assessment interviews to gain input from potential members about needs, thereby decreasing resistance and promoting a sense of group ownership on the part of potential members.
- Presenting the proposal to top managers and obtaining their agreement concerning the group's scheduling, purpose, and goals.
- Making decisions about the size of the group and who needs to be included in the membership. (The ideal group size is five to eight members, although as many as twelve may be included. If the group becomes too large, two groups may be formed to divide responsibilities and coordinate efforts; or the fact that many people need to be included may be an indication that the goals of the group need to be simplified and further narrowed.)
- Identifying other groups, departments, or external stakeholders who may need to be involved in group goals. For example, if the group is focused on an issue of production, do any suppliers or providers also need to have input?

- Organizing practical details for meetings, including arranging a comfortable setting and determining appropriate time frames. This organization also includes coordinating and developing any necessary audiovisual materials. *The more prepared the leader is for the first sessions, the more seriously the members will take the group.*
- Arranging preliminary group discussions to allow members to become acquainted and to orient and prepare them for a successful experience.
- Preparing psychologically for the leadership tasks and meeting with a co-facilitator if appropriate.

Group Members' Functions in the Pregroup Stage

- Including themselves in the discussions concerning the group and its work.
- Learning the facts about the group that might have an impact on them during their tenure.
- Deciding what they feel the outcome of their efforts should be. (Anxiety about the group may be lessened and enthusiasm strengthened if the group members feel that they can prepare. Also, the members will feel a greater sense of control and ownership.)

Initial Stage

During this stage the ground rules are set. The parameters of the group are established. Members identify appropriate issues to be considered as well as those that might be considered in the future. If the group is meeting on a specific production issue, for example, the members determine whether the concerns raised by group members have to do with that issue and whether the group can do anything about those concerns. It is important in this stage to clarify the parameters and narrow the group's focus.

The central issue in this stage is trust. The members are testing the group for comfort and trying to determine identities for themselves. They display high degrees of "socially acceptable" or restrained behavior, and facades may be strong. Negative feelings may arise as the members experiment to see which feelings are acceptable and as they learn group norms, both implicit and explicit. In addition, positive connections may begin to develop. Each member may ask himself or herself questions such as these:

- Will this group make a difference?
- Will it be beneficial to me?
- If I am expected to be honest, will my honesty be used against me if I disagree?
- If I disagree, is it safer to hide my opinion and simply go along with the other members?

The members may slip into problem solving or may attempt to explain away problems to avoid taking risks and identifying their own needs or concerns. They also may focus on other members' personal needs, thereby sublimating their own needs.

Leadership Functions in the Initial Stage

- Laying out general guidelines and teaching the group members how to participate actively (both by example and through didactic information): how to be specific, how to clarify, how to give and receive feedback appropriately. This function may include teaching the basics of group process, including the importance of active listening. (Some instruction may take place during pregroup sessions).
- Providing an activity through which the group members can become acquainted and can share their expectations of the group. "Brainstorming" activities also may be used to identify potential concerns. These concerns can then be prioritized by the group and placed on the group's agenda.
- Assisting members in expressing themselves; pointing out linkages among the members' ideas.
- Clarifying the division of responsibility; helping the members to identify their personal roles in the group.
- Giving positive feedback for member participation.
- Providing structure and direction for the group while allowing for member participation.
- Identifying the members' verbal and nonverbal cues.
- Recognizing and providing an opportunity for discussion of mistrust or misgivings about the group process.
- Stressing the importance of confidentiality regarding discussions within the group. (In identifying problems with the organization, the group members can put themselves at risk. It is imperative that they feel safe to critically examine the organization.)

Group Members' Functions in the Initial Stage

- Establishing a commitment to the needs of the organization, as opposed to purely personal needs.
- Participating in "brainstorming" and other team activities.
- Being responsible for their own reactions. For example, a group member who assumes responsibility says something like "I feel confused about what is happening right now" instead of "This group is confusing."
- Listening.

- Offering suggestions for alternatives if they disagree with the group's focus or procedures.
- Letting go of personal agendas. All members must guard against letting their personal agendas take precedence over group needs. At first the members may not be aware of their agendas, but in time these agendas become clearer.

Transition Stage

This phase in the group's development is marked by the dropping of facades and restrained behavior and may be characterized by challenges to the leader and other group members. Resistance and conflict become more apparent. Members may be experimenting with their group identities and checking to see how much disagreement or conflict will be accepted as well as how it will be handled. This is a critical stage. The leader may feel threatened and overwhelmed, with the sense that everything is falling apart.

Whenever roles or expectations of organizational members are changed, hidden agendas and informal power structures may come to the surface. Although this development may seem like regression, it is actually a sign that the group is advancing.

If the members represent different work areas, resistance may come from the supervisors of those areas, who feel threatened or left out. It is important to remember the "linking" function of the group leader in keeping top management and other organizational groups informed. If resistance is encountered from other managers or supervisors, it might be wise for the leader to try to enlist their support and "expertise."

Leadership Functions in the Transition Stage

- Encouraging and rewarding the open sharing of group members' reactions during meetings.
- Validating feedback while keeping the superordinate goal of the organization in focus.
- Identifying subgroupings and ensuring that no members are taken advantage of or excluded.
- Assisting the members in recognizing their own patterns of defensiveness or resistance.
- Knowing when to direct interventions toward the group or toward individual members. For instance, examples of defensiveness may be presented to the total group rather than directed to one particular person. Also, directing interventions at the total group involves balanced communication and decreases the likelihood of dialogue between group members and the leader.

- Encouraging members to express ideas and feelings in the here-and-now and keeping them focused on the task at hand. Such encouragement keeps the group from digressing into a complaint session about past problems and maintains a focus on finding solutions to current problems.
- Encouraging the group members to be autonomous. The leader should be stepping back, allowing the members to do more and more of the communicating among themselves. The leader's task is to facilitate and to ensure that the communication continues to flow, while allowing the members more freedom in directing the conversation. *If there are disagreements within the group, it is not the leader's responsibility to solve them;* instead, the leader should simply facilitate to ensure that no members are treated abusively in any way.

Group Members' Functions in the Transition Stage

- Moving away from dependence on the leader and establishing more independence.
- Recognizing and expressing personal reactions and/or negative feelings.
- Learning how to confront others or others' ideas in a constructive manner.
- Learning to work through conflicts rather than avoiding them. Members may begin to form subgroups. If conflict is suppressed in a group, it may go more deeply "underground," with members communicating more outside the group. Members have a responsibility to bring outside or covert material to the surface and to assist in making it overt so that it may be processed or dealt with.

Working Stage

This stage of the group's development is indicated by increasing cohesiveness among members, with open communication about different viewpoints. Leadership functions are likely to be shared by the group members; interactions are balanced between and among members, not directed by the leader.

Feedback is given more freely, and it is met with less defensiveness than previously shown. Members display a willingness to work outside of the group to implement changes. They take ownership of their behavior. Also, member empathy is high. The members assist one another in nonjudgmental ways and display greater identity with one another.

Problems at this stage may include a decreasing ability of the group to be self-critical regarding its effectiveness. Group members may have dual goals or purposes: (1) the effectiveness of the group and (2) acceptance by group members. Group members may avoid critical analysis or confrontation for fear of being ostracized.

Leadership Functions in the Working Stage

- Ensuring that the members do not collude to avoid conflict in order to maintain comfortable levels of group cohesiveness.
- Interpreting group behavior to assist the members in attaining deeper levels of understanding.
- Linking members; pointing out the norms of the group, both formal and informal.
- Assisting in clarifying and assessing the goals and accomplishments of the group.
- Encouraging the members to turn new insights and ideas into action.
- Providing the members with needed information and materials to allow them to continue functioning effectively.
- Summarizing group process and interactions and assisting the members in clarifying emerging goals in behavioral terms.
- Helping the members to identify time lines and clarify responsibilities.

Group Members' Functions in the Working Stage

- Providing feedback, confrontation, and support to one another. The members monitor one another's feedback and work toward keeping one another involved.
- Taking turns in assuming leadership behaviors; directing topics, communication flow, and the assignment of responsibilities.
- Monitoring to ensure that the group does not become too comfortable with familiar relationships and that members continue to challenge one another when necessary.

Final Stage

One of the reasons for clearly specifying the objectives of the group at the outset is to be able to tell when it has served its purpose and needs to disband. If the urgency of the problem that brought about the group has lessened, energies may be lost. It is important to remind the members why the group was formed, to point out its accomplishments, and to stress the fragility of those accomplishments if actions are not carried through.

A number of questions need to be answered at this stage of group life:

- If new procedures have been put in place, are the responsibilities clear?
- Are there ways of monitoring the ongoing results or suggestions of the group?

- Are other support systems in the organization aware of their responsibilities in connection with the group's work?
- If the group was formed to deal with a human resource issue, has the human resources department been informed of the recommendations of the group?
- Has this department responded to the group's suggestions, given alternatives, or made a commitment to the suggested actions?
- Is top management aware of the accomplishments of the group and willing to support or at least respond to the group's suggestions?

As these questions illustrate, the group leader's linking function is again important at this stage.

The final stage brings about the possibility of another issue. Certain group members may feel that their concerns have not been attended to, and now time is running out. It is important to respond to their concerns and to assign them to future groups or include them in discussion. The members must know that the work of the group is only a beginning and that a much more important demonstration of the group's effectiveness lies before them in their behaviors and actions outside the group.

Members are likely to pull back, anticipating the end of the group. They may be feeling some sadness over that ending, or they may worry about being able to continue their new-found levels of communication.

Leadership Functions in the Final Stage

- Assisting in clarifying and summarizing group goals.
- Assisting members in dealing with any unfinished business.
- Reinforcing changes that the members have made.
- Ensuring that the members have information about resources to enable them to make desired, identified changes.
- Assisting the members in operationalizing changes, determining how they will put identified goals into action. This function may involve establishing member contracts or giving "homework" assignments.
- Providing the members with opportunities to give one another feedback.
- Re-emphasizing the importance of maintaining confidentiality; continuing to respect the rights of others outside the group.
- Summarizing, integrating, and consolidating what the members have achieved in the group.
- Providing more leadership, direction, and structure to decrease anxiety and to solidify group goals.

Group Members' Functions in the Final Stage
- Clarifying personal and group goals to which the members have committed.
- Completing any unfinished business.
- Clarifying the direction/decisions of the group.
- Evaluating the impact of the group.
- Making suggestions regarding future groups.
- Realizing that the group is not an end in itself and that most of the work identified within the group must take place outside.

Postgroup Stage

Although the critical postgroup stage is often overlooked, it may be the most important of the group-development stages. The group's major contribution to the organization is likely to occur during this stage. The impact of the decisions or actions of the team must be assessed in the wider context of the organization's systems and subsystems. Obstacles to group action need to be identified, attended to, and removed if possible. Also, work during this phase may provide information that will prove valuable in establishing future groups in the organization.

A concern at this stage is that if members have problems implementing the group's approved recommendations or if they lose patience, they may become frustrated and subsequently view the entire group process as negative. The ultimate effectiveness of a group is not shown in its process or in how it ends; it is shown in what it is able to accomplish once the group experience has been completed. The group is only a beginning.

Leadership Functions in the Postgroup Stage
- Administering a postgroup assessment to help determine the group's long-range impact. This assessment should be done in multiple, longer-term follow-up stages.
- Using the information from the group to help bring about needed changes for member effectiveness.
- Making sure that resources are available for desired changes.
- Encouraging the members to continue to find some avenue of support outside the group process.
- Providing follow-up group sessions, if needed.
- Using information from the group (other than personal) in future planning of groups and as a source of needs assessment.
- Meeting with the co-facilitator, if one exists, and individually with group members to assess the overall impact and effectiveness of the group.

- Assisting the members in using identified measures of change.
- Using information to identify future training/skill building.

Group Members' Functions in the Postgroup Stage
- Finding ways of reinforcing new behaviors without the support of the formal group.
- Keeping records of changes, progress, problems, so that they can monitor the effectiveness of the group.
- Continuing relationships with one another to support individual programs for change.

SUMMARY

Traditional, autocratic leadership styles are obsolete in organizations in the United States. Although there is a place for decisive leadership at the top, the value of worker involvement and contribution must be fostered. Changes in work environments and technical developments require organizations that are proactive and responsive to change. And responsiveness depends on creative, effective communication skills—skills that are often overlooked if not covertly and even overtly discouraged.

The use of groups in the work place provides an avenue for enhancing communication skills, worker resiliency, and the effectiveness of organizations. Groups can foster more realistic job analysis, employee and job evaluation, assessment of training needs, increased motivation, and increased awareness of changes in the work environment. Groups must be considered as more than a "quick fix" or a fad, however. In order to manage groups effectively, organizations must train both supervisors and nonsupervisory personnel in the stages of group development and in ways to exploit the full potential of groups. As shown in Table 2, a number of instruments and structured activities can be useful in providing necessary training during the various stages of group life.

REFERENCES

Argyris, C. (1991). Teaching smart people how to learn. *Harvard Business Review, 69*(3), 99-109.

Beckhard, R. (1972). Optimizing team-building efforts. *Journal of Contemporary Business, 1*(3), 23-32.

D'Aprix, R. (1982). *Communicating for productivity.* New York: HarperCollins.

Veres, J.G., Locklear, T.S., & Sims, R.R. (1990). Job analysis in practice: A brief review of the role of job analysis in human resources management. In G.R. Ferris, K.M. Rowland, & M.R. Buckley (Eds.), *Human resource management: Perspectives and issues* (pp. 79-103). Needham Heights, MA: Allyn and Bacon.

Table 2. Useful Learning Resources for Each Stage of Group Development

Stage	Instrument*	Experiential Learning Activity**
Pregroup	Organization Diagnosis	Color Me: Getting Acquainted
Initial	Feedback Rating Scales	A Note to My Teammate: Positive Feedback
Transition	Conflict Management Style Survey	The Hundredth Monkey: Shared Mind-Sets
Working	Group-Growth Evaluation Form	Stating the Issue: Practicing Ownership
Final	Self-Assessment Inventory: Behavior in Groups	Organizational Structure: A Simulation
Postgroup	The Individual-Team-Organization Survey: Conscious Change for the Organization	Supporting Cast: Examining Personal Support Networks

*All instruments can be found in the *Instrumentation Kit,* San Diego: Pfeiffer & Company, 1988.
**All learning activities can be found in *The 1992 Annual: Developing Human Resources,* or *The 1993 Annual: Developing Human Resources,* J. William Pfeiffer (ed.), San Diego: Pfeiffer & Company, 1993.

Patrick J. Ward, Ph.D., is president of Organizational Counseling and Development, Inc., and contracts with United Information Services and Technical Resources Incorporated of Washington, D.C., to provide staff and management-development assistance for agencies with federal grants. He also serves as an adjunct professor for Nova and Barry Universities. He has developed training programs and organization development interventions for manufacturing, hospitality, and healthcare industries, as well as for state and federal agencies. His area of interest in research over the last several years has been in management and employee development in relation to strategies for continuous quality improvement. Dr. Ward is a member of the American Society for Training and Development and the Association for Quality and Participation.

Robert C. Preziosi, Ph.D., is the associate dean and a professor of management education with the School of Business and Entrepreneurship at Nova University in Fort Lauderdale, Florida. He is also the president of Management Associates, a consulting firm. He has worked as a human resources director, a line manager, and a leadership-training administrator and has consulted with all levels of management in many organizations, including AT&T, Dade County Public Schools, Southern Bell, and a large number of hospitals and banks. In 1984 he was given the Outstanding Contribution to HRD Award by the American Society for Training and Development (ASTD); in 1990 he received the Torch Award, the highest leadership award that ASTD gives.

USING MENTORING FOR PROFESSIONAL DEVELOPMENT

J. Barton Cunningham

INTRODUCTION

The mentoring process can take place in either a formal or an informal context. Levine (1985) estimates that formalized mentoring programs probably only constitute about 3 to 4 percent of the mentoring that is actually occurring. Informal mentoring, by far the more prevalent form, typically occurs when a protégé just happens to be chosen by a mentor who possesses much greater experience and expertise. This phenomenon is frequently described as "being in the right place at the right time to be noticed by the right person."

However, formal mentoring programs, in which the organization assigns or matches mentors and protégés, are rapidly increasing in popularity in both the public and the private sectors. In a survey conducted in eight countries (Murray & Owen, 1991), 18 percent of those surveyed (sixty-seven companies) had some kind of formal mentoring program. Most reported that these programs were generally successful and that they planned to continue them.

In view of the reported success of formal mentoring programs, organizations would be well advised to consider them. In implementing a formalized mentoring program, however, an organization needs to resolve several issues: how to identify mentors and prospective protégés, how to develop a learning culture for succession planning and employee development, and how to recognize the skills and characteristics that people need in order to learn. This article provides a perspective on facilitating a formal mentoring process and developing a culture for mentoring. It describes the benefits of mentoring, discusses why informal mentoring and performance-appraisal systems are insufficient ways to develop employees, pinpoints some criteria for a successful mentoring program, and then discusses how to set up a mentoring program.

THE BENEFITS OF MENTORING

Mentoring offers benefits for the organization, for mentors, and for protégés. For example, it is critical for an organization to develop managerial and leadership talent among the ranks. Although it is true that organizations can easily recruit people from outside to fill their managerial needs, most organizations recruit from within. Recruiting from outside the organization not only can negatively affect morale and organizational loyalty but also can introduce new people who conflict with the organization's culture. Introducing new managers or employees into an organization is analogous to the introduction of new strains of bacteria into the body: Some strains can strengthen the immune system, but others can be dangerous. Similarly, in some cases new people in an organization can be a very positive influence, but in others the results may be catastrophic to the culture.

Obviously, the process of promoting from the ranks involves much more than choosing and promoting the most talented technical specialists. Talented line workers may possess high levels of skill in their areas of technical expertise, but such competencies are quite different from those required to create and manage teamwork within a work group. The process of developing competent leaders requires an awareness of the organization's personnel needs as well as mechanisms for developing managerial potential and ability (Sveiby & Lloyd, 1987).

Mentoring programs recognize that on-the-job experience and coaching are valuable ways to develop managerial capabilities. When people in organizations are asked to indicate the ways in which they learned most, they rarely mention university courses, management seminars, or on-the-job training. Rather, they mention on-the-job experience. This finding coincides with research indicating that effective leaders are most often "able to identify a small number of mentors and key experiences that powerfully shaped their philosophies, personalities, aspirations, and operating styles" (Bennis & Nanus, 1985, p. 188).

Mentoring also offers obvious benefits for protégés. A young, new employee, for example, forms an occupational identity and relationship with other employees during the initial stages of his or her career. This is the period during which questions of competence and ability to achieve future occupational dreams are most salient. The employee must learn how to function effectively within the organization by developing technical, interpersonal, and political skills as well as a sense of competence in his or her work. The necessary skills and a sense of competence are acquired primarily through interaction and feedback, and mentoring can be extremely useful in this acquisition process.

In addition, mentors benefit from the mentoring experience. During mid-career the more experienced employee is likely to be reappraising accomplishments and reassessing goals. Entering into a mentoring relationship with a new, ambitious worker provides the senior employee with an opportunity to redirect his or her energies into creative and productive endeavor. It also provides an opportunity to participate vicariously in another person's resolution of the challenges associated with a succession of difficult career stages. In addition, if the protégé is young, the mentor can help that young person to meet the challenges of early adulthood. A related benefit is that the protégé may enable the mentor to see issues, situations, and conditions in a new light.

WHY INFORMAL MENTORING AND PERFORMANCE-APPRAISAL SYSTEMS ARE NOT ENOUGH

Although informal mentoring has always occurred and will continue to do so, there are several reasons for not waiting for mentoring to "just happen" (Gray, 1983):

1. *A very small percentage of motivated and capable employees ever receive informal mentoring.* Often excluded from mentoring are women and minorities, groups that in many cases require the assistance of mentors the most. Instead, it is frequently the case that an organization either consciously or unconsciously endeavors to groom specific types of employees with distinct backgrounds for key management positions. This form of succession planning is often undertaken in order to reinforce the organization's cultural norms, traditions, and underlying value system. However, this approach can perpetuate an "old boys' network" whereby "who you know" is more important that "what you know."

2. *Capable people who do not receive informal mentoring frequently feel envious of those who do and, as a result, feel bitterness toward the organization.* These negative by-products of informal mentoring can severely undermine the credibility of the merit principle within the public sector. Employees may perceive that career opportunities are determined in large part on the basis of one's "connections" rather than on the basis of one's perseverance, dedication, and acquisition of requisite skills.

3. *When human potential goes unrecognized and undeveloped, everyone loses.* Employees end up resigning or working far below their potential and capacity because they feel that no one is truly concerned about them or their career expectations. In turn, the organization may lose valuable human resources that are capable of making significant contributions.

Performance-appraisal systems also do not measure up to formal mentoring programs. They cannot foster an employee's psychological growth in the same way that mentoring can, nor can they provide the opportunity to associate and identify with those who have experience, skill, and power. This deficiency may be due, in part, to the fact that many performance-appraisal systems are highly judgmental in nature and tend to inhibit meaningful two-way communication between a manager and an employee. Also, these systems are not always used in a regular and ongoing manner to facilitate employee learning and development; they may be used for evaluations alone. In addition, they are frequently perceived as the exclusive responsibility and prerogative of management, because management frequently establishes the performance criteria, standards, and objectives along with the evaluation schedule and location.

CRITERIA FOR A SUCCESSFUL MENTORING PROGRAM

Interviews with nine mentors and thirteen protégés suggested the following criteria for successful formal mentoring programs:

1. The program must have the support of top management.
2. Mentors and protégés must be carefully selected.
3. Mentors and protégés must undergo an extensive orientation program emphasizing the development of realistic expectations concerning the relationship.
4. The responsibilities of mentors and protégés must be clearly stated.
5. Minimums of duration and frequency of contact between mentors and protégés must be established.
6. The program should recognize and take into account the skills and characteristics required of mentors and protégés. (See "Developing an Awareness of Mentoring Skills" in this article.)
7. The program should recognize that the mentor-protégé relationship flourishes when the mentor and protégé share responsibility for the relationship; when there is regular, structured contact between mentor and protégé; when the mentor and the protégé respect each other; and when challenging and substantive issues and protégé assignments are dealt with.
8. The program should recognize that there are benefits for mentors, for protégés, and for the organization.
9. The program should recognize the advantages of the mentoring experience, including the development of plans for employee development and employee succession.
10. The program should also recognize the possible drawbacks to the mentoring experience, such as perceived favoritism and exploitation of mentor and protégé (Cunningham & Eberle, in press).

The successful mentoring program is one that takes these findings into account and includes plans to use and develop the skills and characteristics of both mentors and protégés, to foster the appropriate atmosphere and climate, to publicize and promote the benefits for program participants, to maximize the advantages of mentoring, and to minimize the drawbacks.

HOW TO ESTABLISH A MENTORING PROGRAM

To establish formal mentoring, an organization first assesses its needs for mentoring and then designs and implements a mentoring program. Many of the steps involved in assessing needs and in designing and implementing a program can be undertaken during a conference or a series of meetings attended by managers and possibly some nonmanagerial employees representing the different functions of the organization. In such a conference, task subgroups can meet and discuss the various topics within each of the planning steps. Subsequent steps of the planning process leading to program implementation are undertaken after the task subgroups report their results to the total group.

Assessing the Organization's Needs for Mentoring

The initial steps of establishing a mentoring program are concerned with assessing the need for such a program: (1) identifying the organization's personnel needs, (2) developing a mission statement, and (3) establishing an organizational philosophy. If the conference participants determine that particular skills must be developed to meet future needs, that employee development is part of the organization's mission, and that the organizational philosophy supports mentoring, then proceeding with a mentoring program is appropriate.

Identifying the Organization's Personnel Needs

In assessing whether the organization really needs a mentoring program, first the conference participants must take a good look at the organization's personnel needs in the future and must determine the methods that the organization will use to meet these needs. This form of personnel or succession planning is dependent on defining the organization's future environment and identifying the skills that will be needed most in that environment. Both the external and the internal environments should be defined. Figure 1 offers a sample analysis of one organization's external and internal environmental trends. Four types of skills should be considered as necessary resources in connection with what is or will be happening in both environments:

1. *Problem-solving skills.* These skills are designed to help the organization raise questions about its strengths and weaknesses. The purpose of identifying and analyzing strengths and weaknesses is to determine and interpret present directions as well as future directions that may be possible with a more organized and deliberate plan. These skills are generally used after the problem or need has been thoroughly defined.

2. *Adaptive skills.* Unlike routine problem-solving skills, which are used to resolve only immediate organizational issues, adaptive skills incorporate new ideas from outside the firm.

3. *Coordinative skills.* These skills are brought to bear in improving the administrative system to keep up with new technologies and with changes of staff.

4. *Productive skills.* Productive skills focus on the regular, ordinary requirements for the survival and stability of the organization. They are generally used to help the organization to produce its products and/or to provide its services.

EXTERNAL ENVIRONMENT

1. **Technological Change.** The rapidly changing technological environment will hasten and aid the decentralization process. Technology improvements will provide the means for less direct centralized operational control and will permit effective decentralized functional control, while at the same time enabling senior management to obtain timely and usable financial information for decision making.
2. **Demographic Change.** The "baby boom" will slow down the rate of career progression and in-crease the need for "career development," that is, changes in work assignment through lateral transfers.
3. **Economic Change.** Free trade zones will result in increased competitiveness in most countries. This competitiveness will increase the rate of change in the economy.

INTERNAL ENVIRONMENT

1. **Technological Change.** The focus of technology implementation will continue to shift from automating what we are currently doing to developing new and better ways of doing things and to improving the range and quality of services provided. Additional staff training in the use of computer technology will be required if we are to realize the full potential of existing and future computer hardware and software.
2. **Human-Resource Change.** The company has a good mix of age groups and should not be faced with a sudden turnover due to retirements. It will be an ongoing challenge to keep performance and morale up in a climate of increasing work loads, change, and uncertainty. There is a risk of cutbacks and freezes, particularly if there is a downturn in the economy.
3. **Work-Load Change.** The work load will continue to increase, and the work will become less routine.

Figure 1. Sample Environmental-Trend Analysis

Different and often-conflicting needs and values are inherent in each of these skill areas. In a typical manufacturing organization, for example, these differences may manifest themselves in interdepartmental "warfare": The production department, which depends on productive skills, may fail to understand and appreciate the constant modification of products and plans that characterizes the research and development department, which relies on adaptive skills. Such differences are a reflection of the conflict inherent in the tasks acted out by the different subsystems.

At certain times in an organization's life, it may be necessary to highlight certain skills over others. For instance, at times it may be appropriate to develop skills that assist in changing and adapting. Also, changes in one functional area (in one subsystem) will affect other areas. Thus, after a major change, it might be appropriate to emphasize problem-solving skills.

In most cases, the conference participants will be able to forecast skill responses to environmental trends by brainstorming answers to four questions:

- What skills will we need to respond to future changes?

- What skills will we need to improve our internal management?
- What skills will we need to improve our internal efficiency and cost effectiveness?
- What skills will we need to improve our maintenance and repair?

Those who participate in the conference can prioritize these skills in terms of the degree to which they will be required and the degree to which they are now present in the organization.

Developing a Mission Statement

An organization's mission statement describes its justification for existence, what it is in business for, the unique aim that sets it apart from others. If the mission statement establishes the organization's commitment to employee development, then the organization can support mentoring; if such a commitment is determined to be inappropriate and is absent from the mission statement, then a mentoring program is inappropriate. Figure 2 offers an example of a mission statement that incorporates employee development and, therefore, supports mentoring. To begin constructing a mission statement, the conference participants should answer the following questions:

- *Who* are the customers or client groups?
- *What* makes the organization distinct?
- *Why* do we have the goals and motivators that we have?

The objectives of the Government Branch of Accounting and Reporting are to achieve goals of excellence in service, accounting, and financial reporting and to create the working environment that will accomplish these goals.

Excellence in service is striving to meet the needs of our clients—taxpayers, Treasury Board, ministries, suppliers to government, etc.—in a manner that is efficient, effective, and friendly.

Excellence in accounting and financial reporting is ensuring that there is an effective system for accurately recording government expenditures, revenues, assets, and liabilities on a timely basis and ensuring that financial information produced from records is accurate, timely, understandable, and useful to the reader.

The skills, abilities, and dedication of our staff are our most valuable resources. This belief is supported by our commitment to enhancing the knowledge, skills, and experience of our people and by encouraging risk taking, greater two-way communication, more decision making, a greater sense of trust at all levels, and a better work environment overall.

We want our clients, as well as each staff member, to regard the Branch as professional, innovative, fair, efficient, and responsive and as providing leadership in the areas of our accountability, expertise, and responsibility.

Our objective is to promote consultation, teamwork, and cooperation with our clients and with one another.

Our goal is to become the Canadian model for service, accounting, and reporting in public sector financial administration.

Figure 2. Example of a Mission Statement That Incorporates Employee Development

- *Where* are our facilities and markets?
- *How* are we carrying out production, marketing, sales, and distribution?
- *What* skills do we need?

The participants in the conference also need to conduct what is called a SWOT analysis. The acronym SWOT stands for Strengths, Weaknesses, Opportunities, and Threats. An analysis of these four areas provides a perspective on the organization's internal and external environments. The ideas of conference participants are particularly valuable in identifying the opportunities and threats impacting personnel development. Consequently, brainstorming and other idea-generation activities should be used to identify situations and trends that the organization will have to respond to in the short and long term as well as to pinpoint strengths and weaknesses in terms of resources and procedures. To conduct a SWOT analysis, the conference participants answer questions such as these:

- What are the organization's personnel strengths and weaknesses?
- What are some opportunities and threats connected with the development of our staff?

Establishing an Organizational Philosophy

The test of an organization's commitment to establishing a mentoring program is whether that organization would rather develop its staff from within or obtain people from outside. To determine whether the organization is committed to developing from within, the conference participants should generate a philosophy statement, which describes the organization's values or the broad, general beliefs that it feels are realistic, credible, attractive, and desirable. Such a statement is one tool for developing an organizational culture; if the statement promotes a culture that emphasizes development from within, then the organizational culture will foster mentoring. The following is an example of an organizational-philosophy statement that expresses the desire to develop from within:

> Of all the environmental influences in our organization, the most powerful ones are personal relationships.
>
> Of all relationships, it is the manager/employee relationship that leaves the deepest impressions and has the greatest effect on us.
>
> Fundamental to the work of this organization is a respect for the development of the employee through guidance. We believe that training should respond to our needs.

To construct a statement of organizational philosophy, the conference participants should answer the following questions:

- What are our values regarding achieving the organization's mission and service to customers or clients?

- What are our values and beliefs regarding employee development?
- If we want to encourage development from within, what are the mentor's responsibilities? What are the protégé's responsibilities?

The process of articulating a philosophy statement, like that of generating a mission statement, is just as important as the resulting words. The opportunity for thorough discussion should be provided so that the conference participants can learn what values others find important. Debate should be encouraged, and ultimately the participants should reach consensus.

After the conference participants have identified the organization's personnel needs, developed a mission statement, and established an organizational philosophy, they should review these issues before proceeding to design and implement a mentoring program:

- What environmental needs do we have that justify the need for a mentoring program?
- Are top-level executives prepared to commit time and energy? In what ways?
- At this stage what is the scope of the program with regard to target group, functional areas, hierarchical levels, duration, and size?

Designing and Implementing the Mentoring Program

Mentoring programs vary widely in terms of their formality. Perhaps the most important rule of thumb that the conference participants can follow is to make the program flexible and voluntary. The following steps encourage the design and implementation of such a program: (1) selecting mentors and protégés, (2) developing an awareness of mentoring skills, (3) creating an action plan for the mentoring program, (4) making the plan work, and (5) monitoring and evaluating the program.

Selecting Mentors and Protégés

Mentoring programs are more successful when people are not required to participate but do so because of their commitment to their career and life goals. This principle is necessary in order to ensure that only employees who are sincerely motivated, interested, and committed will participate in the program.

If employees are not willing to participate in their own career development, some investigation is warranted. Those who are reluctant may not trust the program's objectives or the people involved, or they may not understand the program. Alternatively, the conference participants might need to look at the people they are recruiting.

There are various ways in which the conference participants can recruit mentors, ranging from solicitation of volunteers to nomination by executives. One of the best strategies is to ask each potential protégé to nominate three people whom he or she thinks would make good mentors. When one of the three is matched with a protégé, the other two may be asked to be members of the mentor pool and considered by other potential protégés.

Developing an Awareness of Mentoring Skills

Obviously, there are certain skills and characteristics required of mentors and protégés, just as there are certain requirements of the parties of any coaching relationship (Murray & Owen, 1991). The following are skills and characteristics that mentors must have:

- Knowledge of the organization;
- Technical competence;
- Exemplary supervisory skills;
- Status and prestige;
- Personal power and charisma;
- Willingness to be responsible for someone else's growth;
- Personal security and self-confidence;
- Willingness to trust;
- Ability to generate trust;
- Openness;
- Ability to communicate effectively;
- Innovativeness;
- Willingness to share credit;
- Patience and tolerance;
- Ability to be introspective;
- Accessibility; and
- Willingness to take risks.

Some of the more important mentor assets are personal security and self-confidence, accessibility, the ability to generate trust, and openness to sharing experiences.

Protégés need these skills and characteristics:

- Desire to learn;
- Interest in people;
- Orientation toward a goal;
- Conceptual ability;
- Initiative;
- Ability to be introspective; and
- Assertiveness.

In addition, the nine mentors and thirteen protégés who were interviewed suggested that the mentoring relationship is best cultivated under the following conditions involving mentor and protégé behavior:

1. *Shared responsibility.* Mentors emphasized the importance of protégés' formulating their own strategies and solutions to problems prior to engaging the advice and wisdom of their mentors. Mentors also stated that protégés must recognize the interactive nature of the mentor-protégé relationship and that protégés have a responsibility to challenge their mentors' preconceived ideas and positions.

2. *Regular, structured contact.* Protégés placed substantial value on meeting regularly with mentors for specific periods of time; regular, structured meetings gave them needed access to their mentors. Mentors were more concerned with the quality of the interaction that took place during their meetings with protégés than they were with the frequency and duration of those meetings; consequently, they tended to emphasize the importance of creating a safe and supportive atmosphere that is conducive to open communication. The "quality" of interaction, as defined by mentors, implied the provision of appropriate psychological reassurance and affirmation, especially during periods of struggle and crisis.

3. *Mutual respect.* Mentors perceived mutual respect as encompassing respect for the protégé's desire to learn. However, mentors also emphasized the importance of each person's demonstrating respect for the professional and personal integrity of the other.

4. *Challenging and substantive issues and assignments for the protégé.* Mentors felt they should make sure that protégés develop an understanding of the broad, philosophical and conceptual issues that impact both them and the organization. Both mentors and protégés stated that mentors must teach certain necessary skills and career strategies and must help to ensure that protégés receive work assignments that are challenging and stimulating.

It is probably not possible to find all of the characteristics of the ideal mentor or protégé in a single person, nor is it possible to construct the ideal environment for mentoring. However, at the outset of the mentoring relationship, it is a good idea for a mentor and a protégé to prioritize the skills and characteristics that are most important for them to have and then to prioritize the elements of the relationship they desire. On the basis of this prioritization, it should be possible to construct a relationship that meets the established priorities. The conference participants may find it useful to conduct a group-orientation session for mentors and protégés for the purpose of assisting these people in identifying the skills and characteristics they find most important.

Creating an Action Plan for the Mentoring Program

The action plan is a list of steps to take in order to reach the objectives of the program. Although creating an action plan does not guarantee that the best means for achieving objectives will be selected, it increases the chances of success. Furthermore, the very act of planning is useful in that it may reveal that the original objectives have to be adjusted.

The conference participants can create an action plan by following this procedure (Bryson, 1988; Murray & Owen, 1991):

1. *Determining ways in which mentors and protégés can acquire needed skills.* The conference participants should choose practical alternatives that provide a range of ways to learn skills. Two particularly useful alternatives are training programs and coaching. Another important consideration is that management must be willing to allow mentors and protégés to practice skills on the job. Regardless of the alternatives chosen for teaching skills, feedback must be a component; no skills can be acquired without adequate feedback.

2. *Identifying the negative factors that might keep a mentoring program from being successful.* The conference participants should identify potential difficulties that may be faced. It is important, however, to avoid associating those difficulties with a particular person or group of people. Lack of training, low morale, poor management skills, and other people-related deficiencies should be seen as problems to be solved, not as failures. Once these difficulties have been identified, the conference participants can determine actions to take to ameliorate them.

3. *Identifying the positive factors that might drive toward success in a mentoring program.* Several conditions or situations might be useful in implementing a successful mentoring program and strengthening the mentor-protégé relationship. These factors can be tangible (the plant, inventory, market share, salary levels, patents) or intangible (quality of management, employee loyalty, public support). The qualities of certain people might also be important strengths. The conference participants should pinpoint such factors and determine ways to capitalize on them.

4. *Choosing proposals and projects to implement the program.* Each proposal or project should correspond to one of the objectives of the program. The conference participants can begin by brainstorming proposals or projects and then discussing the possibilities, choosing those that are most feasible.

The initial proposals and projects will probably be vague and much larger in scope than is necessary. To test the feasibility of any one of them, the conference participants may want to talk to various people, look for examples of similar situations in other settings, and in general check to see if the idea will work within the organization.

5. *Identifying action steps and resources needed.* After the proposals and projects are outlined, the conference participants must determine specific action steps to be taken, who will take them, deadlines for all steps, and the resources (money, people, and equipment) needed to carry them out. The people who are assigned to each step can then identify the means to accomplish that step.

6. *Establishing criteria for judging the accomplishment of program objectives.* The criteria chosen by the conference participants should, in effect, serve as standards that mentors and protégés can use to focus their development. A good way to start in establishing criteria is to consider what the project will look like when it is fully developed and successful: How will mentors and protégés be functioning? What kind of career progress will protégés be making?

Making the Plan Work

The six steps of creating an action plan should help to crystallize the roles and responsibilities of mentors and protégés, the goals of the program, the philosophy that mentors and protégés will use in working together, the skills they will try to use, the expectations they will have, and the methods they will use to report progress.

At this point the conference participants might want to prepare a suitable form to post to assist people in volunteering to participate in the mentoring program. This form should include information such as name, current location, education, experience, reasons for interest in mentoring or being mentored, type of mentoring relationship wanted, amount of time available for mentoring activities, and any constraints (Bryson, 1988; Murray & Owen, 1991). The rewards offered for participating will have a major impact on the success of the program. The surest way to encourage people to take the roles of mentor and protégé seriously is to tie these roles to the performance-appraisal process.

The conference participants also may want to have mentors and protégés summarize their roles and expectations in a document of expectations. Although formulating documents may sound formal and bureaucratic, such documents do provide a framework for discussing expectations, values, goals, and roles.

Various strategies or tactics can be used for implementing the mentoring plan: educational and training activities (in listening, problem identification, problem solving, and so on), communications and briefings, and changes in the organizational structure and the reward system. Generally, these strategies help to manage the process of change.

Monitoring and Evaluating the Program

Periodically it is appropriate to summarize the major outcomes and results of the mentoring program, including problems encountered, positive aspects of the experience, and areas in which changes might be needed. This kind of evaluation is conducted for the purpose of improving the program as opposed to determining whether the program is effective. It might be thought of as a series of systematic, information-gathering activities that facilitate the organizational change to a mentoring environment. In this sense, then, evaluation is not a separate activity that takes place after the program has been implemented; rather, it occurs at various stages of the intervention.

When monitoring and evaluating the program, it is useful to review some of the issues considered early in the process, before the decision was made to design and implement the program:

1. Will voluntary participation work here?
2. Are there enough mentors?
3. How will we recruit mentors?
4. How will we reward mentors and protégés?
5. How do we encourage and make it easy for people to volunteer for the mentoring program?
6. What will we include in the document of roles and expectations for mentors and protégés?
7. How can we guard against obstacles to success?
8. How do we orient mentors and protégés?

SUMMARY

The most important criterion of a healthy mentoring program is that it involves people appropriately in assisting personnel development. In any mentoring process, a critical mass of people is necessary to ensure implementation. The critical mass consists of those individuals or groups whose active support will ensure that the program becomes an important element in employee development. Their number may be small, but it is critical (Cunningham, 1993).

It would be unrealistic to maintain that mentoring will work in all organizations. There are circumstances in which the process is unusable. For example, mentoring is not suitable in an organization whose senior executives refuse to consider the input of organizational members or in an organization in which a union forbids its members to participate. Because the mentoring approach described in this article is built on participation, only companies that encourage employees to participate actively should consider instituting a formal mentoring program.

REFERENCES

Bennis, W., & Nanus, B. (1985). *Leaders: The strategies for taking charge.* New York: Harper & Row.

Bryson, J.M. (1988). *Strategic planning for public and nonprofit organizations.* San Francisco: Jossey-Bass.

Cunningham, J.B. (1993). *Action research and organizational development.* New York: Praeger.

Cunningham, J.B., & Eberle, T. (in press). Characteristics of the mentoring experience: A qualitative study. *Personal Review.*

Gray, W.A. (1983). *Challenging the gifted through mentor-assisted enrichment projects.* Bloomington, IN: Phi Delta Kappa Educational Foundation.

Levine, H.Z. (1985). Consensus on career planning. *Personnel, 62,* 67-72.

Murray, M., & Owen, M. (1991). *Beyond the myths & magic of mentoring: How to facilitate an effective mentoring program.* San Francisco: Jossey-Bass.

Sveiby, K.E., & Lloyd, T. (1987). *Managing knowhow.* London: Bloodsbury.

*J. **Barton Cunningham** is a professor in the School of Public Administration at the University of Victoria, Canada. Currently (until 1994) he is teaching at the School of Accountancy and Business at Nanyang Technological University in Singapore. Dr. Cunningham completed a doctoral degree in public administration at the University of Southern California and was a Visiting Scientist at the Tavistock Institute of Human Relations in London, England, in 1980 and 1981. He has lectured in various organizations and universities in North America, Great Britain, and Southeast Asia. In addition, he has just completed a book entitled* Action Research and Organizational Development, *published by Praeger, and has coedited a casebook entitled* Quality of Working Life.

THE ENNEAGRAM: A KEY TO UNDERSTANDING ORGANIZATIONAL SYSTEMS

Michael J. Goldberg

The Enneagram is a system that describes nine different worldviews: the ways that people or groups think, act, feel, and, most especially, relate to one another. The system draws on traditions that are centuries old, and it is a powerful and elegant approach to character and culture.

Each of the Enneagram's nine worldviews is quite distinct. Each engenders characteristic values, blessings, and predicaments, and each suggests appropriate interventions and development. Each framework is not so much a pathology (although it can be that) as a pathway through life with adventures and distractions likely along the road, and with attendant lessons, resolutions, and metamorphoses.

Simply being conscious of one's own perceptual style—one's automatic habits—has profound implications. A person who sees others as being on a different journey can begin to forgive them their trespasses. Recognizing those on a similar journey can evoke shock or sympathy. In this way, the Enneagram purports to teach compassion.

The Enneagram also describes the worlds that others live in—their interior reality. Therefore the system is particularly imaginative at interpreting relationships, at understanding how one style will get along with another, the nature of the difficulties the two styles are likely to have, and the opportunities for partnership and co-creation.

ORIGINS OF THE SYSTEM

The Enneagram, a nine-pointed figure enclosed in a circle (Figure 1), is quite old and the origins are obscure. The Greek philosopher Pythagoras used this very diagram—one of the "Pythagorean seals"—as part of his sacred geometry, which used numbers for their meaning rather than for arithmetic. From Pythagoras the tradition passed through Plato, Plotinus and the neo-Platonists, into Judaism by way of Philo, and into Christianity by way of Pseudo-Dionysius. Closely associated with the Gnostic and Stoic traditions, the work traveled north with the Orthodox Church, east to Arabia, and west to influence the Kaballah in Spain and France. In each case the Enneagram became a part of a secret and sacred mystical teaching about the nature of things.

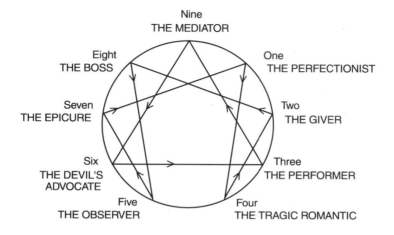

TOWARD ACTION, AWAY FROM SECURITY
(TOWARD STRESS, AWAY FROM NONSTRESS)

Figure 1. The Enneagram*

A 17th century Jesuit mathematician and diarist, Athanasius Kircher, writing at the Vatican, judged the Enneagram to be precisely equivalent to the Kaballah's Tree of Life, the central map of Jewish mysticism. Kircher inscribed a similar nine-pointed figure on the frontispiece of his book, published in 1665.

The controversial Armenian-Russian mystic George Ivanovitch Gurdjieff is identified with the Enneagram, but he never explained it as a personality system. Gurdjieff did say that the Enneagram was the final arbiter of esoteric knowledge: Two people could meet and draw the Enneagram, and both would immediately know who was to be the student and who was to be the teacher.

Oscar Ichazo, a philosopher and teacher originally from Bolivia, developed the applications to personality of what he called the Enneagon in the 1950s and 1960s as part of his larger theory, which is taught as the Arica system. In recent years, the Enneagram has become immensely popular with a broad audience of psychotherapists, human resource professionals, clerics, and educators. This article applies the Enneagram work to groups and organizations.

THE NINE POINTS OF VIEW

The Enneagram describes nine points of view, which appear as personalities, group styles, or organizational cultures. Point of view shapes our experience of

---

* Copyright © by Helen Palmer. Used with permission.

life, including how decisions are made, how conflict is resolved, what is valued, and how obstacles are overcome. The following sections describe each of the nine types, using the names designated by Helen Palmer (Palmer, 1988).

1. The Perfectionist

Perfectionists can be critical, idealistic, and judgmental; these people make decisions with an internalized "single correct standard" in mind. Their constant zealous sermonizing, teaching, and monitoring of others may make people feel criticized and rejected, but their anger is turned inward on themselves even more. Pleasure takes a distant back seat to perfectionism. At their best, these upright, fastidious, high-energy 1's are honest and idealistic, with superb powers of criticism; they can be fine mentors, selfless humanitarians, and astute, moral heroes.

2. The Giver

Givers can be prideful, seductive, manipulative, vivacious, and sometimes sweet; they work to be indispensable to others as a path to love and influence. These are the powers behind the throne, with exquisite radar for the moods and preferences of others. Relationships are central, especially with strong authorities who might offer powerful solutions. Others may sense that 2's flatter and give in order to get adulation back. Givers can be high energy and proactive, genuinely sensitive, helpful and humble, and exuberantly engaging; they can bring out the best in others.

3. The Performer

Performers can be enthusiastic, efficient, high performing, and competitive, seeking to be loved for what they accomplish. Because 3's are concerned with image and approval, others may see them as facile, artificial, superficial, and insensitive. Performers tend to confuse who they are with what they produce. Evolved 3's can be charismatic leaders; efficient, practical problem solvers; and accomplished team players. They get things done.

4. The Tragic Romantic

Tragic Romantics can be melancholic, artistic, flamboyant, elite, explosive, and intense. They long for past and future loves, while living a passionate life filled with panache, elegance, and good taste. They make decisions based on the shifting chemistry of mood. Those around them see recurrent crises, invidious comparisons, and endless dissatisfactions. Because 4's are filled with deep feeling, they can be highly empathic, romantic, and stylish doyens of the creative.

5. The Observer

Observers can be emotionally detached, penurious, and wise, seeking to observe life from a safe and protected distance, buffered by accumulated knowledge and information. They camouflage themselves and minimize needs, preferring independence to satisfaction and self-sufficiency to relationship. Emotional and business interactions are seen as a drain. Others may see 5's as withdrawn and greedy, hoarding information as well as themselves. Observers can be excellent decision makers, brilliant analysts, and insightful commentators.

6. The Devil's Advocate

Devil's Advocates can be dutiful and loyal, but also fearful and plagued with doubt. They tend to overfocus on what might go wrong and who can be trusted. Others may be frustrated by their procrastination and paranoia. Constantly on guard, these rational and linear thinkers are at war with their own impulses. They can be imaginative, faithful, sensitive, intuitive, committed, and ultimately courageous troupers for a side or cause, especially the underdog; 6's are terrific at ferreting out hidden motives and pitfalls along the way.

7. The Epicure

Epicures are romancers, idiosyncratic visionaries, and optimistic planners, but also classic Peter Pans who never want to grow up. Magical thinkers, 7's are gluttons for wonderful options and pleasant possibilities but avoid closure, pain, and boring work. Others may experience them as narcissistic and irresponsible. They can be gifted, perceptive, and witty enjoyers of life. Playful idealists, they can become enlightened synthesizers of ideas and networkers of people.

8. The Boss

Bosses can be lusty, powerful, straightforward, intense, and dictatorial. They lack subtlety and restraint and are focused on power and control. Abrasive and ruthless, they believe truth comes out in a fight; they focus on their own strengths and others' weaknesses, which makes them feel invulnerable. Their tendency to excess may repel others. However, 8's can be excellent, bold leaders and empire builders; they often are genuinely protective of the weak in their care.

9. The Mediator

Mediators can be warm, calming, caring, compromising, and sometimes neglectful. They empathize with the needs, enthusiasms, and points of view of their fellows more than their own. Others may be put off by the obsessive ambivalence of 9's, their deliberate pursuit of inessential distractions, and their tendency to passive-aggression. Supportive and easy to be with, evolved 9's reflect and identify with others' positions. They therefore can be excellent counselors, negotiators, and peacemakers. A sense of the global makes them particularly adept at working with the group as a whole.

THE ENNEAGRAM SYMBOL

An Enneagram *fixation* (point or number) does not operate in isolation. Each point is a complex of forces; indeed, each individual number exists only in relation to the others. The Enneagram as a whole describes the psychological pressures exerted by each fixation on the rest, which amount to patterns of behavior, relationship, and transformation.

Stress and Heart

Each fixation is connected to two others by arrows. These arrows describe shifts in perspective that a person with a particular fixation tends to make under certain conditions. Movement *in the direction* of the arrow is to the Stress Point ($9 \rightarrow 6 \rightarrow 3 \rightarrow 9$ in the inner triangle; $1 \rightarrow 4 \rightarrow 2 \rightarrow 8 \rightarrow 5 \rightarrow 7 \rightarrow 1$ in the hexagon). Movement *against the direction* of the arrow is to the Heart Point ($9 \rightarrow 3 \rightarrow 6 \rightarrow 9$ and $1 \rightarrow 7 \rightarrow 5 \rightarrow 8 \rightarrow 2 \rightarrow 4 \rightarrow 1$).

Each Enneagram style goes to its heart point when *integrating*. This is the expansive flow state; there is a feeling of ease, connectedness, creativity, inspiration, integration, well-being, and transformation. Each Enneagram style goes to its stress point when *disintegrating*, a place of frustration, defensiveness, blame, and rigidity. Figure 2 charts the characteristics of each fixation, its stress point, and its heart point.

For example, a 9 has one foot at 3 (its heart point), urging action; the other foot is at 6 (its stress point), counseling caution. Mediators are naturally able simultaneously to see and agree with conflicting sides of a conflict; they tend to feel best when they are proactive, moving, and getting the job done (at 3); when they are stressed they can be paranoid and hesitant (at the low side of 6.)

THE ORGANIZATIONAL ENNEAGRAM

Organizations, like individuals, have different worldviews: the ways that people or groups think, act, feel, and, most especially, relate to one another.

Fixation		Stress Point		Heart Point
1	4	Drama, emotion, tragedy, hopelessness, envy, melancholy, shame	7	New options, fun, good times, fresh ideas
2	8	Bossiness, combativeness, tyranny, steamrolling	4	Life, authentic qualities of self and others, elegance
3	9	Laziness, inability to make decisions, avoidance, distractedness	6	Loyalty, commitment, preparedness, trustworthiness, humaneness
4	2	Hysteria, manipulation, codependence	1	Clear vision, good boundaries, value centeredness
5	7	Mania, disconnectedness, fantasizing	8	Fearless leadership, protectiveness, outer-directed energy, confrontativeness
6	3	Compulsive production, disconnection from people	9	Global vision, empathy, calmness, natural connectedness
7	1	Rigidity, punishment, criticism	5	Inner wisdom, receptivity, observation
8	5	Withdrawal, frozen energy, disconnectedness from others	2	Protectiveness, sensitivity, caring for others
9	6	Accusations, suspicions, defensiveness, paranoia	3	Task orientation, proactivity, high energy, confidence

Figure 2. Movement Dynamics in the Enneagram

The Enneagram asks the central question, "Where does the organization focus its attention?" The answers help to identify the system:

- On quality controls and standard operating procedures (ONE)
- On customer service (TWO)
- On efficiency and competition (THREE)
- On an image as unique, authentic, and enviable (FOUR)
- On secrecy and special knowledge (FIVE)
- On tight management-information systems and what the competition is doing (SIX)
- On innovation (SEVEN)

- On bullying through (EIGHT)
- On avoiding conflict (NINE)

By looking past expressed intention and overt behavior to underlying assumptions and values, the Enneagram focuses on what *really matters* to a working group or an organization. From this, the Enneagram generates powerful paradigms and suggests particular interventions.

ONE Systems

ONE systems are wedded to a plethora of formal policies, standard operating procedures, and strong cultural norms, which precisely describe the way things are done. These may include prominent disciplinary systems, frequent management meetings, dress codes, strict schedules, and even prescribed worker attitudes. The phrase "zero defects" is a byword in a ONE system. A clear and precise conception of the product, service, or activity is central.

On the positive side, industrious, highly organized ONE systems believe that results come from hard work and that hard work leads to perfection. ONEs are ethical, value driven, and detail oriented. A steady focus on self-referenced ideals about products or services means the system will not be distracted by the vagaries of the environment or market or human foibles. Quality, integrity, and thoroughness are their own reward.

On the negative side, rigid adherence to a standard of excellence or ideology ("the right way to do things") means that ONE cultures, though hard working, can be estranged from the external market environment and the bottom line. They lack the flexibility, responsiveness, and spontaneity necessary for true effectiveness, particularly in an unstable market. The system has trouble tolerating ambiguity and differences of opinion. Meticulous trivialities push out the big picture; no one wants to make the big mistake, which stifles creative initiative.

ONE systems are exemplified by Japanese baseball, Electronic Data Systems, the Puritans, Krupp Armaments, and Switzerland.

As an intervention in a ONE system, brainstorming, a pure 7 process, permits alternate, nascent, and possibly imperfect ideas and possibilities to be generated and considered without criticism or judgment (and not understood as failures.) In this way, competing alternative values can be introduced. The "real needs" of the system can be separated from "correct needs" and "shoulds," and applied creativity can be rewarded.

TWO Systems

In TWO systems, the focus is on human relationships and attention to the needs of others. "Extraordinary customer service" is the battle cry, and TWO organizations are the experts at systematically tracking customer needs and meeting them. TWO systems also appear in large organizations in staff functions such as human resources and employee assistance programs, which have authority and influence because the line functions are dependent on them.

On the positive side, TWO systems are participative, "people oriented," and highly adaptable. TWO management and cultures emphasize training, team building, and coaching; they seek to inspire and empower people, discovering the best in them and bringing it out. TWO managers are "servant leaders," who, when they operate without machination, provide the best human-to-human service.

On the negative side, TWO systems can be overinvolved, enmeshed, power hungry, and intrusive, but without being direct about it. "I am only here to serve you, but you can't do it without me, so do what I say." The apparent self-sacrifice has hooks; the coercive demands may or may not be subtle. Decisions tend to be impulsive and frantic. Ironically, TWO systems, although good at meeting the needs of others, may be disconnected from their own real needs.

TWO systems include Scandinavian Airlines System, United Service Organizations (USO), the Salvation Army, and many twelve-step groups.

To align with a TWO system, a consultant needs to appreciate it for how necessary it is. TWO systems benefit from self-inventory, a 4 process. This means delineating the system's unique passionate vision, special gifts, and talents, while being clear about real needs (capacity, finances, procedures, and sentient needs) and the ways of meeting them.

THREE Systems

In fast-moving, competitive, bottom-line THREE systems, the focus is on efficiency, high-profile image, performance, and mastery. Work is specified precisely, as are the measures of success. Success is understood to come from persistence. Timelines are short; feedback comes quickly, and, as masters of the market, THREE systems easily adjust. Decisions are made rapidly, and high activity is the cornerstone.

On the positive side, when tasks are clear and straightforward and the goal is efficient production and marketing of a uniform product or service, the can-do THREE group gets the job done best. Planning and goal-setting are natural, and team players are rewarded. Creativity is the talent for synthesis (making better what already is) as opposed to invention.

On the negative side, THREE systems "sell the sizzle, not the steak." The real emotional needs of employees fall by the wayside, leading to overexertion and burnout. Workers are interchangeable as "role occupants." Pressure is constant; exploitative, opportunistic, or quick-fix solutions and a short-term horizon may lead to problems in the long term.

Examples of THREE systems include McDonald's, est ("a world that works"), Transcendental Meditation, Federal Express, "just-in-time inventory," Hong Kong, and the U.S.A.

Alignment with a THREE system centers around performance and task. Intervening in a THREE system requires confronting the difference between appearance (public image) and reality. It is important to create and reward loyalty (a 6 process) through trustworthy and congruent authority. Leaders must follow through on promises and not pressure their workers beyond reasonable limits.

FOUR Systems

FOUR systems create unique, imaginative, and wonderful products and services that meet elite standards and are a special pleasure to use. Suffused with emotional or traditional symbolism and a sense of being "the real thing," a FOUR organization is often driven by a charismatic leader who acts intuitively and puts his or her personal stamp on everything.

On the positive side, FOUR systems focus not only on their stylish products but also on the humanity and individuality of their employees and customers, which engenders high commitment from those who are on board. Deeply held feelings are more important than abstract principles; immoderate passion is central. FOUR companies tend to prefer their unique high-quality niche to large market share. They want to impose their felt designs on the world, perhaps by being socially active.

On the negative side, there may be dramatic swings between great successes and extraordinary mishaps. FOUR systems may sabotage their gains with rash and impulsive decision making, based more on impression than research. Everything is taken personally; relationships may be oversolicitous or histrionic and sometimes brittle and demanding. Conflict, turbulence, and dissatisfaction ("things aren't what they should be") may be at or just below the surface.

Examples include The Body Shop (natural cosmetics), Nordstrom, Herman Miller, Merchant-Ivory Productions, People for the Ethical Treatment of Animals, Alvin Ailey Company, the Actors Studio, suicide hot lines, emergency veterinary hospitals, and France.

To intervene, a consultant needs to remember that FOUR systems can be intense and emotionally overloaded; note their attraction to volatility and extremism. These systems are well served by 1 processes such as strengthening role, boundary, and system limits; operating with equanimity and balance; clarifying rules and procedures; and eliminating the inevitable, special, private agreements. These processes allow all who are involved to know that the business in rooted in a stability that will not be swept away by arbitrary feeling.

FIVE Systems

FIVE systems frequently are technology or information driven. Experts (or groups of experts) work on their own, with a tendency to be isolated from one another—much like independent contractors—observing, analyzing, experimenting with ideas, theories, systems, and patterns of meaning. Face-to-face management confrontation is avoided.

On the positive side, FIVE systems are masters of the intricate, natural reservoirs for enormous amounts of special information. Profound insights and clear, elegant solutions may emerge, always grounded in the particular; FIVE groups may also be interested in how the pieces relate to the whole.

On the negative side, management may be isolated. Because jobs are fragmented, important tasks or responsibilities can be forgotten. Information tends to be hoarded rather than shared. The organizational structure may be overcompartmentalized, with inadequate communication and coordination; rivalry for power and influence may be found among competing managers and groups. Responsibility is diffused, and meetings are seen as a drain rather than social glue. Team members may see themselves merely as loose collections of individuals. External forces are seen as intrusive distractions.

Examples include research/technology/engineering work groups, many traditional monasteries and convents, the classic penitentiary, Hughes Tool, Tibet, Vipassana Buddhism, historical China, and Finland.

As far as interventions in a FIVE system are concerned, boundaries (of space, time, role, relationship, and task) need to be conscientiously honored. Structures that encourage the sharing of ideas, information, and enthusiasm (8 processes) override the paralysis of the rational. It is important to create a bias to action and to taking bold risks.

SIX Systems

In the SIX system, the world cannot be trusted: Things are not what they seem. Secrets are common. Attention is on hidden motives and meanings. The system struggles with doubting appearances or with excessive credulity. Such cultures delight in high-technology management-information systems, intelligence, and electronics, all of which report to a centralized power group. Loyalty is highly valued; disloyalty means expulsion. Authority issues (the legitimacy of the exercise of authority, for example) are paramount.

On the positive side, SIX groups can be terrific coalition builders; once committed, they are dutiful and stay the course. SIX systems are hyperalert—sophisticated management-information systems abound—and hypervigilant: They are ready for whatever might come along (as long as the problem is on the long list of those contemplated in advance.) Enlightened SIX systems can be models of humanist authority.

On the negative side, strong internal controls, including regular checks of the bona fides of the membership (lie detector tests, performance appraisals, surveillance equipment, cost controls) along with handling of sensitive materials, lead to intrigue, caution, and paranoia. New ideas are viewed with suspicion. Strategies are conservative and reactive.

Examples include the CIA, police forces, criminal gangs, many cults, the Knights Templar (duty, loyalty), Germany, and Disneyland (constant scanning and safe "dangerous" rides).

To intervene in a SIX system, a consultant needs to validate the genuine fears, concerns, and premonitions in the system. This is easy because SIX systems are frequently right about what might go wrong. The system evolves by moving toward 9, when it also includes what might go right, and when the world is experienced without prejudgment. The system relaxes when it moves from projective, rationalist, security-building, fight/flight thinking to tolerating ambiguity and competing agendas.

SEVEN Systems

SEVEN Systems are adhocracies, connecting interdisciplinary ideas, resolutely focused on imaginative and innovative possibilities and the exciting upside (whether called for or not)—and on avoiding the downside, the difficult, the direct confrontation. Options are always kept open. Lengthy business plans are an anathema, as are comprehensive reports. SEVEN organizations may feature small, autonomous project teams or entrepreneurial units, with minimal supervision. Employees may have multiple bosses.

On the positive side, the exciting SEVEN system is ideal when the task requires enthusiastic, high-energy generation of plans, ideas, and options; extreme flexibility, complexity, creativity, and rapid change; and drawing on interdependent experts. Such a system is often the first to pick up on new trends. In these egalitarian systems, people have plenty of room to grow: SEVEN cultures encourage individuality, intrapreneuring, experimentation, and creativity.

On the negative side, SEVEN systems can become fixated and disconnected from reality. Painful problems are discounted or overlooked. These systems attract dabblers, dilettantes, and jacks-of-all-trades, who, in their greed for stimulation and constant change, are not in for the long term and may have trouble with detail and completion.

Examples include 3M Company, ABC Olympic Sports, positive futurists, Atari, W.L. Gore, and Brazil.

To intervene in a SEVEN system, a consultant must join in the sense of enthusiasm, but also take note of the tendency to intellectualize and to avoid decisions. Commitment—especially to agreements, to closure, and to working through difficult issues—grounds the SEVEN system. Seeing things as they are, without positive spin or embellishment, integrates the negatives that were previously disowned.

EIGHT Systems

EIGHT systems focus on the direct and forceful exercise of raw power, without ambivalence or regret. Confrontative, aggressive, and proactive, EIGHT systems see and understand events in black and white, without subtlety. Individuals tend to be stars; managers are tough rather than thoughtful or responsive.

On the positive side, EIGHT systems thrive and are anchors in turbulent, treacherous, or uncertain business environments. They are action oriented, genuinely protective of the weak, willing to use their power and strength for others magnanimously to fight injustice and eliminate obstacles in their way. EIGHT cultures reinforce those who take risks and win.

On the negative side, vengeful EIGHT systems attract bullies, those without sensitivity to depth, shades of gray, or the rights of individuals. Intimidated staff may lack initiative. Sensory excess is common. Cooperation may be hard to come by. Delegation to middle managers is regularly overridden by "The Boss," who may be out of touch because of being told what he or she wants to hear.

Examples include commodities brokers, oil companies, real estate developers, movie moguls, robber barons, and industrial magnates (Andrew Carnegie moved from steel magnate [8] to philanthropist [2]), and Iraq.

To intervene in an EIGHT system, a consultant must honor the system's vision of itself as enforcer of justice and morality. Using 2 themes can sensitize the system to its effect and impact, particularly on individuals, customers, stakeholders. A service audit and the empowering of middle managers are good strategies to employ. System-wide procedural controls and feedback loops restrict the impulse to act immediately, impulsively, and insensitively.

NINE Systems

NINE systems are procedure oriented—they seem to run by themselves. They create a nominally collegial, accommodating, and nonconfrontative atmosphere, reliable in that its past is prologue. Job descriptions are clear and detailed. Satisfied with the status quo, change is slow and deliberate. NINE organizations thrive where there is no real competition. They tend to implode energy, which leads to inertia, but which can be very powerful when released.

On the positive side, NINE organizations are built to cope with overwhelming or numbing input; they do it brilliantly. NINE systems reconcile different and opposing opinions and wide-ranging demands on resources through global vision and equal treatment. At their best they are equanimous, receptive, empathic, and patient.

On the negative side, NINE systems live in a world of little or no feedback, where it is hard to measure the substantive results of one's work. Complacent and noninnovating, NINE work teams insulate themselves from real engagement through habit, routinized solutions, and pleasant demeanors. "Sweet obstinacy" or passive-aggressiveness (such as absenteeism, diffusing responsibility, and failure to complete assignments) masks a deeper refusal to be budged. The "process" of the work is emphasized more than the bottom line. Managers delay major decisions because they are distracted by minor details.

Examples include the U.S. Post Office, public utilities, large bureaucracies, heavily regulated industries, and Polynesia.

To intervene in a NINE system, a consultant may draw on the 3 perspective: Make goals clear and manageable, prioritize, reward successes, and encourage proaction. It is important to avoid overanalyzing and endless ruminating about products or services. A good strategy would be to streamline complicated personnel and decision-making procedures. In a NINE system, real change requires that the choices be framed in terms that demand a manageable response.

CONCLUSION

Organizations are, of course, networks of relationships that are based on shared beliefs, common concerns, and values that create a consensus reality, a context. The Enneagram can be a road map for how living systems frame their cultures and create that context. As such, it is a lodestar for understanding and for change.

REFERENCES AND BIBLIOGRAPHY

Beesing, M., Nogosek, R., & O'Leary, P. (1984). *The enneagram: A journey of self-discovery*, Denville, NJ: Dimension Books.

Bennett, J.G. (1983). *Enneagram studies*. York Beach, ME: Samuel Weiser.

Campbell, R. (1985). *Fisherman's guide*. Boston: Shambala.

Goldberg, M.J. (1993, October 14). "Enneagram Heresies," in *LA Weekly*, p. 1.

Ichazo, O. (1982). *Between metaphysics and protanalysis: A theory for analyzing the human psyche*. New York: Arica Institute Press.

Ichazo, O. (1982). *Interviews with Oscar Ichazo*. New York: Arica Institute Press.

Ichazo, O. (1988). *Letters to the school*. New York: Arica Institute Press.

Keyes, M.F. (1990). *Emotions and the enneagram*. Muir Beach, CA: Molysdatur.

Naranjo, C. (1990). *Ennea-type structures*. Nevada City, CA: Gateways Books.

Naranjo, C. (1993). *Character and neurosis*. Nevada City, CA: Gateways Books.

Palmer, H. (1988). *The enneagram*. San Francisco: HarperCollins.

Palmer, H. (1994). *The enneagram in love and work*. San Francisco: HarperCollins.

Riso, D.R. (1987). *Personality types: Using the enneagram for self-discovery*. Boston: Houghton Mifflin.

Riso, D.R. (1990). *Understanding the enneagram*. Boston: Houghton Mifflin.

Rohr, R., & Ebert, A. (1990). *Discovering the enneagram*. New York: Crossroad.

Webb, J. (1982). *The harmonious circle*. Boston: Shambala.

***Michael J. Goldberg** is an organizational consultant, certified mediator, and teacher of the Enneagram. He has been on the faculty of graduate schools of psychology, management, and law. He leads seminars and consults internationally with managers, work teams, boards of directors, communities, agencies, and organizations, emphasizing interpersonal and group dynamics and systemic change.*

JOURNEY TO EXCELLENCE:
ONE PATH TO TOTAL QUALITY MANAGEMENT

Donald T. Simpson

Total-quality management is a major movement in business and industry. The concept is spreading rapidly through social services, hospitals and health care systems, academic and financial organizations, and other areas of our society. Consumers, clients, audiences, and constituencies—the customers—are more sophisticated than ever. They expect high-quality products and services. They patronize establishments that meet their expectations. Total quality is a genuine trend. It is not a fad. Total quality is a way of organizational life, a cultural phenomenon.

As for any organizational transformation, beginning such a journey is difficult. Some organizations may give up when goals are vague or results not immediate. Understanding the nature of the change helps senior managers, directors, and consultants plan the journey and chart the progress. There are many approaches to total-quality transformation. This article describes one path which is proving successful in both public and private, profit and nonprofit sectors. The process complements sound management practice, such as strategic planning. Every organization is unique. Each is at a different place in transformation to a total-quality culture. Anyone—manager, staff member, board member, or consultant—who works as a change agent must meet the organization and its people where they are in the journey.

TOTAL QUALITY AS ORGANIZATIONAL CULTURE

Organizational culture is more than shared understandings. It is the outcome of all the forces that have shaped the organization in the past and that will determine its future. Culture is the pattern of basic assumptions that the organization has invented, discovered, or developed in learning to cope with the problems of adapting to its environment and integrating itself internally. These assumptions have worked well enough to be considered valid. They are taught to new members as the "right" way to perceive, think, and feel (Schein, 1983). Many patterns of the organization—the way we operate around here—become so ingrained that they are subconscious and therefore not debatable. They are basic assumptions. Other patterns—values—are more explicit and open to discussion.

Total-quality efforts often run against many of the basic assumptions in traditional organizational culture (Figure 1). Until the organization makes basic assumptions explicit, total quality remains a good intention at best, a miserable disappointment otherwise. Management and labor each naturally reinforce behavior that supports their own assumptions and values. The culture often does not reinforce on-the-job use of quality processes. Management, even as it espouses total quality, may consciously or unconsciously suppress quality efforts that present new ways of thinking contrary to the traditional culture. Developing a total-quality organization involves for many establishments a change in culture. Such a transformation requires learning new ways to perceive the world, a paradigm shift. In spite of some anecdotes to the contrary, the process takes time, perhaps three to five years, with committed management and directors. Some organizations will not complete the journey. In a "can-do" national culture, short-term results have traditionally dominated management thinking (Deming, 1982).

THE CRITICAL BEGINNING

Senior management must lead the way. Senior managers must make a conscious, informed decision that the organization will change. They must become role models. In a culture embodying values like empowerment, consensus, teamwork, continuous improvement, and openness to new ideas, good management is more important than ever. Becoming such a role model is not easy, nor is it without risk and pain. But it is necessary. Good intentions are not enough. Management needs a road map, a process by which it can guide the organization into the new world. Acknowledging vulnerability and need for help is the first step in learning. Organizational consultants can provide objectivity, new insights, and needed process skills. Networking with other organizations on their own total-quality journeys is equally important.

A PROCESS MODEL

Through practical experience with large and small organizations, a model of the initial phases of the journey of transformation has emerged (Figure 2). Total quality is a journey, not a destination. The concept implies continuous improvement. The process described here is not a recipe. It is a guide—to be considered, followed, deviated from, and modified as the particular organization, its management team, board of directors, customers, and environment determine. Consultants can help, but management must take responsibility for its own process.

VALUES IN SOME TRADITIONAL ORGANIZATIONAL CULTURES

Bigness Obsession: Success is measured by how big or profitable we are. *Charge what the market will bear, expand, grow in size.*

Departmental View: We measure success by how well this department does. *We're the best; let the rest of the organization do as well as it can.*

Closed System: We know what is true and best in our field. Outsiders cannot understand it, and thus they cannot really contribute. *Reject what was not invented or discovered here.*

Individual Competition: As the pyramid still narrows at the top, we are in competition with one another for fewer and fewer positions as our careers progress. *Sorry if I step on you from time to time.*

Individual Responsibility: I am responsible for my job, you for yours. *If I do better than you, I get promoted or rewarded, and you do not.*

Different Processes: We use what works for this department. *That's the way we have always done it; it works for us.*

Within Tolerance: We believe that there is a certain point at which further improvements are not necessary. *If it isn't broken, don't fix it.*

Short-Term Focus: All we need to do is get through another day, put out the fires, and make a dollar or two. *Tomorrow will have to take care of itself.*

VALUES IN A TOTAL QUALITY CULTURE

Customer Obsession: We exist to meet customer needs. Success and growth depend on satisfied audiences, constituents, and customers.

System View: We consider the organization as a whole, intentionally suboptimizing parts as necessary so that the whole can be optimal.

Open System: We accept new ideas from outside the field and adapt them as appropriate. We encourage creative/innovative approaches.

Teamwork: We work together, sharing, listening, building on one another's ideas without undue attention to awarding individual credit.

Shared Responsibility: We succeed or fail as a team. Each person has a personal commitment to the success of the organization and the profession or field.

Common Process: We know and use the same language and disciplined process in problem solving, planning, and improvement efforts.

Continuous Improvement: We believe that there is no "there," no perfect solution; we are always seeking improvement.

Balanced Focus: Board and staff members balance long-term goals with necessary short-term objectives.

Figure 1. Transformation to Total Quality

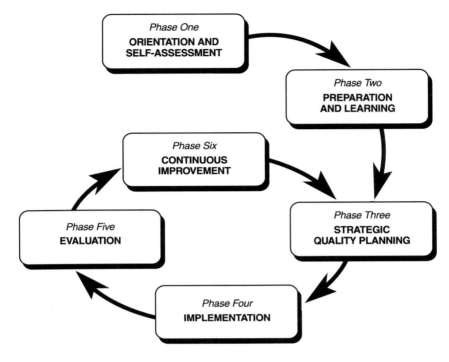

Figure 2. The Journey

The model involves six phases. It is more holistic than it appears. Although depicted as distinct sets of activities, in practice the six phases overlap, and activities begun in one phase often continue or recycle through other phases. Again, every organization is unique. Readiness for change, already established processes, management style, and organizational purpose all suggest adaptations in the basic model. Nevertheless, the model provides a useful road map and a vehicle for examining the role of organizational change toward total quality.

PHASE ONE: ORIENTATION AND SELF-ASSESSMENT

Phase One experientially introduces the organization's senior management team to the concepts of a total-quality culture (Figure 3). The team then makes an informed decision whether to undertake the journey. Through self-assessment, often based on the Malcolm Baldrige National Quality Award Criteria, the team gains an appreciation of critical issues it faces.

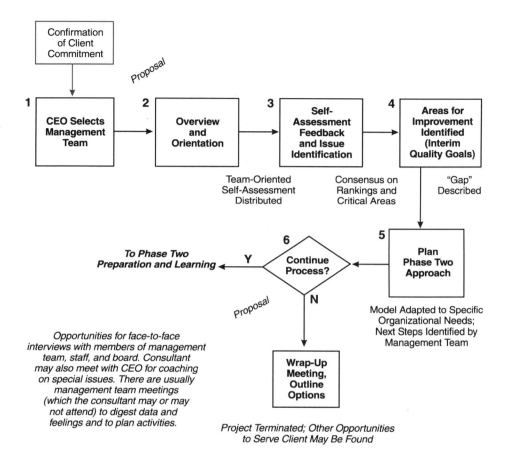

Figure 3. Phase One: Orientation and Self-Assessment

At the culmination of Phase One, the management team:

- Assesses the organization against recognized, established criteria.
- Has a statement of present state, desired state, and interim quality goals.
- Considers options in undertaking a total-quality journey.

The keystone of this initial phase is self-assessment through a comprehensive questionnaire covering recognized criteria for total quality. A quality consultant usually administers the survey, tallies the results, and feeds the information back to the team. The team develops a sense of the issues it faces as it comes to consensus in identifying pressing quality issues. The management team uses the data from the self-assessment to define a gap between the organization's present state and the team's vision of what quality means.

Phase One is necessarily heavy on consultant input, although major decisions, such as the composition of the management team, belong to the organization's executives. Nevertheless, the consultant assures that near the end of Phase One the management team is aware of options. The team makes a decision whether to continue its exploration of total quality.

Phase One is essentially an awareness-building process. How quickly a management team completes this phase depends on its enthusiasm and commitment—and those of the consultant. Phase One should move promptly. An anticipated target time is about two to four weeks.

PHASE TWO: PREPARATION AND LEARNING

Phase Two provides the senior management team with essential knowledge and skills that enable it to undertake a long-term organizational transformation effort. There is also some immediate return on investment—a payoff in using the quality processes—which encourages the team and reinforces total-quality values. In Phase Two, the management team internalizes the basic quality processes and tools in preparation for cascading them through the organization (Figure 4).

At the culmination of Phase Two, the management team:

- Understands and uses the basic quality processes—managers prepare to be mentors.
- Has an interim quality plan.
- Commits itself and the organization to the long-range total-quality journey (strategic quality planning).

Training

Training enables the management team to internalize key quality processes. Some management teams are already quite proficient in the basic processes. Others have had little or no preparation. Through an assessment of its training needs, the team identifies learning experiences that prepare the team for the journey. Training includes:

1. *Team or Individual Training.* Senior managers, in assessing their readiness for embarking on the organizational transformation journey, may determine that they need training either as a team or as individuals. Such training might include team building, benchmarking, facilitation skills, management-style awareness, statistical process control, planning, or

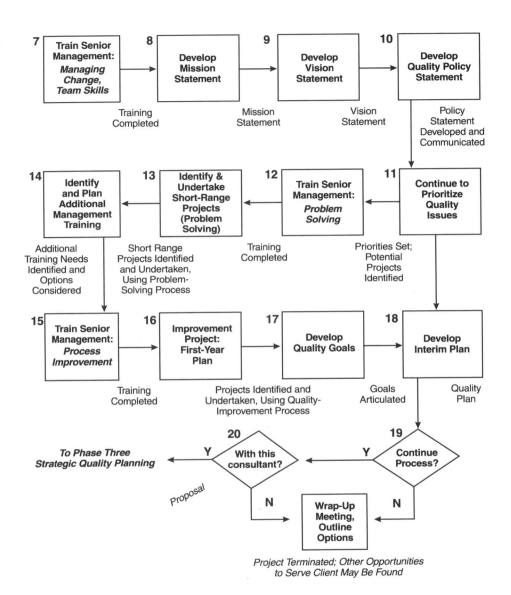

Figure 4. Phase Two: Preparation and Learning

other knowledge and skills. The consultant refers the team or individual managers to appropriate sources (commercial houses, educational organizations, reading programs, network/support groups, and so on). In some cases, the consultant delivers the appropriate training or development experience.

2. *Quality Training.* As senior managers learn and internalize the basic quality processes, they become resident experts—champions and mentors of total quality. Eventually they facilitate the process with action teams, working with the quality consultant to cascade the processes through the organization (Figure 5). The consultant is key to helping the management team assess itself in the use of quality processes.

Quality training should be internalized by senior managers before action teams undertake improvement projects. By thoroughly learning the quality process skills through application, then teaching them to the next staff level, the management team cascades the skills through the organization.

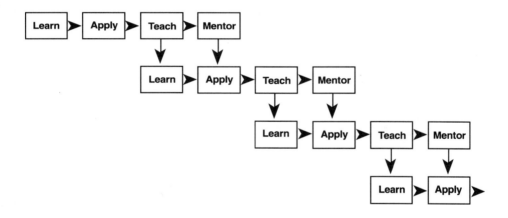

Figure 5. The Cascade Process

The Cascading Process

The cascading process varies. Relatively "flat" organizations may begin training action teams in essential quality skills early, accelerating the process. Senior managers, however, are still the role models, coaches, and mentors.

Although organizations are not transformed overnight, there are practical short-range payoffs to total quality efforts. If some more immediate benefit is not forthcoming, the organization may lose heart. The organization's leadership balances commitment to strategic thinking with quality improvement projects. The relatively short-range projects reinforce quality skills, such as problem solving and process improvement.

Organizational leaders prepare themselves to become champions of total quality and mentors in the quality processes. They learn and habitually use the quality tools. They develop a total-quality mind-set. Eventually, the system becomes self-sustaining. Outside consultants provide essential knowledge and skills and assist the organization in its learning. They also provide an objective view of what is going on in the organization.

For organizations with little experience in long-range planning, the interim (first-year) quality plan is an excellent learning vehicle. Strategic quality plans usually include cascading the quality processes and skills throughout the organization as a whole.

Phase Two is essentially an educational process. The training itself might be expected to take between six and ten days, depending on the management team's present level of expertise. Scheduling the training and assuring its proper application (train→ apply →mentor→ follow-up) could take a significant period of time—six months to a year, depending on readiness and willingness for change.

PHASE THREE: STRATEGIC QUALITY PLANNING

In Phase Three the senior management team plans for long-term organizational change (Figure 6). The team takes the strategic viewpoint in developing a plan that may span as long as five years and will be revised considerably as it unfolds. The eventual goal is to integrate total-quality concepts with organizational practices. The business plan and the quality plan become one.

At the culmination of Phase Three, the management team:

- Continues to use and reinforce the basic quality processes.
- Has a five-year strategic quality plan.
- Continues commitment to the long-range total-quality journey, and develops commitment throughout the organization.

The planning process begins with mission and vision statements. These concise documents provide direction for organizational management. Mission, vision, and policy statements, developed and negotiated in Phase Two, now become the cornerstones of the long-range quality plan. The strategic planning process generally follows this sequence:

1. *Desired Future State.* Through the visioning process the management team develops a detailed description of the desired future state. This desired future statement, along with the vision statement, becomes a "star to steer by." Developing the future scenario calls for creative thinking, a personal vision, and the extrapolation of key trends in the organization and its environment.

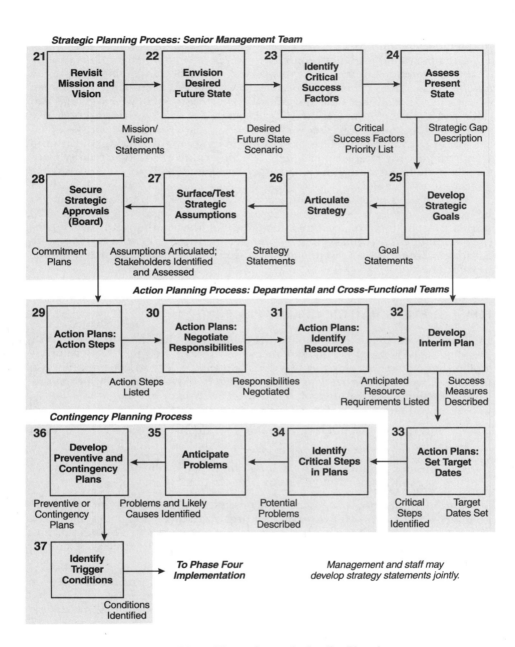

Figure 6. Phase Three: Strategic Quality Planning

2. *Present-State Assessment.* A detailed assessment of the present state provides the base to define the journey. The assessment is based on a review of the Phase One self-assessment, reassessment of quality goals, strategic plans already in place, and feedback from customers and employees.
3. *Planning the Transition.* The management team develops long-term goals and strategy and plans the necessary steps to achieve them. Transition planning also includes responsibility and commitment planning and surfacing/testing of assumptions. Depending on the organization's experience with long-range planning, the quality plan may be integrated with the business plan.

Strategic plans result in action plans, specific statements of how departmental and cross-functional teams will implement the strategic vision. Action plans include negotiated responsibilities, statements of resources needed, success measures, and target dates. The implementation teams review their action plans periodically. An important part of this planning is developing preventive and contingency plans to deal with potential problems that may jeopardize success.

Before action teams can become effectively involved, they must be trained in quality principles and skills. Either the management team members or an outside consultant may take the trainer role. A member of the senior management team, however, is present at each team training session, modeling behaviors, demonstrating commitment, establishing direction and boundaries, and providing process expertise.

Phase Three is essentially a planning process. The planning process may be done in four or five days. Some management teams may go on retreat for this purpose. Most teams, however, distribute planning meetings over four to twelve weeks. The effort may involve others, such as the board of directors, as the team considers organizational direction.

PHASE FOUR: IMPLEMENTATION

In Phase Four the management team implements the strategic quality plan, while continuing progress toward short-range quality objectives along the way (Figure 7).

At the culmination of Phase Four, the management team:

- Has achieved some of its initial quality goals for the organization.
- Has continuously assessed progress through review meetings.
- Continues commitment to the long-term total-quality journey and develops commitment throughout the organization.
- Has successfully cascaded training regarding quality principles and skills through the organization.

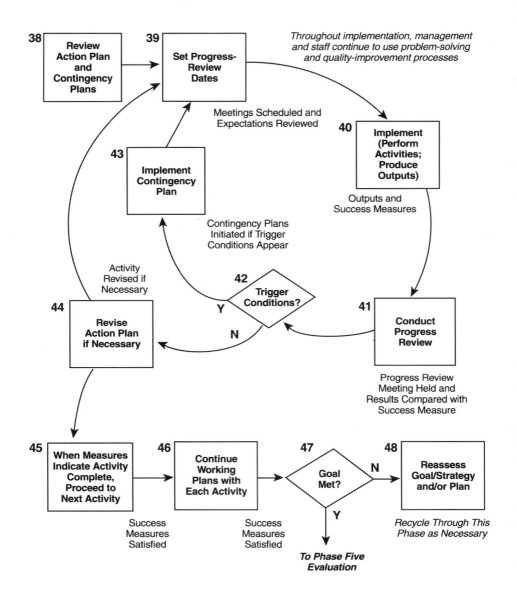

Figure 7. Phase Four: Implementation

In the transition phase, the period between the present reality and the desired future state, the management team directs its energies toward enabling departmental and cross-functional action teams to bring about interim and long-range goals. The management team is involved in activities such as:

- Reviewing action plan progress
- Building commitment
- Training
- Facilitating and coaching action teams in problem solving and quality improvement
- Changing reward systems
- Role modeling

Progress Reviews

An important part of implementation are periodic progress reviews. Plans not reviewed are worthless. Progress reviews focus on the output from each step in the action plans and the target dates. Although the action teams prepare their own review schedules, senior management monitors and supports the process. Teams review plans frequently, so they can address implementation issues while there is time to affect the outcomes. For the management team the questions are: Are we on track? If not, why not? What needs to be changed? Answers to these questions lead the team to appropriate action.

- *Progress as planned.* If progress toward quality goals is on plan, the management team and the action teams have done a fine job of assessing the situation and planning. They might ask, however, if they can do better—upgrade the goal.
- *Progress better than expected.* What has changed? The team may upgrade the goal or reallocate resources.
- *Progress less than expected.* What has changed? The team may reinforce the plan with additional time, effort, people or other resources, or goal expectations may need to be reduced. In some cases, environmental conditions may have made the goal and plan impractical. The team may abandon the goal or replan. Progress reviews take place through regularly scheduled meetings. Face-to-face reviews are more effective than casual phone calls. The coming together of a team enhances commitment and enthusiasm. The team needs to be clear about what results are expected at what point in time. The frequency of review depends on many factors, such as the experience of the team, confidence in the process, and changing environmental conditions.

Phase Four is essentially an execution and monitoring process. Timing depends on the complexity of the plans and the enthusiasm, willingness, and capability of the management team. Implementation is ongoing, as teams update and complete initial plans and develop new ones.

PHASE FIVE: EVALUATION

In Phase Five the management team evaluates progress toward strategic quality goals. Phase Five is not time bounded; it is a continuous process. As each goal is attained, management reassesses the organization in preparation for upgrading the strategic plan. The team begins recycling through the planning process as it evaluates the plan. The desired result of the process is the integration of the quality plan and the organization's strategic business plan. The organization considers total quality as a way of life as it establishes and consolidates the new culture.

Throughout Phase Five activities, the management team and action teams:

- Confirm that a goal has indeed been achieved.
- Examine the process of transition management.
- Feed back the results of the work into the strategic plan for upgrading and revision.

Evaluation is not something the management team does only at or near the end of a strategic plan. Rather, the team builds evaluation into the plan. The organization's leadership selects or develops measures of success so that progress toward the goal can be adequately determined all along the way.

Nevertheless, when a strategic goal is attained or abandoned, a more comprehensive evaluation is appropriate. Evaluation is more than answering the question "Did we achieve our goal?" Evaluation addresses (with the proverbial 20/20 hindsight) other issues: Was the goal appropriate? Was the strategy a wise one? Were the critical success factors and measures correctly analyzed and planned? Did we have the needed data? Was our plan realistic, yet challenging? What would we do differently? Were our customer requirements met? What must we continue monitoring?

The organization begins a higher-level self-assessment. Documentation of progress and processes in the new present state provides data for continuous improvement. Outside audits (customer audits, panels of visitors, or consultants) also provide insight into the effectiveness of planning and implementation efforts. These audits provide an invaluable view of the organization. Evaluation, like implementation, is essentially an ongoing process. Timing depends on the complexity of the plans and the enthusiasm, willingness, and capability of the management and staff. The process continues as initial plans are updated and completed and others take their place. By the time the management team is engaged in evaluation, the organization is beginning to consider planning, implementing, and evaluating for continuous improvement a continuous cycle.

PHASE SIX: CONTINUOUS IMPROVEMENT

In Phase Six the organization approaches subconscious competence: people internalize the concepts of total quality and integrate them into their daily work life. They put principle into practice habitually. Total quality becomes a way of life—just the way things are done around here.

The keystone in Phase Six is customer obsession. Management and labor understand the expectations of their customers. The organization becomes a valued supplier. People take a collaborative approach within the organization and the larger community, facilitated by the quality processes.

The emphasis throughout the organization is not on catching and fixing problems, but on process improvement—preventing poor quality. Employees, empowered to make changes toward enhancing total quality, make decisions appropriate to their part in the total operation and take the initiative to assure continuous improvement. Further, they consider themselves and their department as part of the whole organization, taking a systems view of their work world. Teams and teamwork are the vehicles for continuous improvement. A shared responsibility and sense of cohesion elicit the best thinking from everyone.

Senior management still must lead the way. Managers ensure that the quality processes are being used correctly. They continue to be coaches, mentors, and role models for the new organizational culture. The organization by this time has a common language of quality. People use quality processes such as problem solving and the continuous-improvement cycle to enhance communication and efficiency.

Another aspect in this phase of the process is sharing. A total-quality organization advocates an openness in supporting other organizations in their journeys. Managers find themselves visiting or hosting their counterparts from other organizations, sharing process information and experiences about quality. Sharing expertise is a way of life.

Phase Six is really a continuation of the journey. Like the rest of the total-quality process, it is not bounded in time or scope. Planning, implementing, and evaluating phases become blended as the cyclic process matures. Even when an organization develops what it describes as a total-quality culture, the task is far from complete. By its very nature, the new culture welcomes change as it explores new ideas and new concepts. Change is still uncomfortable, and management must encourage continuous improvement. The question is not "Will the organization change?" It will. Management asks instead, "How is the organization changing, and how do we want it to change?"

SUMMARY

Planning and implementing total quality means changing the organization culture, a relatively long-range approach. Many organizations with the best of intentions falter because they lack a vision or a plan that helps them see and work toward a desired future. The map is not the territory, but a rendering of the terrain. The process model attempts to document one way of beginning the total quality journey and sustaining the effort until it becomes self-reinforcing. This model is certainly not the only route. It is, however, a tested approach, and one that carries a high probability of success.

Total quality is a journey, not a destination. The journey carries its own rewards. The organizations of the future will be total-quality organizations, because others will have no future.

REFERENCES

Deming, W.E. (1982). *Out of the crisis.* Cambridge, MA: Massachusetts Institute of Technology.

Reagan, G. (1992). Total quality management (TQM) inventory. In J.W. Pfeiffer (Ed.), *The 1992 annual: Developing human resources.* San Diego: Pfeiffer & Company.

Schein, E.H. (1983). *Organizational culture: A dynamic model.* Unpublished paper, Massachusetts Institute of Technology, Sloan School of Management, Cambridge, MA.

U.S. Department of Commerce. (1992). *1992 application guidelines: The Malcolm Baldrige national quality award.* Washington, DC: Author.

Donald T. Simpson, Ed.D., *is a management and organization development consultant based in Rochester, New York. His experience includes over twenty-five years of practical work with business, social service, academic, and financial organizations, and local and state governments. Dr. Simpson has conducted extensive training and consulting in total-quality management to help organizations identify and develop areas for productive change. He has a master's degree in mechanical engineering and in adult education and holds a doctorate from The Fielding Institute in human and organization development. His published work appears in recognized journals and handbooks.*

THEME DEVELOPMENT: FINALLY GETTING CONTROL OF THE DESIGN PROCESS

H.B. Karp

A highly talented colleague and close friend recently lost a sizeable training contract for an odd reason. The program was a three-day, management-development public workshop being offered through a prestigious university. At the end of the first day, the workshop was going very well and the participants seemed engaged and satisfied. On the second day of the program, as my colleague was leaving to lunch, the client overheard him say to his partner "What do you want to do when we get back?"

The client was horrified that his welfare was being left in the "lap of the gods." Not having a complete and comprehensive design for a program is extremely risky. It forces the trainer to use his or her talent to develop a program rather than using that talent to achieve an intended outcome. In addition, not having a developed theme for a program heightens the probability that there will be inconsistencies or blank spaces in the design.

A theme is to a training program what a mission is to an organization. It is the beacon that guides the design process easily and effectively. Once a clear theme has been developed and established, the designer of the training program will be better able to set learning objectives and design unique modules that will support the entire learning process.

A clear theme is invaluable as a means of working creatively with the client, with colleagues, and most of all with the program participants. The theme allows the trainers to be uniquely themselves while still supporting the central purpose of the training program. Similarly, if the theme is visible and agreed on among the designers and the client, there will be less resistance from the client to unique or more innovative design suggestions.

In the incident with my friend, a strong program theme had not been established. Had there been a clearly stated and mutually understood theme for the program, his developing a module dealing with current concerns might have been seen as a creative, on-the-spot, design innovation rather than as a lapse of responsibility.

WHAT IS A THEME?

The term "theme" needs to be defined so that it can be distinguished from other training elements such as learning objectives or designs. For our purposes, theme is the unifying element that represents the purpose of the program.

Characteristics of a Theme

Given the preceding definition, a theme has four identifying characteristics: It is *general, clearly understood, unique,* and *results oriented.*

General. The program theme is stated in general terms and is as succinct as possible. The theme provides a rationale that permits the program design to adjust to individual differences. A theme that is stated in general terms (for example, "Assertive Leadership for the Newly Appointed Supervisor") will allow each attending supervisor-participant to develop a unique and specific understanding of that theme within the context of the training program.

Clearly understood. One of the theme's subtle but important functions is to provide a common frame of reference for everyone who is associated with the training program. The client, the program designers, the trainers, the line managers, the HR or financial support people, and the current and prospective participants, all need to have a common and agreed-on awareness of the program theme. The rule of thumb is that the theme should be stated briefly and clearly so that it is understood by everyone.

Unique. The theme's most important function is to give the program its unique and specific purpose. A well-conceived theme conveys an idea of how this training program will fit the needs of the participant. To illustrate, compare the two following program titles: "Basic Non-Parametric Statistics" and "Practical Introductory Non-Parametric Statistics for the Terminally Frightened."

The first title, "Basic Non-Parametric Statistics," is technically correct and does conform to the criterion of clarity. The problem is that there is nothing in the title/theme that differentiates this program from any other course or program being offered on the subject.

The second title is a more unique and precise description of the program. "Practical" says that the focus of the program is on hands-on applications rather than on statistical or mathematical theory. "Introductory" acknowledges that the participants are expected to have little or no prior experience with the subject matter. "Non-Parametric Statistics" clearly identifies the subject matter. And, "for the Terminally Frightened," playfully identifies the target group and acknowledges the concerns the participants may have, and simultaneously sends a very clear message that the participants can expect to have some fun at this program.

Results oriented. Inherent in the theme statement are the criteria for improving performance. Effective themes generally support observable outcomes rather than changes in attitude. That is, even if the learning objective of the program is attitudinal, the theme should keep the focus on outcomes rather than on processes. For example, for a personal growth workshop, a theme and title of "Making Better Choices" would be preferable to "Feeling Better About Yourself." The first title is results oriented; participants can expect to achieve personal growth by improving their decision-making skills. The second title offers only the abstract goal of "feeling better."

Functions of the Theme

The program's theme provides four necessary functions: *criteria for program design, control, a common basis for working together,* and *personalization.*

Provides criteria for program design. From a design standpoint, the theme provides the background from which to draw the design. The stronger and clearer the theme statement, the easier it is to design creatively, without losing the message. This point is particularly useful if there is a team approach being taken to the design and delivery of the program.

Training is an art form in any of its aspects. Except possibly for beginners who are trying to learn the rudiments of training through emulation, no two trainers use the same methods, the same designs, or interact with the participants in the same manner. A strong theme provides the basis for resolving differences of opinion and creativity among trainers, and it also makes it safer for creative differences to emerge and be considered.

Provides essential control. The program's theme protects the training program from becoming a conglomeration of unrelated activities, games, and pieces of information. An experienced trainer knows that there are two sure-fire ways of losing a group. The first is to bore them, and the second is to only entertain them.

The participants have usually given up something of value to attend the program (for example, they have paid fees, taken time away from their jobs, given up vacation time, and so on). This implies that the participants have come to the program having made sizeable investments. It is essential that the participants leave feeling that there was a reasonable return on their investments. The theme's guidelines allow the trainer to design creatively, knowing that everything that is put into the design will support the learning objectives of the participants.

Provides a common basis for working together. Once the theme is surfaced, stated simply and clearly, and mutually agreed on, there is a commonality of understanding among all the individuals who are connected with the program. The needs, concerns, and perspectives of the client, the trainers, the participants, the support people, and so forth, are all going to be somewhat unique and different. The stronger the one common thread of understanding, the theme, the easier it will be for individuals to negotiate with and support one another, as well as the program itself.

Personalizes the design. Anybody with a good speaking ability, an attractive appearance, and a little self-confidence can follow a script and conduct what appears to be an effective training program. This is common practice and some adequate training is being conducted in this manner today. So long as the group is large enough and the message simple enough to discourage difficult individual questions and participant confrontation, it will continue.

The professional trainer, on the other hand, is a person with a message. How the theme is phrased is as much a statement of how the trainer sees the world and how he or she uniquely contributes to it as it is a statement of what is important to the client.

The theme is the one place that allows the trainer to place his or her signature on the training effort. For example, suppose that a large corporation has regionalized its training strategy. Each region is required to conduct a program entitled "Increasing Supervisory Effectiveness" and to cover the same topic areas, but each region has latitude in how to design and present the program. One trainer's theme statement is "A Collaborative Approach to Increased Productivity." A second trainer's theme is "Increasing Self-Reliance in the First-Line Supervisor."

It is quite reasonable to assume that both programs could cover the same material and meet the learning objectives of the corporation superbly, while providing observably different and unique training experiences. The highest probability is that the participants would be getting the best possible exposure because each program was developed from the respective trainer's area of expertise and personal commitment. Most people are familiar with this phenomenon having been exposed to multiple sections of the same course in high school or college.

Developing the Theme

Themes originate from many sources. Three of the more common sources are *initial contacts, needs analyses,* and *learning objectives.*

The initial contact. Suppose a prospective client begins the first conversation with a trainer by explaining that supervisors are not holding the people they manage accountable. The trainer then may develop the following program theme from this conversation, "Developing Strong Supportive Supervision." The trainer may alter the program theme once he or she has learned more about the situation, but a preliminary theme can be established.

The needs analysis. A trainer may be asked to perform a needs assessment concerning a drop in performance. While working on the needs assessment, he or she discovers that the drop in performance may not be due to the workers' incompetence, but to their unwillingness to ask their supervisors questions and to take reasonable risks. The real problem may be restrictive or harsh management. The trainer must then shift the focus from technical training to supervisory training and perhaps develop a new theme such as "Increasing Supervisory Options for Developing Collaborative Effort."

The learning objectives. When the training program begins, what the participants want or need individually is related to—but always somewhat different from—the learning objectives developed by the trainer. Listening to the participants' individual learning objectives before the program format is disclosed gives the trainer an opportunity to hear what they want and then tailor the theme to the participants' specific needs.

For example, in asking the participants what they would like at the beginning of a supervisory training program, several of the participants might mention that they are having problems dealing with the inappropriate behavior of their subordinates. Although this issue was not covered in the trainer's original objectives, it is possible to cast the training program materials (communications, feedback, conflict management, and so on) within this context. The trainer may revise his or her theme to include a sub-theme such as "Increasing Your Comfort in Dealing with Difficult People."

Theme Statement

There are three elements embedded in every theme statement: *what the content is, who it is for,* and *what is unique.*

What the content is. This is the statement that clearly says what the training program is about. This element is usually expressed in one or two words such as "leadership," "training skills," or "parametric statistics."

Who it is for. The theme should identify the target group. This is necessary for setting the appropriate level of intensity or complexity of design for the program. This is expressed as newly appointed supervisors, nonfinancial managers, or experienced mental health professionals.

What is unique. This element is what gives the theme its particular and specific character and differentiates it from every other program. This is expressed as "A systems approach to...," "...from the Gestalt perspective," or "A layman's view to...."

The theme of the program should be clear and observable as an integral part of the program. In most cases it can be included in the title of the program, either as the sole title, or as a subtitle.

CONCLUSION

It is practically impossible to design a program or module outside the context of a theme. Working with a theme is a process with which most trainers are already familiar. The theme needs to be developed and established before beginning to work on the design of the training program. A clear and precise theme will allow the trainer to maintain control of the design process by making sure that each element in the format supports the purpose of the program, the client's objectives, and the trainer's need to make a singular and important professional contribution.

H.B. Karp, Ph.D., *provides training and consulting services, public seminars, and in-house programs through his organization, Personal Growth Systems, in Virginia Beach, Virginia. His specialties are team building, supervisory/leadership development, motivation, conflict management, and working with power and resistance. Dr. Karp's background is in organizational psychology, organization development, human motivation, and Gestalt applications to individual and organizational growth. In addition to many articles, he has written* Personal Power: An Unorthodox Guide to Success.

EVALUATING THE EFFECTIVENESS OF TRAINING PROGRAMS

Patricia Boverie, Deanna Sánchez Mulcahy, and John A. Zondlo

Change is everywhere. It is inescapable. Hardly a day goes by without news of the new world economy or the shift from a production to a service orientation. Indeed, change is necessary to survive in an uncertain world. Also, today's business environment is highly competitive. Because of the sweeping effects of change and competition, a great deal of interest has been placed on higher education and lifelong learning. Consequently, business is turning to training in order to cut costs and increase productivity among employees. In fact, according to Fulmer (1988) and Eurick (1985), in 1985 the United States corporate training and education efforts were estimated to cost 40 to 60 billion dollars annually, which is close to the amount spent on post-secondary education.

However, in the rush to train and educate people, many organizations have failed to treat the evaluation of such training as a priority. At best, the evaluation of training has been a perfunctory task with little analysis and usefulness. Yet evaluating the effectiveness of costly training efforts is paramount to the success of any program. This article reviews the current HRD literature addressing the evaluation of adult and workplace training programs, based on Donald Kirkpatrick's (1979) evaluation steps.

FACTORS AFFECTING ADULT EDUCATION

Before discussing the evaluation of training, it is important to explain the elements that serve as an impetus for adult education and workplace training. Merriam and Caffarella (1991) identify three major areas of change that influence adult learning:

- Demographic changes;
- Economic changes; and
- Technological changes.

Demographic Changes

One of the changing elements of demographics is age. According to Merriam and Caffarella, there are more Americans aged sixty-five and older than there are Americans aged twenty-five and younger. The aging of the population will continue well into the next century, and the demand for quality adult education will rise accordingly.

The rapid growth of cultural and ethnic diversity in the U.S. is another changing element of demographics. The United States is now experiencing a wave of immigration, primarily from Asia and Latin America, that parallels the influx of Europeans at the beginning of this century. By the year 2000, minorities are expected to compose 29 percent of the U.S. population (Merriam & Caffarella, 1991). In order to tap this valuable resource, employers will need to provide specialized training to help these people adjust to the American workplace.

Economic Changes

Economic changes are also having and will continue to have an impact on adult learning and training. Many experts, such as Naisbitt and Aburdene (1990), contend that the economies of the world are now interdependent. Consequently, major companies are allowing, encouraging, and sometimes subsidizing their employees' education in order to become more competitive and to increase their chances for survival in a world economy.

Another critical economic change is the shift from a manufacturing economy to a service economy, which has produced a change in the job market and has affected the kind of training that employees need. Moreover, changes in the composition of the U.S. work force itself are influencing training. For example, since World War II women have become an integral part of American organizations.

Technological Changes

Finally, the advancements in technology will continue to shape and define adult training needs, primarily because of the advent of the personal computer. Computers have revolutionized every aspect of corporate education, allowing people to produce, analyze, and manipulate data with greater ease than before. By some accounts (for example, Apps, 1988), every seven years the amount of information generated in the world doubles. Furthermore, about half of the information that most professionals learn will be outdated in about five years.

The implication of technological advancements is that learning is a lifelong proposition. Not only will there be a demand for training to keep up with technological advancements, but there also will be a demand to retrain the millions of Americans who will be displaced because of such advancements.

WHY EVALUATE?

Although for many years trainers have attempted to evaluate their programs, until quite recently there has not been a bona fide effort to use valid and reliable methods to conduct such evaluations. Furthermore, some trainers gather data for evaluation but do not analyze those data for trends or use them to improve existing training programs. Such an oversight can be costly, especially in light of the billions of dollars that have been spent and will continue to be spent annually on training efforts as a result of the demographic, economic, and technological changes just discussed.

It is important to remember that effective evaluation is multifaceted. All of the literature recognizes the importance of evaluation in terms of client orientation and economic return. In other words, most researchers in the field understand that clients, whether they are those who have hired the trainer or those who have participated in the training, must be satisfied with that training. If clients do not perceive a return on their investment, whether measured in terms of time or dollars, they may not be willing to continue to invest in training.

LEVELS OF EVALUATION

There are several components to an effective evaluation program. One of the most comprehensive and widely referenced models of evaluation is Donald Kirkpatrick's (1979). The four levels of this model are as follows:

- Reaction;
- Learning;
- Behavior; and
- Results.

The balance of this article reviews the current research on evaluation in light of Kirkpatrick's model.

Level 1: Reaction Evaluation

Reaction is the term that Kirkpatrick uses to refer to how well the participants liked a particular training program. Evaluation of participants' reactions consists of measuring their feelings; it does not include a measure of actual learning. Kirkpatrick contends that although the evaluation of reactions is an easy measurement, many trainers do not follow these five essential steps for accurate measurement:

1. Determine what information is desired.

2. Devise a written "comment sheet" that includes items determined in the previous step.

3. Design the sheet so that reactions can be easily tabulated and manipulated by statistical means.

4. Make the sheets anonymous.

5. Encourage the participants to make additional comments not elicited by questions on the sheet.

Although Kirkpatrick suggests that participants should feel free and be encouraged to make additional comments, he also contends that this type of qualitative data is extremely difficult to analyze. Thus, it is difficult to discern any patterns or trends in order to revise the training program.

Other researchers have different perspectives regarding the evaluation of participants' reactions. For instance, Antheil and Casper (1986) state that participant reaction is a measure of "customer satisfaction" indicating the level of effectiveness and usefulness of the training program at the time the participants are experiencing it and sometimes weeks or even months afterward. However, they are careful to stress that data collected regarding participant reactions reflect participant opinions and should not be considered proof of learning.

To determine what training-evaluation tools were being used by industry, Fisher and Weinberg (1988) of Bell Communications Research, Incorporated (Bellcore) conducted a phone survey in March of 1986. The data indicated that the typical instrument to gather information regarding reactions was a "short, quickly constructed, open-ended questionnaire" (p. 73). This "happy sheet" (p.73), as Fisher and Weinberg refer to it, provided subjective impressions and no data that could withstand statistical analysis or measures for reliability. Because there was no adequate tool for evaluation, the Bellcore System developed a new instrument with items addressing the trainer's behavior, the participant's experience, and other issues phrased as open-ended questions.

This questionnaire, like most such instruments, focuses on participant reactions—not learning or the transfer of learning. For instance, one item on the questionnaire reads, "The course presented useful information" (p. 76). The participants are then asked to rate the statement on a Likert scale. Fisher and Weinberg (1988) warn that while this questionnaire does provide a "general estimate of a particular course's success based upon the views of the participants" (p. 75), the data may be somewhat inaccurate because participants have a tendency to report what a trainer wants to hear. Also, some questionnaires have poorly constructed questions or items that predispose participants to respond in predicted ways.

Some trainers and researchers feel that measurements of participant reactions are inaccurate and counterproductive. For instance, Conway and Ross (1984) found that participants have a tendency to underestimate their pretraining skills and overestimate their posttraining skills in an attempt to justify participating in the training. Their research is consistent with research in the field of social psychology indicating that people have a strong need to justify their behavior and actions and consequently may alter their opinions and their interpretation of past events. Therefore, if trainers continue to use participant reactions as the sole means of evaluation—and management continues to allow such use—the outcome can be misleading and extremely costly.

Carnevale and Schulz (1990) go a step further. They claim that "participant reactions are easy to collect but provide little substantive information about training's worth" (p. s-15). They also claim that because data concerning participant reactions do not reveal the actual learning that has taken place, those data do not accurately indicate the return on investment for training efforts. They state that because of such unreliable data, many trainers have stopped using reaction sheets. However, Carnevale and Schulz go on to say that most trainers believe participants' favorable reactions are crucial to a program's success and that participants whose reactions are favorable tend to be more receptive to the material and consequently more likely to use it on the job.

Dixon (1987, p. 108) claims that "the use of participant reaction forms can cause more problems than benefits for the training function of an organization." This statement is especially true when participant reactions are the only evaluation method used. Dixon contends that three major problems result from the use of reaction forms:

1. *The expectation that training must be entertaining.* Because reaction sheets measure how the participants felt about the training, the trainer may tend to emphasize participant enjoyment during the training rather than substantive information. As a trainer is often rewarded with high marks when the participants enjoy themselves, this relationship between evaluation and participant enjoyment can become a vicious cycle. The trainer's ratings are also a major factor in the rewards that the trainer receives from management or the client organization: renewal of a contract or a promotion. Obviously, under these circumstances the use of a reaction sheet can lead to a conflict of interest.

2. *Faulty instructional design.* The term "faulty instructional design" refers to a questionnaire design that asks for information that participants cannot legitimately provide. As Dixon (1987) states, the art of questionnaire design is to ask questions for which a participant can give informed responses.

3. *The perception that learning is passive rather than active.* This perception refers to the common belief that it is the trainer's responsibility to ensure that participant learning occurs. Measuring how well this responsibility has been met with a reaction sheet is problematic, as a reaction sheet asks questions about the trainer's performance and the course design without asking about the participants' efforts to learn. Dixon emphasizes that evaluation and learning are not complete unless both functions have been measured. Ultimately, it is the responsibility of the trainer to provide information and the responsibility of the participant and the trainer to process the information. Reaction sheets rarely take into account the participant's role as part of the training program.

Level 2: Learning Evaluation

According to Kirkpatrick (1979), the second level of analysis in the evaluation process is that of learning. Kirkpatrick defines *learning* as the "principles, facts and techniques that were understood and absorbed by the participants" (p. 82) and identifies the following guidelines or standards for evaluation in terms of learning:

- Each participant's learning should be measured by quantitative means.
- A pretest and posttest should be administered so that any learning can be attributed to the training program.
- The learning should be measured by objective means.
- When feasible, a control group should be used so that comparisons can be made with the actual training group.
- When feasible, the evaluation results should undergo statistical analysis so that learning can be viewed in terms of correlation and/or levels of confidence.

Obviously, evaluation of learning is much more difficult to measure than reaction. According to Kirkpatrick's guidelines, a knowledge of statistical procedures is essential for accurate and meaningful measurement.

Endres and Kleiner (1990) state that pretests and posttests are necessary when evaluating the amount of learning that has taken place. Without a point of comparison, the measurement of learning at the end of the training program will not reveal exactly how much knowledge has been obtained from the training experience. Although paper-and-pencil tests are the most frequently used tools to measure knowledge, there are other means for gathering this kind of data.

For instance, when simulations, role plays, or demonstrations are used to measure knowledge, the trainer can use before-and-after situations in which participants can demonstrate or perform the knowledge and techniques that they have learned. This information is consistent with Kirkpatrick's research on the measurement of learning. In fact, like Endres and Kleiner, Kirkpatrick maintains that simulations and demonstrations can closely approximate the participants' work environment and can help them relate the learning in meaningful ways, especially when specific job skills are the focus of the training.

According to Carnevale and Schulz (1990), the measurement tools used to evaluate learning should reflect each training program's particular objectives. Also, measures of learning changes may be taken during or at the end of a training session. Carnevale and Schulz warn that such a measure of learning changes "may indicate that a program's instructional methods are effective, but it doesn't show whether or how participants' new learning will be applied on the job" (p. s-16).

A useful process for reviewing items on a measurement tool that evaluates learning has been suggested by Cantor (1990):

1. Determine the acceptable task level by objective.
2. Determine whether each objective is adequate.
3. Identify the items associated with each objective.
4. Determine whether the items match the objectives.

These steps are consistent with the instructional systems design method and will help ensure that items will be reliable and valid means for determining whether learning has occurred.

Research by Antheil and Casper (1986, p. 58) indicates that "evaluation of learning at this level closely resembles testing" and most often takes the form of paper-and-pencil tests. They suggest that the typical measurement tool includes gathering pretest and posttest data to determine the amount of learning that has been acquired. They also stress that skill demonstrations in a learning situation merely indicate whether a participant *can* use the skills—not whether he or she *will* use them.

Level 3: Transfer-of-Learning Evaluation

Kirkpatrick's third level in the evaluation model is *transfer of learning*. In the HRD literature there are relatively few examples of studies that have specifically attempted to assess the transfer of training skills or knowledge to the job. Even Kirkpatrick (1979, p. 86) warns that "evaluation of training programs in terms of on the job behavior is more difficult than the reaction and learning evaluations...." As a result, much training is delivered without a plan for measuring the transfer of training.

Kirkpatrick goes on to suggest a framework for evaluating training programs in terms of behavioral changes:

1. A systematic appraisal should be made of on-the-job performance on a before-and-after basis.
2. The appraisal of performance should be made by one or more of the following parties (the more the better):
   - The participant:
   - The participant's superior(s);
   - The participant's subordinates; and/or
   - The participant's peers or other people who are familiar with the participant's performance.
3. A statistical analysis should be made to compare before-and-after performance and to relate changes to the training program.
4. The post-training appraisal should be made three months or more after the training so that the participants have an opportunity to practice what they have learned. Subsequent appraisals may add validity to the study.

5. A control group (of people who did not receive the training) should be used.

Antheil and Casper (1986) propose a comprehensive evaluation model based on Kirkpatrick's four levels, which they call "program effects levels." Their three-step procedure for implementing the model is as follows:

1. Discuss the focus and goals of the evaluation study with the identified evaluation audience.
2. Design and implement data-collection strategies aimed at tapping one or more levels of program effects. These strategies should reflect the audience's expressed needs for information.
3. Communicate evaluation results to the audience through a process that incorporates various user needs and abilities to learn from and use results. Encourage joint interpretation of the data.

Antheil and Casper (1986) emphasize the importance of collecting and presenting the information in a way that will be meaningful and relevant for the specific audience involved. This level of evaluation not only assesses the performance of the person who receives the training, but also provides valuable feedback to those involved in redesigning existing training programs or in designing programs to meet future needs. This information is also useful to those who will be evaluating the effectiveness of the overall training program.

The collection of qualitative as well as quantitative data is encouraged by Antheil and Casper. They suggest logs, diaries, and observer narratives, for example.

Endres and Kleiner (1990) use Kirkpatrick's model in suggesting an approach to evaluating the effectiveness of management training. They caution against relying on in-house performance-appraisal systems as the primary measure of transfer of learning, as it is difficult to separate the effects of training efforts from those of other factors. Instead, they suggest setting initial performance objectives and monitoring accomplishment of those objectives after training. They offer an example in which participants write personal and professional objectives at the end of the training experience. These objectives are then sent to the participants approximately a week after the training. Two months later they are sent again, and the participants are asked to comment on their performance against these objectives. A certificate of completion for the training is issued only after each participant's feedback is secured.

Like Kirkpatrick, Endres and Kleiner suggest multidimensional on-the-job evaluations, including feedback from the participant, his or her subordinates, and peers. "By using all three forms of feedback," they say, "the builtin biases of the evaluator can be reduced as the number of evaluators having different perspectives is increased" (p. 6).

Finally, they remind evaluators that other factors can impact the effectiveness of management training and development, including the manager, the trainer, the organization, and the environment. As they state, "All four are complex creatures" (p. 7).

Nanda (1988) also looked at the transference of supervisory skills following training programs and found that most supervisory-training programs are knowledge based. However, to be of value to the trainee and the organization, that knowledge must result in a change of attitude, followed by a change in the supervisor's behavior. Unfortunately, the impact of most supervisory-training programs does not go beyond knowledge and awareness. One factor that often inhibits transference of learning is the organizational climate, which may be inconsistent with what is taught in the training program. This inconsistency often renders such training programs entirely ineffective. As Nanda (p. 28) says, "perhaps changes in attitude among top managers are key to the skill development of supervisors."

The instrumental impact of the on-the-job environment is consistent with Bandura's findings in the studies that led to the development of Social Learning Theory. Bandura (1965) found that any learning that may have been gained by observing the behavior of models was completely wiped out by the subsequent incentives received for the performance of a specific response, leading him to conclude that "mere exposure to modeling stimuli does not provide sufficient conditions for imitative or observational learning" (p. 593).

Kelly (1982) starts with the assumption that typically only 10 percent of a company's training transfers skills to the job. What happens to the other 90 percent of training? She suggests that 40 percent is lost because the training function is often isolated or peripheral: "Therefore, management, who views anyone paid to do a peripheral job as a peripheral person, will not bring that person's ideas into the workplace" (p. 102). An additional 40 percent, she suggests, is lost because most trainers or management educators do not build transfer into the training programs. Finally, 10 percent may be lost when the course designer does not deliver the training.

For skills to be transferred to the job, Kelly believes that they must be built into the training "before the first specific behavioral objective is chosen, before the first course activity is imagined or before a packaged product is selected" (p. 104). In other words, the course should be designed with the specific intent of transfer to the actual job situation.

Kelly's comment stresses an important point. In order to study whether skill transfer related to training has in fact occurred, one must establish a baseline of current skills or knowledge before the training occurs. For example, six months after a two-day workshop on supervisory skills, Swierczek and Carmichael (1985) conducted a survey in which they attempted to measure whether participants in the workshop actually used the learned skills. They found that they were hampered by the lack of baseline information: "Therefore the results cannot be linked definitively to the workshop" (p. 97). Of course, following a good process for instructional system design would suggest pretesting, both to establish such a baseline as well as to determine the need for training in the first place.

Mahoney (1980) suggests that management training be evaluated using three criteria:

- Targets—working on relevant issues;
- Time—working efficiently; and
- Transfer—producing results on the job.

To optimize transference of management training, Mahoney suggests that a manager who wishes to train subordinates in supervisory skills should conduct a series of working meetings on specific issues. The issues selected should be ones that have been identified by the subordinates (thus meeting the "targets" criterion). Next, Mahoney suggests that the training be divided into a series of half-day segments. One criticism of training is that it takes too much time both for the participant and for the manager/trainer. However, if the working meetings are limited to four to eight times per year, they represent only a 1- to 2-percent investment of each subordinate's time (thus meeting the "time" criterion). Finally, Mahoney suggests that training be designed with an "action-research" process in mind. With proper selection of training topics and content, the manager's subordinates will actually take their jobs with them to each training session. Thus, "the job and the training are separated only by the training setting, not by process and not by content" (p. 29) (thus meeting the "transfer" criterion).

A synthesis of the literature reviewed here suggests the following ten guidelines for designing training that ensures transfer:

1. Build a plan for transfer into the training program from the outset.
2. Make sure that the work environment provides positive incentives to apply the skills gained in training.
3. Consider the audience—the people who will use the evaluation results. Collect data and report results with the audience in mind.
4. Set initial performance targets based on the training needs identified in the assessment phase.
5. Use specific topics that are relevant and job related.
6. Use the work-group manager or supervisor to deliver the training whenever possible.
7. Keep training sessions short.
8. Ensure that practice during the training sessions clearly matches the on-the-job situation.
9. Plan for the assessment of skill transfer to be multidimensional, including the participant as well as the participant's subordinates, peers, and supervisor(s) whenever possible.
10. Do not consider the training to be complete until transference has been evaluated.

It is interesting to note that if transfer of learning is considered at all, this consideration usually occurs after the training has been designed or even delivered. However, most of the guidelines suggested above should be followed during the design phase.

Level 4: Results Evaluation

Kirkpatrick's fourth level of evaluation is *results* or impact on the organization. Attempting to measure results is not for the fainthearted! Although measuring training programs in terms of results may be the best way to measure effectiveness, Kirkpatrick himself (1979, p. 89) points out that "there are...so many complicating factors that it is extremely difficult if not impossible to evaluate certain kinds of programs in terms of results." The separation of variables to measure how much of the improvement is due to training is extremely difficult. Instead of offering a specific formula, Kirkpatrick simply reports anecdotal efforts to measure results. He does applaud attempts by researchers such as Likert to use qualitative data in measuring results, but he laments the fact that current research techniques are essentially inadequate and that progress in this area is slow.

Zenger and Hargis (1982) recommend experimental-research designs using pretesting and posttesting of experimentally trained groups with untrained control groups. However, outside an ideal laboratory environment, this approach is not without its challenges.

Ban and Faerman (1990) report on their attempt to measure both skill transference and results following an intensive, twenty-four-day advanced supervisory-training program. They had hoped to study impact with an experimental design by surveying a control group of managers who had not participated in the training program. However, they had to abandon this part of their study because of logistical problems. They conclude that "the literature on training evaluation may be too optimistic in recommending experimental or quasi-experimental design for many field situations" (p. 278).

Similarly, Trapnell (1984, p. 92) remarks that "impact evaluation is not a science" because of the number of variables other than training that may affect long-term results. Despite this comment, though, Trapnell encourages the use of available secondary data, such as savings resulting from reductions in downtime, accident rates, absenteeism, customer returns, assembly-line rejects, staff turnover, and employee grievances.

In an update to Zenger and Hargis's 1982 article, Kelly, Orgel, and Baer (1984) recommend quasi-experimental designs based on samples and groups that exist naturally in the work environment. An example would be two similar departments, one that receives training and one that does not. Rather than evaluating performance differences statistically and presenting those statistics—which, according to them, few people really understand—they suggest demonstrating results visually through graphic presentations.

The literature offers an account of at least one attempt to apply an econometric model to the evaluation of costs and benefits of training. Schmidt, Hunter, and Pearlman (1982) adapted "linear-regression-based decision-theoretic equations" to estimate the dollar impact of "intervention programs designed to improve job performance" (p. 333). The models they used were originally developed to estimate the dollar impact of valid selection procedures on work-force productivity. Typical studies on the value of selection procedures are highly statistical. However, "in general, organizational decision makers are less able to evaluate these statistics than statements made in terms of dollars" (p. 334). The model developed depends on a number of key assumptions, several of which must be inferred or estimated because they are not typically available from prior research.

Using their model, Schmidt, Hunter, and Pearlman estimated the value of a training program for one hundred programmers at more than one million dollars. In general, they hypothesized that "the economic impact or intervention programs may be greater than industrial/organizational psychologists have realized" (p. 340).

Using Schmidt, Hunter, and Pearlman's procedure, Sheppeck and Cohen (1985) propose a somewhat less statistical "utility" formula:

$$\text{UTILITY} = \text{YD} \times \text{NT} \times \text{PD} \times \text{V} - \text{NT} \times \text{C, where:}$$

- YD = years of duration of effect on performance;
- NT = number of employees trained;
- PD = performance difference between trained and untrained employees;
- V = "value"—the standard deviation of job performance in dollars; and
- C = cost per trainee.

This formula still depends on estimates for several variables. The most obscure is the concept of "value," a statistic that is not readily available for most jobs. Sheppeck and Cohen provide several suggested estimates of "value" based on the few actual studies reported in the literature, but they suggest that Schmidt, Hunter, and Pearlman's range of 40 to 70 percent of annual salary is a reasonable estimate when actual figures are unknown. They suggest further studies in a variety of occupational settings to develop more precise, job-specific estimates for each of these variables.

Given the difficulty of results evaluations and the relative lack of objective, valid tools to use, are they worth pursuing? McEvoy and Buller (1990) suggest not only that it would be wise to think twice about pursuing such evaluations but also that not all training is results oriented. They describe their attempts to conduct a comprehensive, four-step evaluation of their training for developing executive leadership, which is similar to Outward Bound. They found that training is often used for purposes other than achieving a measurable impact on the performance of an individual employee or the organization. For example, sometimes training is seen as a perquisite for performance that has already been judged successful or as a cultural "rite of passage" that all those hoping to advance must complete. In these cases the value of the training is more symbolic than technical.

McEvoy and Buller even went so far as to use a utility formula similar to that described by Sheppeck and Cohen to assess the dollar impact of their program for one of their clients. Using the most conservative assumptions for the model, they still estimated a net benefit of over a half-million dollars! They decided not to share the estimate with the client—because they did not think the client would believe it. The formula is not at all intuitive, and they reasoned that sharing the figure would hurt their credibility rather than help it.

These studies suggest that evaluation training on the basis of results or organizational impact may not be the ultimate measure. In the years since Kirkpatrick proposed his model, little has been added in the way of specific, valid tools to objectively measure training impact. Most promising are the quasi-experimental methods suggested by Kelly, Orgel, and Baer (1984) using graphic representations of hard data. Unfortunately, we may see few examples of this approach in the literature, as it lacks the scientific rigor that most journals favor.

It would also be a good idea to conduct further studies in a greater variety of occupational settings to determine reasonable, more precise estimates of performance differences between trained and untrained employees as well as value (that is, the standard deviation of job performance in dollars between trained and untrained employees). This research, however, may have some ethical hurdles to cross if it involves consciously withholding training from some people.

SUMMARY

Kirkpatrick's (1979) four levels of training evaluation—reaction, learning, transfer of learning, and results—are still a useful framework for considering evaluation techniques, as evidenced by the frequency with which they are referenced in the current training-evaluation literature. This article has offered a review of recent contributions in the literature as they pertain to Kirkpatrick's four levels.

The experience reflected in the literature suggests that trainers incorporate at least the first three levels routinely in the design of training programs. In fact, many authors emphasize the importance of considering early in the design process how each level of evaluation will be addressed. The ability to track and report regularly on the effectiveness of training programs beyond participant reaction (that is, to documentation of learning, behavioral changes, and transfer of learning) can be critical to the success of a training program. It can also cement organizational recognition of the value of training and can help to ensure continued support.

Kirkpatrick's fourth level of evaluation, results, is still difficult to measure. The difficulty here, as Kirkpatrick himself points out, is the ability to separate training from the multitude of other variables that can impact long-term performance. The econometric and utility models reviewed here may be statistically elegant but are not sufficiently intuitive to warrant widespread application. This fact suggests opportunities for further research into alternative approaches and methodologies for addressing results. The more qualitative, quasi-experimental approaches involving action research, critical incidents, and similar methods appear promising. These approaches offer the advantage of observing and documenting the impact of training activities at the site. The authors hope that the journals that target adult educators and organizational trainers will recognize the value of these approaches and will share studies based on such methods.

As can be seen from the existing literature, more research in the field of training evaluation is necessary. In fact, evaluation is paramount to the success of any training program. Training not only must be cost effective but also must teach participants skills and concepts that they can readily use in their organizations after the training has been completed.

REFERENCES

Antheil, J.H., & Casper, I.G. (1986). Comprehensive evaluation model: A tool for the evaluation of nontraditional educational programs. *Innovative Higher Education, 11*(1), 55-64.

Apps, J.W. (1988). *Higher education in a learning society.* San Francisco: Jossey-Bass.

Ban, C., & Faerman, S.R. (1990). Issues in the evaluation of management training. *Public Productivity & Management Review, 8*(3), 271-286.

Bandura, A. (1965). Influence of models' reinforcement contingencies on the acquisition of imitative responses. *Journal of Personality and Social Psychology, 1*(6), 589-595.

Cantor, J.A. (1990). How to perform a comprehensive course evaluation. *Performance & Instruction, 29*(4), 8-15.

Carnevale, A.P., & Schulz, E.R. (1990, July Supplement). Return on investment: Accounting for training. *Training & Development Journal,* pp. 51-531.

Conway, M., & Ross, M. (1984). Getting what you want by revising what you had. *Journal of Personality and Social Psychology, 47*(4), 738-748.

Dixon, N.M. (1987). Meet training's goals without reaction forms. *Personnel Journal, 66*(8), 108-115.

Endres, G.J., & Kleiner, B.H. (1990). How to measure management training and development effectiveness. *Journal of European Industrial Training, 14*(9), 3-7.

Eurick, N. (1985). *Corporate classrooms.* Princeton, NJ: Carnegie Foundation.

Fisher, H.E., & Weinberg, R. (1988). Making training accountable: Assess its impact. *Personnel Journal, 67*(1), 73-77.

Fulmer, R.M. (1988). Corporate management development and education: The state of the art. *Journal of Management Development, 7*(2), 57.

Kelly, A.I., Orgel, R.F., & Baer, D.M. (1984). Evaluation: The bottom line is closer than you think. *Training and Development Journal, 38*(8), 32-37.

Kelly, H.K. (1982). A primer on transfer of training. *Training and Development Journal, 36*(11), 102-106.

Kirkpatrick, D.L. (1979). Techniques for evaluating training programs. *Training and Development Journal, 33*(6), 78-92.

Mahoney, F.X. (1980). Targets, time, and transfer: Keys to management training impact. *Personnel, 57*(6), 25-34.

McEvoy, G.M., & Buller, P.F. (1990). Five uneasy pieces in the training evaluation puzzle. *Training and Development Journal, 44*(8), 39-42.

Merriam, S.B., & Caffarella, R.S. (1991). *Learning in adulthood.* San Francisco: Jossey-Bass.

Naisbitt, J., & Aburdene, P. (1990). *Megatrends 2000: Ten new directions for the 1990s.* New York: Morrow.

Nanda, R. (1988). Organizational performance and supervisory skills. *Management Solutions, 33*(6), 22-28.

Schmidt, F.L., Hunter, J.E., & Pearlman, K. (1982). Assessing the economic impact of personnel programs on workforce productivity. *Personnel Psychology, 35*(2), 333-346.

Sheppeck, M.A., & Cohen, S.L. (1985). Put a dollar value on your training programs. *Training and Development Journal, 39*(11), 59-62.

Swierczek, F.L., & Carmichael, L. (1985). The quantity and quality of evaluating training. *Training & Development Journal, 39*(1), 95-99.

Trapnell, G. (1984). Putting the evaluation puzzle together. *Training and Development Journal, 38*(5), 90-93.

Zenger, J.H., & Hargis, K. (1982). Assessing training results: It's time to take the plunge. *Training and Development Journal, 36*(1), 10-16.

Patricia E. Boverie, Ph.D., *is an assistant professor of training and learning technologies at the University of New Mexico. She teaches courses in adult learning theory, training, critical thinking, and team and group development. Her current research interests include examining efficacy in groups, team development, the evaluation of delivery systems, educational change and reform, and the examination of adult-study skills. In addition to her teaching responsibilities, she has a consulting practice.*

Deanna Sánchez Mulcahy *received her Master's degree in training and learning technologies from the University of New Mexico in 1992. She currently works at the university and is a private tutor of adult learners. In addition, she has worked with Centerline Enterprises and Zia Imports as a training and management consultant.*

John A. Zondlo is the director of leadership training and development for Presbyterian Healthcare Services, an integrated healthcare delivery system headquartered in Albuquerque, New Mexico. His responsibilities include overall coordination of a leadership-development program for more than three hundred managers and supervisors across the organizational system. He has more than twelve years of experience in health-services administration and is a Fellow in the American College of Healthcare Executives.

WHY JOB AND ROLE PLANNING IS CRITICAL TO THE FUTURE[1]

Edgar H. Schein

Job and role analysis and planning are becoming increasingly important activities because work and organizations are changing at an ever more rapid rate, and all the indications are that work will become more fluid and will involve more complex relationships with others in superior, peer, and subordinate roles. The following are what I believe are some of the most important trends and their consequences for the nature of work. These trends all interact in complex ways and must be treated as a single system of forces, even though they are described one at a time.

STRUCTURES ARE BEING REEXAMINED

Organizations worldwide are reexamining their structures and engaging in "downsizing" or "rightsizing." In order to remain competitive in an increasingly global marketplace, organizations are discovering the need to be concerned about perpetual improvement and stringent control of costs. This has led to a wave of layoffs and restructuring of organizations. As a result, many jobs have simply disappeared, and work has been reallocated and redesigned so that a smaller number of people can perform it.

The possibilities inherent in the creative use of information technology, especially "groupware," have opened up new ways of thinking about work and jobs (Johansen, Sibbet, Benson, Martin, Mittman, & Saffo, 1991; Savage, 1990). The way in which people will be connected to one another will vary and will require all kinds of new relationships. Strategic job and role planning will be a primary tool for assessing and reassessing those relationships.

BOUNDARIES OF ORGANIZATIONS, JOBS, AND ROLES ARE CHANGING

Globalization, new technology, and "rightsizing" have loosened the boundaries of organizations, jobs, and roles. At the organizational level, we see in many industries a loosening of the boundaries between suppliers, manufacturers, and

---

[1] Adapted from *Career Survival* by Edgar H. Schein, 1993, San Diego, CA: Pfeiffer & Company.

customers (Kochan & Useem, 1992; Scott-Morton, 1991). By using sophisticated information-technology tools, customers can directly access a company's sales organization, specify in detail what kinds of products or services they require, and get immediate prices and delivery dates from the computer (Davis & Davidson, 1991). As such systems become more common, not only do the roles of purchasing agent and salesperson become much more ambiguous, but also a chain reaction occurs throughout the organization that necessitates the redefinition of order processing, marketing, and even design and manufacturing.

At the same time, the automation of everything from secretarial work to complex production processes makes all kinds of jobs much less manual and more conceptual. Operators who work in automated refineries, nuclear plants, paper mills, and other such organizations know as much about the running of their plants as the managers do. This knowledge creates new power relationships. The role of management becomes more ambiguous as managers no longer have the power of knowing things that their subordinates do not know. It is especially important for managers to discover that their relationships to their production workers fundamentally have changed and that workers have come to occupy a much more central position in the role network.

OPERATIONAL ROLES ARE FEWER

As work becomes technically more complex, fewer people will work in operational roles and more people will work in the service and staff roles that support the operation. The goal of automation generally is to reduce head count, but the result typically is more of a redistribution of workers. Fewer operators are needed, but more support services are needed. The total cost of the operation ultimately may not change much, but the kinds of work that are performed will change radically. The relationships between sets of workers will, therefore, change in unknown ways. Operators have greater immediate responsibility for doing things right, but the programmers, systems engineers, and maintenance engineers have greater ultimate responsibility to keep the systems running—to keep the computers from "going down." Management becomes more of a coordinating and liaison function and less of a monitoring and control function. Peers in service roles come to be seen as much more central in the role network than they have been previously.

STRESS LEVELS ARE INCREASING

As conceptual work increases and job and role boundaries loosen, anxiety levels will increase. Human organisms depend on certain levels of predictability and stability in their environments. Although we all have needs for creativity and stimulation, we may forget that those needs operate against a background of security, stability, and predictability (Schein, 1992).

As organizations face increasing competitive pressures, as jobs become more conceptual, and as levels of responsibility in all jobs increase, we will see levels of stress and anxiety increase at all levels of the organization. Formalization and bureaucracy have been one kind of defense against such anxiety, but have the kind of work that needs to be done in the information and knowledge age requires more flexibility and innovation, thus making more anxiety an inevitable result.

An increasing role for management will be the containment and working through of anxiety levels, although it is not at all clear by what individual or group mechanisms this will occur. When people are anxious, they want to be with others, so one of the most important functions of groups in organizations is the management of shared anxiety. The increasing emphasis on groups and teams that we hear about may be the result not only of the growing complexity of work but also of the growing anxiety levels attending work.

The concept of sociotechnical systems has been promulgated for several decades, but as we project ahead, it would appear that it becomes a more important concept than ever (Ketchum & Trist, 1992). One cannot separate the technical elements of a job from the social elements, as the network analysis in job and role analysis and planning is intended to illustrate. It also should be noted that job and role analysis and planning, when carried out regularly in a group setting, can be an anxiety reducer in that employees and managers can share their concerns about the loosening of boundaries and role overloads and conflicts while, at the same time, beginning to resolve them.

"FLAT," PROJECT-BASED ORGANIZATIONS ARE EMERGING

In the process of "rightsizing," organizations are (1) reexamining their hierarchical structures, (2) moving toward flatter structures, (3) relying more on coordination mechanisms other than hierarchy, and (4) "empowering" their employees in various ways. In the flat, project-based organization of the future, power and authority will rotate among different project leaders, and individual project members will have to coordinate their own activities across a number of projects with different leaders. Operational authority will shift rapidly from one project leader to another, and individual employees may find themselves working for several bosses simultaneously. At the same time, as knowledge and information are more widely distributed, employees will become empowered *de facto* because, increasingly, they will know things that their bosses do not know.

However, hierarchy is fairly intrinsic to human systems, so we will probably not see the abandonment of hierarchical structures so much as a change in their function (Schein, 1989). For example, broad hierarchical categories such as civil-service grades, degrees of partnership in a law firm, or levels of professorial rank may continue to serve broad career-advancement functions but may not be good guides as to who will have operational authority over a task or project. Respect for people and the amount of influence they exert will have more to do with their operational performance than with their formal rank, and hierarchy increasingly will be viewed as a necessary adjunct to organizational life rather than its prime principle.

Power and authority will derive from what a person knows and what skills he or she has demonstrated. Because conceptual knowledge is largely invisible, the opportunities will increase for misperception or conflicting perceptions of who knows what and who should be respected for what. This development will make the exercise of authority and influence much more problematic, which, in turn, will increase anxiety levels in organizations. By bringing groups together to do job and role analysis and planning, one can help to contain this anxiety and, more importantly, overcome the limitations of traditional job analysis, which attempts to evaluate the level of each job. One can speculate, in this regard, that pay will be tied more to formal rank, length of service, and number of skills that an employee has than to the particular job he or she is doing at any given moment.

DIFFERENTIATED AND COMPLEX ORGANIZATIONS ARE EMERGING

Organizations are becoming more differentiated and complex. With the rapid growth of technology in all fields of endeavor, the number of products and services available is increasing. At the same time, growing affluence and more widely distributed information about products and services are creating more demanding consumers. Organizations are, therefore, having to respond by becoming more able to deliver more different kinds of products and services faster, in greater variety, and in more different places all over the globe.

One of the major consequences is that the organizations that make the products and/or deliver the services have to be more differentiated and complex. That, in turn, means that there will be more different kinds of occupational specialists who must be managed and whose efforts must somehow be tied together into a coherent organizational whole. Many of these specialists are neither motivated nor able to talk to one another, which creates special problems of integration of effort (Schein, 1992). The highly specialized design engineer working in the research and development end of the company often has little in common with the financial analyst whose specialty is the management of the company's investment portfolio or the personnel specialist who is concerned with the most recent affirmative-action legislation. Yet all of these and many other specialists contribute in major ways to the welfare of the total organization, and their efforts have to be integrated. Such integration cannot take place unless all the specialists and managers involved become conscious of one another as stakeholders and begin to make an effort to respond to one another's expectations.

Beyond this, senior management must begin to worry about and plan for the specific career development of such specialists, because many of them will be neither able nor willing to go into managerial positions (Schein, 1990). Such developmental planning cannot occur without a clear understanding of the role networks within which these specialists operate and the involvement of those employees in planning their own development.

SUBUNITS ARE BECOMING MORE INTERDEPENDENT

In order to produce a complex product or service effectively over a period of time, the many subspecialties of the organization will have to be coordinated and integrated, because they are simultaneously and sequentially interdependent in a variety of ways. For example, if the financial department does not manage the company's cash supply adequately, there is less opportunity for capital expansion or research and development (R & D); on the other hand, if an engineering design sacrifices some elements of quality for low cost, the result may be customer complaints, a lowered company reputation, and the subsequent decreased ability of the company to borrow money for capital expansion. In this sense, engineering and finance are highly interdependent, even though each may be highly specialized and neither may interact with the other directly.

Sequential interdependence is the more common situation. The engineering department cannot design a product or service if R & D has not done a good job of developing the concept or prototype; in turn, manufacturing cannot build the product if engineering has produced unbuildable designs; and sales and marketing cannot do their jobs well if they have poor products to sell. Of course, R & D cannot get its concepts right if marketing has not given it clear descriptions of future customer needs, and the process innovations that occur within manufacturing often influence both marketing and engineering in terms of the types of products that are thought to be conceivable and feasible (Thomas, 1993).

These types of interdependence always have existed within organizations, but as specialization increases, interdependence also increases because the final product or service is more complex and more vulnerable to the malfunctioning of any its parts. Nowhere is this clearer than in computer products or services. The hardware and software have to be designed properly in the first place and then implemented by a variety of specialists who serve as the interfaces between the final users and the computer system. If any of the specialists fails to do his or her job, the entire service or product may fail.

Job and role analysis and planning are designed to reveal these interdependences through analysis of the role network and the identification of key stakeholders. What often is most surprising as one does the analysis is the large number of stakeholders whom one must take into account simultaneously. And, as one looks ahead, that number is growing, so the skills involved in dealing with multiple stakeholder expectations become more and more central to organizational performance (Rosell, 1992).

ORGANIZATIONAL CLIMATES ARE BECOMING MORE COLLABORATIVE

One major effect of the recognition of increased interdependence is that competition between organizational units or individuals is perceived as potentially destructive. Teamwork and collaborative/cooperative relations increasingly are touted as necessary to get the job done. This trend runs counter to the external marketplace philosophy that competition is a good thing, but it increasingly is seen to be a necessary adaptation within organizations, even if *interorganizational* relations continue to be competitive.

If this trend is worldwide, one will begin to see more evidence of interorganizational collaboration as well, not for political reasons but for practical reasons of technological necessity. Increased levels of coordination will not be achieved by more centralized planning, as was attempted in the communist/socialist economies, but by more distribution of information and decentralization, which will permit the various units to coordinate among themselves. However, for this self-managed coordination to occur, not only must information be widely available, but all of the actors in the system must be able to decipher their roles in it. The same information can be framed and interpreted in many different ways. For collaboration and cooperation to work, common frames of reference must be established, and that process will involve organizational members in much more group- and team-oriented activity. Building shared frames of reference also increasingly will become a primary task of leadership (Rosell, 1992; Schein, 1992).

This trend poses a particular dilemma for managers whose own careers have developed in very competitive environments and who simply do not have the interpersonal competence to redesign their organizational processes to be more supportive of collaborative relations. I have met many a manager who pays lip service to "teamwork" but whose day-to-day style sends clear signals of not really understanding or supporting the concept, with the predictable consequence that this person's "team" does not function as a team at all. Unfortunately, both the manager and the subordinates may draw the erroneous conclusion that it is the teamwork *concept* that is at fault rather than their failure to *implement* the concept. Once they understand the nature of the network they are in, they can do a better job of implementation. Thus, the very activity of job and role planning, when carried out in a team, becomes an important team-building function.

LATERAL COMMUNICATION CHANNELS ARE INCREASINGLY IMPORTANT

Closely connected with the need for more collaborative work is the need for information to flow laterally between technical specialists rather than going through a hierarchy. For example, some companies are putting the product-development and marketing departments closer to each other geographically and stimulating direct contact between them rather than having higher levels of management attempt to translate marketing issues for the development people. The customer, the salesperson, and the marketing specialist in a complex industry such as electronics all probably know more about the technical side of the business than the general manager does and, therefore, must be brought into direct interaction with the designer and engineer if a usable product or service is to result.

Jay Galbraith (1973) has argued very convincingly that the information-processing needs of organizations based on task complexity and environmental uncertainty are, in fact, the major determinants of organizational structure and that hierarchical structures work only so long as task complexity and uncertainty are fairly low. Lateral structures such as project teams, task forces, ad hoc committees, cross-functional organizational units, and matrix management become more common with increased complexity and uncertainty.

Technological possibilities and consumer demands are driving toward greater complexity, and information technology will make it possible for organizations eventually to adapt by creating the kinds of lateral communication that will make coordination, integration, and genuine teamwork possible.

Here again, managers face a novel situation because of the likelihood that their own careers have been spent in organizational settings dedicated to principles of hierarchy and chains of command. In such "traditional" organizations, communication with people outside the chain of command is discouraged and punished. Not only will the organizational reward system and climate have to shift to encourage lateral communication but, in addition, managers will have to be trained to create lateral structures and to make them work. Job and role planning will facilitate this trend by showing how many of the key stakeholders are neither superiors nor subordinates but peers in interdependent relationships.

SOCIOCULTURAL VALUES ARE CHANGING

In this section, I will refer mostly to trends that have been observed in the United States.

More Value on Individualism and Individual Rights

People are placing less value on traditional concepts of organizational loyalty and the acceptance of authority based on formal position, age, or seniority and are placing more value on individualism and individual rights vis-à-vis the organization. Increasingly, people are demanding that the tasks they are asked to perform make sense and provide them with some challenge and opportunity to express their talents. Increasingly, people are demanding that the rights of individuals be protected, especially if the individuals are members of minority groups or are likely to be discriminated against on some arbitrary basis such as sex, age, disability, religion, or ethnic origin. Increasingly, people are demanding some voice in decisions that affect them. These developments are leading to the growth of various forms of industrial democracy, participative management, and worker involvement in job design and corporate decision making. From the point of view of the employing organization, worker involvement makes sense to the extent that the trend toward specialization of tasks is occurring. For many kinds of decisions, it is the worker who has the key information and who, therefore, must be involved if the decision is to be a sound one. Thus, employee "empowerment" has taken on almost fad status.

Changes in How Success Is Defined

People are placing less value on work or career as a total life concern and less value on promotion or hierarchical movement within the organization as the sole measure of "success." More value is being placed on leading a balanced life in which work, career, family, and self-development all receive their fair share of attention. Success increasingly is defined in terms of the full use of all of one's talents and in contributing not only to one's work organization but also to one's family, community, and self. Careers are built on different kinds of career anchors, and the measure of success and advancement varies with whether or not one is oriented toward the managerial, technical/functional, security, autonomy, entrepreneurial, service, pure challenge, or lifestyle anchor (Schein, 1990).

Equal Employment Opportunities

People are placing less value on traditional concepts of male and female sex roles with respect to both work and family. In the career and work areas, we are seeing a growing trend toward equal employment opportunities for men and women, a breaking down of sex-role stereotypes in regard to work (for example, more women are going into engineering, and more men are going into nursing), and a similar breaking down of sex-role stereotypes in regard to proper family roles (for example, more women are becoming the primary supporters, and more men are staying home to take care of children, do the cooking, and clean the house). Our society is opening up the range of choices for both men and women to pursue new kinds of work, family roles, and lifestyles. Two of the major changes have been the "dual-career" family in which both husband and wife are committed to career development and the single-parent family. These changes are forcing organizations to develop new personnel policies and are forcing social institutions to develop new options for child care.

One of the most important elements of job and role planning is to determine the positions of spouses or significant others, children, and friends in the role network and as key stakeholders. As dual careers and single parents become more common, one will see complex, overlapping role networks in households, requiring more complex, adaptive solutions both at work and at home.

Focus on the Environment

People are placing less value on economic growth and are placing relatively more value on conserving and protecting the quality of the environment in which they live. Assessing the impact of technology is becoming a major activity in our society. We see increased willingness to stop progress (for example, reluctance to build the supersonic transport or to allow our airports to admit existing SSTs; an abrupt halt to highway construction in the middle of a city; and refusal to build oil refineries, even in economically depressed areas, if the environment would be endangered). However, as we saw in the early 1990s, if a recession continues, economic-growth values resurface, and conflict increases between the need to protect the environment and the need for jobs.

Organizational Generation Gap

These value changes and conflicts have created a situation in which the incentives and rewards offered by the different parts of our society have become much more diverse and, consequently, much less integrated. We see this most clearly in the organizational generation gap—older managers or employees who operate from a "Protestant work ethic" versus young employees who question arbitrary authority, meaningless work, organizational loyalty, restrictive personnel policies, and even fundamental corporate goals and prerogatives.

As options and choices have opened up and as managers have begun to question the traditional success ethic, these managers have become more ready to refuse promotions or geographical moves, more willing to "retire on the job" while pursuing family activities or off-the-job hobbies, and more likely to resign from high-potential careers to pursue "second careers" that are perceived to be more challenging and/or rewarding by criteria other than formal hierarchical position or amount of pay.

IMPLICATIONS OF THESE TRENDS

What all this means for the managers of tomorrow is that they will have to manage in a much more "pluralistic" society, one in which employees at all levels will have more choices and will exercise those choices. Managers not only will have to exhibit more personal flexibility in dealing with the range and variety of individual needs they encounter in subordinates, peers, and superiors, but also will have to learn how to influence organizational policies with respect to recruitment, work assignment, pay and benefit systems, working hours and length of work week, attitudes about dual employment of couples, support of educational activities at a much higher scale, development of child-care facilities, and so on.

With respect to all these issues, the manager will be caught in the middle among several key stakeholders, including the following:

1. Government agencies, with respect to discrimination (on the basis of sex, age, race, disabilities, and other characteristics), environmental issues, and occupational safety issues;
2. Community-interest groups, with respect to equal rights, environmental protection, product quality and safety, and other forms of consumerism;
3. Stockholders, who are eager to maintain an efficient and profitable operation and a fair return on their investments;
4. Competitors, who also are caught in the struggle to meet the challenges of a changing work force;
5. Employees—whether unionized or not—who are anxious to improve the quality of working life, create flexible corporate policies, provide challenging and meaningful work, and be responsible "corporate citizens"; and
6. Family and self in terms of a need to maintain a balanced life.

Role ambiguity, role overload, and role conflict are likely to be chronic conditions, and the processes of setting priorities and negotiating with different stakeholders are likely to be perpetual rather than one-time activities. Boundaries of all kinds will be perpetually defined and redefined, and anxiety levels around those activities periodically will be very high. We see this at the national level in the tension resulting from globalization on the one hand, and the breaking up of countries into ethnic or cultural units on the other hand, even if those units will have a difficult time surviving economically as nations.

THE FUTURE AS SEEN FROM 1994

The trends identified previously are themselves not stable. In fact, if there is anything to be learned from the last few decades, it is that our ability to predict is declining rapidly. The management of "surprise" is the order of the day. For example, we cannot really predict the future economic impact of the Asian bloc of countries (especially China) or the future behavior of the European Economic Community. We cannot predict the rate at which the formerly socialist or communist countries will become politically or economically viable and, when they do, what impact that will have on the global scene.

We cannot predict the rate at which information and biotechnology will evolve low-cost products and services that will fundamentally change the nature of work, the nature of organizations, and the nature of life itself. The potential ethical issues implicit in bioengineering boggle the mind.

On the political front, we cannot predict the outcome of the simultaneous trends toward globalization and fractionization into smaller, ethnically pure countries. As of this writing, the roles of the United States and of the United Nations remain unclear and unpredictable in conflicts between nations and in aid to starving nations.

Within the U.S., we cannot predict the impact of the Clinton presidency, what will happen to the budget deficit, how health-care costs will be brought under control while health-care delivery is improved, how our educational system will be revitalized, and how we will solve the racial problems in our inner cities. Our current systems of governance are strained and possibly not up to the tasks facing us.

What all of this means is that we must become *perpetual learners*. As a growing number of observers and analysts have noted, it will be the ability to learn that will make the difference in the future (Michael, 1992; Peters, 1987; Rosell, 1992; Senge, 1990). If we cannot cope with surprise and develop new ways of framing problems and new responses, we will lose. Ultimately, this challenge puts more emphasis on dynamic processes, on learning to live with perpetual change, and on developing the diagnostic skills that permit us to see what is needed.

It is this need for dynamic processes that leads us back to job and role analysis and planning. Projecting this need to the extreme suggests that job and role planning should become virtually a perpetual activity that is integral to the management process itself. Every time there is a new project or a new assignment, the manager and his or her subordinate should do a truncated version of job and role planning to ensure that there is consensus on what will need to be done and who will need to be involved. Job descriptions will become dynamic documents, perpetually renegotiated as the work of the organization changes in response to changing environmental circumstances.

Perpetual job and role planning will require much higher levels of interaction among members of the organization, especially between managers and their subordinates. On the one hand, such an increase in meetings will increase frustration because of the time these meetings will take, but, paradoxically, people will discover that meetings are the best way of coping with the increasing anxiety that future jobs and roles will precipitate. Job and role planning will provide opportunities for supportive role negotiation that will reduce anxiety while, at the same time, increasing our conceptual understanding of what we must do to best fulfill our own needs and those of the organization.

REFERENCES

Davis, S.M., & Davidson, B. (1991). *2020 vision.* New York: Simon & Schuster.

Galbraith, J. (1973). *Designing complex organizations.* Reading, MA: Addison-Wesley.

Johansen, R., Sibbet, D., Benson, S., Martin, A., Mittman, R., & Saffo, P. (1991). *Leading business teams.* Reading, MA: Addison-Wesley.

Ketchum, L.D., & Trist, E. (1992). *All teams are not created equal.* Newbury Park, CA: Sage.

Kochan, T.A., & Useem, M. (Eds.). (1992). *Transforming organizations.* New York: Oxford University Press.

Michael, D.N. (1992). Governing by learning in an information society. In S.A. Rosell (Ed.), *Governing in an information society.* Montreal, Quebec: Institute for Research on Public Policy.

Peters, T.J. (1987). *Thriving on chaos.* New York: Alfred A. Knopf.

Rosell, S.A. (Ed.) (1992). *Governing in an information society.* Montreal, Quebec: Institute for Research on Public Policy.

Savage, C.M. (1990). *Fifth generation management: Integrating enterprises through human networking.* Maynard, MA: Digital Press.

Schein, E.H. (1989). Reassessing the "divine rights" of managers. *Sloan Management Review, 30*(3), 63-68.

Schein, E.H. (1990). *Career anchors.* San Diego, CA: Pfeiffer & Company.

Schein, E.H. (1992). *Organizational culture and leadership* (2nd ed.). San Francisco: Jossey-Bass.

Scott-Morton, M.S. (Ed.). (1991). *The corporation of the 1990s.* New York: Oxford University Press.

Senge, P.M. (1990). *The fifth discipline.* New York: Doubleday Currency.

Edgar H. Schein, Ph.D., is a Professor of Management at the Massachusetts Institute of Technology and was chairman of the Organization Studies Group from 1972 to 1982. Dr. Schein served as a group trainer for the NTL Institute and has been a consultant in organization development, management development, and organizational culture for companies throughout the United States and Europe. He is the author of the best-selling Career Anchors *materials published by Pfeiffer & Company and is the author of numerous other books.*

CONTRIBUTORS

Steven E. Aufrecht, Ph.D.
Associate Professor
Public Administration
School of Public Affairs
University of Alaska
3211 Providence Drive
Anchorage, AK 99508
(907) 786-1908

Arlette C. Ballew
Senior Developmental Editor
Pfeiffer & Company
8517 Production Avenue
San Diego, CA 92121
(619) 578-5900

Charles A. Beitz, Jr., D.P.A.
Chair
Department of Business and Economics
Mount Saint Mary's College
Emmitsburg, MD 21727
(301) 447-5396

Patricia E. Boverie, Ph.D.
Assistant Professor
Training & Learning Technology
College of Education
University of New Mexico
EOB 105
Albuquerque, NM 87131
(505) 277-2408

Robert T. Brill, Ph.D.
Assistant Professor of Psychology
Department of Psychology
Moravian College
1200 Main Street
Bethlehem, PA 18018
(215) 861-1316

J. Barton Cunningham, Ph.D.
Professor
School of Public Administration
University of Victoria
Victoria, British Columbia V8W 2Y2
Canada
(604) 721-8059

Linda Eschenburg
Principal
Eschenburg Associates
3403 San Pedro
Tampa, FL 33629
(813) 837-9961

Michael J. Goldberg, J.D.
Principal
Enneagram Systems
P.O. Box 825
Venice, CA 90294-0825
(310) 285-2259

Paula Grace
President
Paula Grace Consulting & Training
576 Wisconsin Street
San Francisco, CA 94107
(415) 826-6644

Bonnie Jameson
Consultant
1024 Underhills Road
Oakland, CA 94610
(510) 832-2597

H.B. Karp, Ph.D.
Personal Growth Systems
109 82nd Street
Virginia Beach, VA 23451
(804) 425-8203

The 1994 Annual: Developing Human Resources

Manfred F.R. Kets de Vries, M.B.A., D.B.A.
Raoul de Vitry d'Avaucourt
Chair of Human Resource Management
Department of Entrepreneurship and
  Leadership
INSEAD
Boulevard de Constance
Fontainebleau 77305
France
  (1) 60-72-43-68

Joann Keyton, Ph.D.
Department of Theatre &
  Communication Arts
Memphis State University
143 Theatre & Communication Arts
  Building
Memphis, TN 38152
  (901) 678-2565

Robert William Lucas
Manager, Training
American Automobile Association
1000 AAA Drive
Heathrow, FL 32746-5063
  (407) 444-7520

Danny Miller, Ph.D.
Research Professor
Ecole des Hautes Etudes Commerciales
5255 Avenue Decelles
Montreal, Quebec H3T 1V6
Canada
  (514) 340-6380

Catherine J. Nagy
Training and Development Manager
Human Resources Department
Francis Scott Key Medical Center
4940 Eastern Avenue
Baltimore, MD 21224
  (410) 550-1777

John E. Oliver, Ph.D.
Professor and Head
Department of Management and
  Information Systems
Valdosta State University
Valdosta, GA 31698
  (912) 245-2236

Udai Pareek, Ph.D.
1 Yamuna Path
Swaj Nagar West
Jaipur 302 006
India
  91-141-550700 or 91-141-550065
  Fax 91-141-550119

Steven R. Phillips, Ph.D.
Assistant Professor
Department of Communication Studies
University of Montana
Missoula, MT 59812
  (406) 243-4293

Robert C. Preziosi, D.P.A.
Nova University
School of Business and Entrepreneurship
3301 College Avenue
Fort Lauderdale, FL 33314
  (305) 475-7690

Marian K. Prokop
Senior Editor
Pfeiffer & Company
8517 Production Avenue
San Diego, CA 92121
  (619) 578-5900

Virginia E.B. Prosdocimi, Ph.D.
Consultant
Casemasce di Todi
Perugia 06059
Italy
  (075) 8947639

Gaylord Reagan, Ph.D.
Independent Management Consultant
Reagan Consulting
04 Hackberry Court, #3106
Bellevue, NE 68005
(402) 292-0723

John A. Zondlo
Director, Leadership Development
Presbyterian Healthcare Services
1100 Central Avenue SE
Albuquerque, NM 87102
(505) 841-1536

Deanna Sánchez Mulcahy
Admissions Office
Student Services Center
University of New Mexico
Albuquerque, NM 87131
(505) 277-2526

Edgar H. Schein, Ph.D.
Professor of Management
Massachusetts Institute of Technology
Room E52-583
Cambridge, MA 02139
(617) 253-3636

Donald T. Simpson, Ed.D.
10 Mulberry Street
Rochester, NY 14620
(716) 442-6501

Michele Stimac, Ed.D.
Professor
Graduate School of Education
 and Psychology
Pepperdine University
400 Corporate Pointe
Culver City, CA 90230
(310) 568-5613

D. Allan Tyler
5617 Hulvey Terrace
Alexandria, VA 22306
(703) 765-6080

Patrick J. Ward, Ph.D.
Organizational Counseling
 & Development
5011 SW 109 Avenue
Miami, FL 33173
(305) 274-0539

The 1994 Annual: Developing Human Resources